85 0013609 X

KU-745-452

57004075

WRITING FOR TELEVISION
IN THE 70's

Writing for Television in the 70's

MALCOLM HULKE

ADAM & CHARLES BLACK LONDON

FIRST PUBLISHED 1974
BY A. AND C. BLACK LIMITED
4, 5 AND 6 SOHO SQUARE LONDON WIV 6AD
© MALCOLM HULKE 1974
ISBN 0 7136 1469 2

*All rights reserved. No part of this publication may be
reproduced stored in a retrieval system, or transmitted,
in any form or by any means, electronic, mechanical,
photocopying, recording or otherwise, without the
prior permission of A & C Black Limited.*

PRINTED AND BOUND IN GREAT BRITAIN BY
REDWOOD BURN LIMITED
TROWBRIDGE AND ESHER

Contents

Thanks

The author wishes to thank all the following people for their marvellous help and advice. Without them this book would still have been written, but wouldn't be so good. In fact, without some of them the job would have been much easier, albeit the result less accurate.

Mari Allan, *broadcaster*
Roderick Allen, *copywriter*
Ken Ashton, *producer-director-writer*
Jack Barton, *director*
Alfie Bass, *actor*
Richard Bates, *producer*
Keith Best, *weatherman*
Paul Best, *copywriter*
Eric Brown, *police inspector*
Sid Colin, *writer*
Michala Crees, *writer*
N. J. Crisp, *writer*
Gerry Davis, *writer-editor*
Terrance Dicks, *writer-editor*
Frank Duesbury, *press officer*
Sheila Eidelstein, *secretary*
David Ellis, *writer*
Margaret French, *casting director*
Terence Frisby, *writer and actor*
Nina Froud, *literary agent*
A. S. Gruner, *production and distribution executive*
Willis Hall, *writer*
Caroline Heller, *union official*
Andrew Hemming, *librarian*
Charlie Hewitt, *press officer*
Robert Holmes, *writer*
John Jacobs, *head of drama*
Ivor Jay, *writer*
Penry Jones, *administrator*
Harry W. Junkin, *writer-editor*
Barry Letts, *producer*
Peter Ling, *writer*
A. R. Lucas, *barrister*
George Markstein, *script editor*

Adrian Mitchell, *writer*
Mike Murphy, *press executive*
Alan Nicholson, *administrator*
Sarah Newman, *secretary*
Elizabeth Orpin, *press officer*
Eric Paice, *writer*
Lauraine Palmeri, *journalist*
Carol Parker, *lecturer*
Tony Parker, *writer*
Colin Pearson, *copywriter*
R. D. Pendlebury, *administrator*
Cecil Petty, *producer-director-writer*
Allan Prior, *writer*
Ken Pugh, *videotape engineer*
Terence Rattigan, *writer*
Colin Rogers, *script department head*
Alan Sapper, *union general secretary*
Lisa Scheu, *Redakteurin*
Ann Scott, *script editor*
Stephen Sedley, *barrister*
Leslie Sewell, *marketing consultant*
Rosemary Anne Sisson, *writer*
Dennis Spooner, *writer-editor*
Liz Stern, *stage manager*
John Stevenson, *writer*
S. A. Strauss, *professor of law*
Stephen Sylvester, *union general secretary*
Bob Symmonds, *press officer*
William Trevor, *writer*
Harvey Unna, *literary agent*
Robin Wade, *script department head*
Reg Watson, *producer*
Betty Willingale, *senior script unit assistant*
Ted Willis, *writer*

Chapter 1

WHAT YOU DON'T KNOW YOU DON'T KNOW

Legend has it that a busy American ambassador to Rome asked the Pope whether it would be possible to get to know that city in a day's sight-seeing. The Pope said: "In a day, you can see everything." The ambassador said, "If I dedicated a month to it, would I really get to know Rome?" The Pope said, "In a month, you might get to know a little of Rome." The ambassador persisted and asked, "What if I gave up a whole year to get to know Rome?" The Pope threw up his hands in horror: "What can anyone possibly learn about Rome in only a year?"

The more we learn about a complex subject, the more we realise there is to learn. And we can only start when we acknowledge that there *is* something to learn in the first place. Television comes flooding into our homes day and night. Everything about it seems to be totally exposed. In some of the chat shows, not even the cameras are concealed. So, if we aspire to any kind of writing at all, this friendly, chummy medium is obviously the one for us. No doubt there are a few bits of technical know-how that are necessary. But basically, all we have to do is write a story, send it to someone, and the television people will make it right to go into a couple of million homes by the end of the week.

Writing for television isn't like that at all. It is a craft in its own right. Just as the poet automatically thinks in terms of metre, so does the television writer think of how many characters he may use and how many sets. Of course he thinks creatively, but it is a creativity firmly set within the size of a prescribed canvas.

There are people, both in the British Broadcasting Corporation and in the Independent Television companies, whose job it is to make scripts 'work' (practical) in a television sense. These are the script-editors. But their time is valuable, and they are only going to add their expertise to scripts which are already written basically in television terms.

So, if you want to write for television, you must learn the craft; and what you don't know yet is how much you don't know about it. Because of its homely familiarity, television may seem as exposed as the cogs and springs of a French mantelpiece clock. But a better analogy is the iceberg, with one eighth revealed and seven eighths concealed. However, anyone with reasonable intelligence should quickly grasp the fundamentals.

Television writing in this country falls into two main categories, freelance and staff*. Freelance writing covers plays, episodes in series, serials, situation comedy, and the like. Staff writers are employed for the news, commercials, some documentaries, and what is called presentation. Since the usual way to break into television is by way of freelance writing, most of this book will be devoted to that category.

Like any other industry, television has its own vocabulary. In this book, the first use of a technical term will be in single quotation marks, followed by a bracketed explanation. If you get lost, there is a glossary at the end. Two terms, however, need explanation right from the start: the difference between 'producer' and 'director'. When television drama began it was all 'single shot' plays (a work of drama having no relationship with any other works of drama being transmitted; also called 'one off' plays). The man in charge was called a producer, the term still used in radio drama. With the development of 'series' drama (a succession, usually weekly, of dramatic works, each a complete story in itself, but depicting the same heroes and heroines) and 'anthology' drama (a succession of plays, all using original characters, but thematically connected), each episode had to have its own man in charge: so he became known as the director (a term borrowed from the film industry), and producer was reserved for the person in charge of the series as a whole. Therefore, the director directs the actors' rehearsals and the work of the cameramen; the producer is the administrator, with a number of directors working under him. The script editor is the buffer between the producer and the writers.

---

*I am using the term 'staff writer' to mean people with long-term contracts (say, three months to five years), who have an office, a secretary and, if very lucky, a reserved place in the studio car park. However, from an income tax and Social Security viewpoint, they may still be technically freelance. MH

There is a quaint carry over from former times in that at least in BBC circles the director's right-hand-woman is still officially known as the 'producer's assistant' (or PA). Even in this comparatively new institution of television, tradition, like lichen on rocks, has started to take hold.

Chapter 2

THE ELECTRONIC STUDIO

Sydney Newman, much-quoted one-time Head of Drama at BBC Television, once said: "Television is the highest form of drama, made almost impossible by electronics." You will soon see why.

There are three forms of television production used in the United Kingdom these days: live (the news, weather, some chat shows and some sport), tape (with and without editing—this will become clear later on), and TV/film. In Chapter 9 you will learn about TV/film, which is an industry within an industry. Here we shall concentrate on electronically produced television, which has its historical roots in radio. So let us start there.

A radio studio is a room with one or more microphones, plus various ingenious devices for making sound effects. If the play has a small cast, only one microphone is used. A play with a large cast will use two or more microphones, and the actors will be broken down into groups. For a scene in a public house, all the actors making drinking sounds might be grouped around the first microphone. For the next scene, say in a hospital ward, all the actors hired to cough or moan or ask for bed pans will be grouped around the second microphone. As the first scene (the pub) ends, the technicians will fade down on the first microphone and simultaneously fade up on the second microphone as the hospital characters start their moaning and groaning.

Whereas the radio microphone picks up sound waves which it turns into electrical impulses that can travel through wires and eventually be radiated through the atmosphere to people with receivers, the television camera picks up light waves and turns them into electrical impulses that can be transmitted. When the world's first regular public television service started, in Britain in 1936, we can imagine how simple it all was. The actors had to bunch themselves together so that

12

all would be 'in shot' (the viewing area of a camera). It was, as one wit put it, radio with occasional pictures. But simple as it all was, it had one fundamental difference from radio: it cost much more money.

The actor who had previously attended radio studios in his gardening hat and Oxford bags now had to be dressed to fit his part, because he was going to be seen. And there had to be sets, furniture, 'props' (short for 'properties', meaning small items which go to 'dress' a set, e.g. telephone, pictures on the mantelpiece, etc). Above all, it took much more time to produce a television play because the actors had to learn their lines by heart during many days of rehearsals. Whereas a one hour radio play could be rehearsed and produced in one day, one hour of television drama was suddenly claiming seven or ten days of the time of a lot of fairly expensive people. Still, with only one camera, and only one microphone to be hung over the heads of the actors, the cost of technicians' time could not have been very much. But single-camera production wasn't to last for long.

Imagine a scene in those very early days, where two actors are performing before the single camera. They must keep very close together, even though the play requires them to detest each other. But what could happen if there were two cameras in the studio? Immediately we have all sorts of possibilities. Camera 1 can remain holding its steady 'two shot' (two actors seen 'in frame' on the screen), while Camera 2 can be so angled that it holds on one of the actors in close up. Just as the radio producer could fade from one microphone to another, so with two cameras the television director could 'cut' (change what the viewer is seeing) from one view of the scene to another. So as this 'two hander' (a scene with two characters) progressed, cutting from two shot to close up, the director could present to the viewer a more interesting overall visual impression.

Two cameras also meant that plays could be produced using more than one set—again more cost, but well worth it. While Tom and Dick played out their scene in the living room set they could be seen by Camera 1; then, the moment they had finished, the director could cut to Camera 2, which was already focussed on Harry and Jennifer who were waiting for their 'cue' (a word or signal to motivate an actor to a certain action) to start acting out their scene in the dining room. During this second scene, Camera 1 could be quietly wheeled (they ran on bicycle wheels in those days) into position to see what was going to take place between the vicar and the lady organist in the vestry set, which would be Scene 3. But we are now back to one camera per scene, defeating the object of the extra camera. To make a reasonable visual impression, two cameras are needed *per* scene. Therefore, with continuous action production, a minimum of four cameras was required, two in action and two ready to go into action. Four cameras is the usual number you will find in studios today.

In those early days, no-one had discovered how to record the electrical impulses coming from television cameras. If anything went wrong during a production, the audience saw it. In the first play by Eric Paice and myself, *This Day in Fear*, produced in 1959, a scene between Billie Whitelaw and Patrick McGoohan included the surprise appearance of one of the 'extras' (small part actors) who wandered across the space between the window of the supposed first floor bedroom and the 'drop' (canvas curtain with picture of houses across the street), startling viewers with his seeming levitation act.

VTR (video tape recording) started to come into use in the early 1960's. A VTR machine may be compared with an ordinary domestic tape recorder, except that it records the electrical impulses of vision as well as sound, the tape used is eight times wider, the running speed is 15 inches per second (compared, say, to $3\frac{3}{4}$ i.p.s. or $7\frac{1}{2}$ i.p.s.), and the minimum capital outlay is about £80,000. It can take up to 10 seconds of running time for all the electronic systems to synchronise; so, to keep a safe margin, it is common practice to take a 15 second run-up to make sure that the machine has completed stabilisation. However, there is now a new type of VTR machine coming on the market which can 'lock up' (stabilise, be ready for use) in less than one second.

The great advantage of VTR was that a show to be transmitted at evening prime time could be recorded during the morning or afternoon. This spread the use of valuable studio space. It also meant that if something catastrophic happened, such as the set collapsing about the actors' ears, they could rewind the tape and start all over again. In those early days they had to re-start right from the opening credits. Very soon, however, laborious methods of editing became available, but these involved physically splicing the tape. There was a lot of guess work in editing: the technician had to run through the recorded tape, watching on a monitor for the moment when, for instance, the star began to forget her lines, then stop the machine, close his eyes, snip, and pray. Nowadays video tape is electronically edited with ease, although it still takes time, and time costs money.

In the days before tape editing was possible, a television writer had to avoid ever showing a character at the end of one scene and in the beginning of the next. If it was necessary for the same actor to be in two following scenes, the writer had to devise a 'bridge' (the meaning of that term will become apparent shortly). In most television drama these days, directors do not expect writers to bridge the characters. But there are still some shows where it is necessary, and you would hardly be a competent television writer if you didn't know how.

So let us now enter a television studio where a play is to be produced. It will be recorded of course, but the recording will be in one continuous sequence of scenes without 'tape pauses' (i.e. no editing).

A studio may be as small as a living room (for the news, weather, or presentation links), or as large as a football pitch. For drama, the bigger the better. Looking up we see that the ceiling is obscured by a wall-to-wall grid from which hang hundreds of powerful lights. About half way up the walls we see a gallery; at one or two points, metal steps like a ship's ladders run from the floor to the gallery. On a level with the gallery we see in one corner some windows and doors, and these lead into 'the box' or 'the fish tank', otherwise the director's control room. We shall take a look in there in a moment.

The sets are arranged all round the studio floor like Frontier wagons readied for attack. They arrived in a prefabricated state immediately after the sets for last night's production were 'struck' (dismantled), and they were assembled overnight. In its simplest form, a set is a three walled room: the non-existent 'fourth wall' faces into the centre of the studio floor where the four cameras are. The viewfinder of each camera is a miniscule television screen, so that the cameraman can see exactly what his camera is shooting. Each camera is linked by cable to a socket in the wall, and by this means the television electrical impulses are conveyed to the director's control room. In addition to the cameras, there are the sound booms, tall contraptions on wheels. The sound man stands on a cat-walk that encircles the sound boom, and from that position he can manoeuvre the 'fishing rod' (boom, from the end of which hangs a microphone).

In his control room, the director sits before a bank of switches, buttons, flashing lights and microphones. On the wall facing him are the four monitor screens which show whatever the four cameras are looking at. Above the four monitors is a bigger screen called Output*.

---

*Usually there are two output screens, the main one in colour and a subsidiary one in 'B/W' (black-and-white) to show the director how people with B/W sets will see the show. Some studios also have a screen showing an artificially degraded picture, which may be in colour or B/W, so that the director can be aware of how his show is likely to be viewed in the majority of homes. It is probable that most viewers in Britain tolerate very poor reception because they have never seen the superb picture quality of closed-circuit studio monitor screens.

Corner of a typical television studio. Note the gallery and the windows of the 'fish tank' or director's control room. We see here the kitchen and John's office. Note the 'backing' to the doorway to the kitchen. The sound boom stands between the first two cameras.

By manipulating switches, the vision mixer, who also sits at the console, can put onto the output screen any of the pictures coming in from the four cameras. Thus the cuts are made: the sequence of cuts put onto Output is what will be seen in viewers' homes. Also at the console is the director's assistant (by microphone she tells the cameramen, who all wear earphones, which will be the next camera shot according to the camera script), the inlay operator (responsible for special optical effects), and the technical manager (who is in charge of the technical side of the entire studio: he and the cameramen and other technicians 'belong' to the studio, whereas our director and his actors just have the use of the studio for this particular production). There are two lesser control rooms to either side of the main one: one for sound, the other for lighting. As the action moves from scene to scene, different sets must be lit, or the degree of lighting changed. As soon as a scene is over, the lights above that set will be switched off, not only to keep down costs (the amount of electricity consumed is colossal) but also to keep down the temperature of the studio. The technicians in the sound control room are there to produce music or sound effects when required during the production.

Somewhere else in the studio complex, perhaps many floors and corridors away, are the VTR machines, to which the output circuit is linked. The VTR people may simultaneously be taping the output from a number of studios where productions are taking place.

Down on the floor, the actors are now taking their places for 'the run' ('the VTR', or otherwise the production). They have already had two or three technical rehearsals and at least one 'full dress rehearsal' (complete production). Even so, as they take their places in the sets, set builders are making last minute improvements, the people from the make up department are hurriedly adding final dabs of powder to noses that may be too shiny in the bright lights, and the floor manager can be seen conveying last minute instructions from the director. The floor manager is the on-the-floor ambassador of the director throughout the video tape recording, because the director must remain in his control room. The floor manager wears earphones that are connected to a tiny radio receiver clipped to his belt: by this means he can hear everything the director says, while maintaining complete mobility to move around and pass on the director's instructions.

The studio clock is showing that it is near to starting time. While the director issues last minute instructions to his floor manager and cameramen, the producer is down on the floor being charming to all

17

the cast and wishing them good luck. Then it is time, and the director's assistant says into her microphone, "Run telecine opening titles. Go grams!" On the telecine screen, which is next to the four monitor screens, we see the pre-filmed opening credits. And now we go into our first scene.

Over the next few scenes, our point of interest is how the writer found ways to bridge John from one set to another. In each case, the writer has given the actor just enough time to scuttle round the backs of the sets so that he can be in one continuous-action scene after another.

```
MINE IS NOT TO REASON

by

John Smith


1.  INT.  KITCHEN.                        DAY.


MODERN.  SUBURBAN.  CLEAN AND TIDY.
JOHN, DRESSED READY TO GO TO WORK, IS
EATING TOAST, DRINKING COFFEE, READING
THE MORNING NEWSPAPER.  MARY, IN NIGHTIE
AND DRESSING GOWN, IS MAKING MORE TOAST.

MARY:          There'll be more toast
in a minute.

JOHN:          No time.

HE GOES ON READING.  FROM OFF WE HEAR
THE LETTER BOX FLAP.  JOHN, STILL READING,
MOVES TO GO.

JOHN:          I'll go.

MARY:          You eat your toast.

SHE GOES.

MARY:          And watch mine!

SHE EXITS.  JOHN IS ABOUT TO GO AND
WATCH HER TOAST, BUT SOMETHING CATCHES
HIS EYE IN THE PAPER.  HE GOES ON
READING A MOMENT.  THEN HE SNIFFS,
RUSHES TO THE GRILL, PULLS OUT A PAN
OF BLACKENED BREAD.  MARY ENTERS,
AN UNOPENED LETTER IN HAND.  SHE SNIFFS.
```

MARY: All right, don't watch
mine.

JOHN: Sorry.

MARY: Only the one. It's for
you.

SHE GIVES HIM THE ENVELOPE, THEN THROWS
AWAY THE BLACKENED BREAD AND STARTS AGAIN.
HE OPENS THE ENVELOPE, LOOKS.

JOHN: The garage. Two pounds
for that new fan belt. (CHECKS WATCH)
I'll have to fly.

JOHN EXITS TO HALL. THROUGH OPEN DOOR
WE CAN SEE HIM PUTTING ON HIS TOPCOAT.

MARY: What time will you be
back?

JOHN: The usual. About six.
Honestly, two pounds!

HE PAUSES TO CONTEMPLATE, THEN REMEMBERS
AND RUSHES BACK IN AND PECKS MARY ON THE
CHEEK.

JOHN: See you tonight. 'Bye.

JOHN EXITS. MARY PUTS MORE BREAD UNDER
THE GRILL. THEN WE HEAR THE FRONT DOOR
BANG. SHE WAITS A MOMENT, THEN TAKES
FROM HER DRESSING GOWN POCKET AN
UNOPENED LETTER, OPENS IT, STARTS TO
READ. SHE FROWNS, AND SITS AT THE
KITCHEN TABLE. AS SHE READS ON HER
HAND SHAKES A LITTLE, AND SHE STARTS
TO CRY.

2. INT. JOHN'S OFFICE.   DAY.

MODERN, SOULLESS. JOHN IS DICTATING
TO HIS SECRETARY, KATE.

JOHN: ...We have made the most
exhaustive enquiries into the nature of
your query –

KATE SQUIRMS.

JOHN: What's wrong?

KATE: You don't make enquiries
into the nature of a query. You might
make enquiries into the nature of a
problem. Even then, you could say 'make
enquiries into the problem'.

INTERNAL PHONE BUZZES. JOHN LIFTS.

19

JOHN: (INTO PHONE) John Morgan...
Oh, good morning, Mr Gillick...   Yes,
fine, thanks... Yes, I could if you
wish. Straight away?... Certainly.

JOHN CRADLES THE PHONE, RISES.

KATE: End of dictation?

JOHN: For the time being. (MOVES
TO GO, PAUSES) You know what I want to
tell these twits.   Why don't you just
write it yourself, and have done?

HE GOES.

3. INT. MR GILLICK'S OFFICE.   DAY.

SAME DECOR AS JOHN'S OFFICE, BUT BIGGER.
WE OPEN CLOSE ON GILLICK AT HIS DESK, IN
FULL SPATE.

GILLICK: And what's more, John,
we've really got to tackle this problem.
Get down to hard tacks, the real nitty
gritty. All I ever hear from the despatch
department is talk, talk, talk. If they
can use ten words when only two would do,
they will. Now I want to see what you
can do to rouse up their ideas a bit,
bring them into the Twentieth Century,
kicking and screaming if necessary. It's
the sort of thing I know you can do, John.
So how about it?

WIDEN SHOT TO SHOW JOHN SITTING OPPOSITE
GILLICK.

JOHN: Where do you think I
should start?

GILLICK: Go down there and give them
hell. We've got to compete in world
markets, or we'll end up as someone's
colony.   You don't want that beautiful
little boy of yours to have to speak
Japanese, do you?

JOHN: We haven't got any
children, sir, not yet.

GILLICK: And more's the pity, John.
I often think to myself, where would I be
today if I hadn't had my children to strive
for.

JOHN: I thought you inherited the
firm from your father?

GILLICK: I know what some people
                  (MORE)

20

GILLICK: (CONTINUED) think about
inherited wealth, John. But communism
will never come to this country, not
while there are ravens in the Tower.
Now what about it?

JOHN: I'll get along there
straight away.

GILLICK: Good man! Excellent
fellow –

KNOCK ON THE DOOR.

GILLICK: Come in!

PORTER ENTERS, SEES JOHN IS WITH GILLICK.

PORTER: Oh, I'm sorry.

GILLICK: John was just leaving.

JOHN RISES TO GO.

JOHN: I'll be there within the
hour. (TO PORTER) Good morning, sir.

JOHN EXITS. GILLICK IMMEDIATELY BECOMES
VERY BUSINESSLIKE.

GILLICK: Well?

PORTER: They're willing to offer
our shareholders an extra five pence.
So it looks like they'll take us over.

GILLICK: I see. But I wonder if
they've got any idea what they're going
to take over?

PORTER AND GILLICK LOOK AT EACH OTHER –
AND SMILE.

4. INT. DESPATCH OFFICE.   DAY.

SCRUFFY. FROM OFF WE HEAR MACHINERY,
LORRIES. JOHN, IN TOPCOAT, IS TALKING
WITH THE MANAGER, MARSHALL, WHO HAS ON
A BROWN OVERALL.

MARSHALL: We can't deliver if we
haven't got the stocks.

JOHN: What's the root of the
problem.

MARSHALL: Head office.

JOHN: You mind if I take a look
round?

        21

```
MARSHALL:        Want to catch the lads
playing pontoon?

JOHN:            I hope not.

MARSHALL:        Be my guest.

THEY GET UP TO GO.

JOHN:            With you out of here,
what happens if that phone rings?

MARSHALL:        There's an extension to
a girl in the next office.  You'd know if
you dropped down here sometimes.  Okey?

JOHN:            Yes.  Okey.

MARSHALL:        After you, then, squire.

THEY EXIT.
```

Note how John was bridged from scene to scene. At the end of
Scene 1 we held on Mary, which gave John time to get behind his desk
for Scene 2. There was nothing to hold on at the end of Scene 2, so we
opened with a close shot of Gillick talking, not widening the shot until
John had had time to enter the set and sit down. At the end of Scene 3,
we got John out early and continued the scene with Gillick and Porter,
again giving John time to get into the next set.

Note, too, that all the bridges related to plot or to character. Mary's
letter must be important to the story. So must Mr Gillick's loqua-
ciousness.

Of course fewer problems are presented if you construct your play
so that characters do not have to appear in one scene after another.
We could have opened with John and Mary in their kitchen, then
gone to Gillick and Porter having their talk about the take-over; and

then we might have gone to John's office where he is dictating to Kate, and his being summoned on the phone to Gillick's office. There is usually more than one way to tell a story, and the television writer must think of the way which will work best within the technical limitations of the medium.

As was explained earlier, bridging is not nowadays a necessity on most major drama productions owing to the ease of tape editing. With editing, we could cut Scene 2 with John taking Mr Gillick's phone call, and go straight to John sitting facing Mr Gillick in Scene 3. In this way, we could give the production greater pace (pace is one of the most distinctive characteristics of TV/film compared with tape productions). But it would mean stopping the tape at the end of Scene 2, and setting up (i.e. getting John and Gillick in position, etc.) Scene 3 before starting again. Some directors prefer a great many stops and starts, believing they get a technical production almost as good as the movies. Others favour large chunks of continuous action (not necessarily the entire play, but groups of scenes in sequence) believing they get better, more realistic, performances from their actors. There is also the time factor. Depending on the length of the play, a director and cast will spend six to ten days rehearsing in rehearsal rooms where the walls of their sets-to-be are marked on the floor with coloured sticky tape, and all the props are make-do; this will be followed by one or two days of technical rehearsals in the studio with their real sets and props, and with the cameras. If it is a one-hour (really 50 minutes) play, perhaps only the final three hours of studio time will be allocated for the actual recording. If the director has too many tape pauses in his production schedule, those three hours of valuable studio time can slip through his fingers like sand. Union rules are strictly adhered to, and if the production over-runs its agreed stopping time, a great deal of overtime money may have to be paid out; there is that factor, plus the need of the scene shifters to clear the studio of one lot of sets in order to build sets for another show that will be produced tomorrow. So fairly long sequences of potentially continuous action are favoured by some directors in preference to too many tape pauses, not only for artistic reasons explained above but also for these practical considerations. When you are writing for electronic television, don't run away with the idea that you are writing for the movies. You will see now why the lock up speed of a VTR machine was explained to you. Each time the tape is stopped it has to be started again—and that's 15 seconds of studio time while everyone waits for the phone call from the VTR engineers to say that the machine is now rolling again. Additionally, if there are too many re-takes (recording the same scene again) because the actors can't remember difficult speeches, or a prop gun fails to fire, or a suitcase lid that should open gets jammed, or a camerman fails to get exact focus, or someone in the studio coughs, then they can run out of tape; and it can take up to 20 minutes for a new tape to be wound onto the machine allocated for the production. No doubt all this will change during the lifetime of this book, but it hasn't changed yet. The lesson for you as a television writer is to keep it simple. What 'simple' means will become more apparent as you read through this book.

With some producing organisations there is nowadays a system called rehearse-and-record. The cast still have their six to ten days in the rehearsal room, but the difference lies in the use of the two days in the studio. With normal productions, the first day and a half in studio are spent with the cast running through the play and the cameramen learning to get them in shot for their various moves and speeches (i.e. technical rehearsals), followed at the end of the second day by the coalescence of both cast and cameras into the video tape recording. With the rehearse-and-record system each scene is dealt with separately, and not necessarily in story sequence. When the combined work of both cast and cameras is perfected with a particular scene, that scene is then recorded on tape, and work starts on the next scene.

Whether a show is produced truly live, or with edited tape, or by the rehearse-and-record system, it is all very difficult, and there are a frightening number of things that can go wrong. It is up to you, as the writer, to help things to go right by providing the team with a script that, while using all the resources that are available, doesn't overstrain them.

Chapter 3

SOME LIMITATIONS

Frank Muir and Denis Norden once made an amusing film to explain the differences between writing for television and writing for the cinema screen. They started by showing a 'clip' (short piece of film) from the cinema epic *Zulu*, in which thousands of Zulus attacked some score of Welsh guardsmen. Real artillary fired cannon balls, spears were seen to pierce Welsh chests, blood flowed everywhere, and hundreds of men were shown in mortal combat. It was one of the big production moments from the film, and must have cost the producer tens of thousands of pounds. Muir and Norden then showed how that moment would be presented in a television production. The film cut to Lance Percival and Roy Kinnear, both in soldiers uniforms with pith helmets, inside a very small tent. Kinnear was peeping out through a slit in the tent wall. He said: "There's ten thousand Zulus out there, wave after wave of them." Percival just put his head in his hands and moaned, "I can't look! I can't look!"

Huge sums of money can be spent on a major motion picture because everyone who sees it is going to spend quite a bit of money to have the pleasure. Television production has to exist on licence fees and advertising revenue, and although these amount to millions of pounds the money has to be spread over a fantastic number of transmission hours per year. Thinking economically is an integral part of the television writer's craft.

The income cake has to be cut many different ways. As well as drama there are sport, chat shows, the news, weather forecasts, documentaries, schools, and a great deal more. Each department of a television organisation must have its annual share. Then, within each department, the share has to be broken down into quarters of the year or into series of programmes. Finally each programme gets its share, and by now you really have come down to the crumbs. So a drama producer about to produce one one-hour play knows that he has only so much money to spend, and no more.

Each set in a play costs money to design and build; therefore every set must be important in storytelling terms. In the script example on page 18, it would have been a great temptation to the writer to show Mary finding two letters on the mat in the hall, and hiding one in her pocket. However, the writer knew that he had no further story-use for the hall, so he held the camera on John in the kitchen and gave him a little bit of 'business' with the toast to cover Mary's absence ('business' means almost any kind of activity, such as setting a table, pouring drinks, loading a rifle; not to be confused with a 'move', which means the actor moves himself from one part of the set to another, or makes an entrance or exit).

With sets it is important to get good value for money. If you want the main reception room of an embassy, with expensive draped curtains, chandeliers, a marble mantelpiece, and sufficient space for ten couples to waltz, this may be all very agreeable to your producer provided you make real story-use of it. What *not* to do is to use it for only five seconds while the butler enters, finds the missing pair of gloves, and exits. If you want a ballroom, then have a ball. But better if the set is also used for the assassination of the archduke, the return of the round-the-world voyager, the prelude to the adultery between the ambassador's wife and the first secretary, and the plotting of the war between Bosnia and Serbia.

For a one hour play, restrict yourself to not more than five main sets plus three or four 'cornerpieces' (a small section of corridor, a telephone kiosk against a brickwork drop, or some other very small acting area). When you remember that some of the best stage drama has been contained within a single set, the use of four or five sets is not ungenerous. The actual nature of your sets can seriously affect the budget. Television studios have store rooms full of contemporary furniture and props. But once you embark on foreign-looking interiors, 'period' homes, or futuristic control rooms, costs soar because things may have to be made or bought specially for the one production and probably can't be used again. ('Period' means any time in the past).

Consider costumes. Most television plays depict contemporary times. So, most of the actors and actresses wear their own clothes. But the moment the script calls for clothes of another period in history, the production organisation has to supply these, and that is going to eat into the budget; the clothes must either be made or hired. Even contemporary uniforms can be costly. Uniforms for policemen, nurses, railway porters, and some soldiers will be no problem because the studio will have these in store. But prison uniforms could cost a lot to have made (solution: set your scene, if possible, in the remand wing where prisoners wear their own clothes). It would also be costly to have a number of people dressed as coastguards, or beefeaters, or in the habit of a particular order of nuns.

Actors cost money. It is part of the television writer's craft to create stories which can be told through a minimum number of characters. For a one hour play, try to keep down the number of main speaking parts to eight or fewer, plus half a dozen lesser roles. Don't forget that some of the finest drama has used very few actors. It's what they *say* that counts, not how many there are of them. It is also important *how* they say it, and acting ability varies enormously from one member of that profession to another. So do their fees. No matter how well you have written your play, the newspaper critics and the public will judge it by the overall production, and if mediocre actors cannot do justice to your lines your play will suffer. It is far better if you conceive a story with very few characters, so that the producer will have plenty of money available to hire the best talent he can find. Actor's Equity, the actors' trade union, has agreements with both the BBC and the ITV Contractors about minimum rates of pay; these minima require certain definitions regarding the actors' roles. There is little point in quoting actual money earnings here because with rising costs any figures given in this book are likely to become out of date fairly soon. But it is good for you to understand these categories, so that you will not unnecessarily upgrade what might be an 'extra' to a 'walk-on', or a 'walk-on' to an 'actor'.

Actors Performers with or without lines who are involved in the development of the story.

Walk-ons A walk-on is an identified non-speaking performer who at the precise time that his movements are recorded has a direct acting relationship with an actor who is simultaneously performing his part as set out in the script. A walk-on may also perform individually in a special function peculiar only to the trade he is supposed to represent, e.g. a bus conductor collecting fares; a policeman on point duty; a bartender serving drinks. Walk-ons may say a few *unscripted* words germane to what they, or other people, are doing, at the request and discretion of the director. Therefore a bus conductor could say "All fares, please", or a policeman might say, "Move along there", but *such dialogue must not appear in the script.*

Extras A person or a member of a group contributing to the overall authenticity and atmosphere of the scene (e.g. drinkers in the bar, diners in a restaurant). They may be dressed in clothing identifiable with a particular trade or calling (e.g. chorus girls, soldiers). Extras can be used for community singing, provided it is a well-known song or hymn so that the words do not have to be specially learned.

To anyone outside the profession, those definitions must read like a fiendish trade union conspiracy to impose restrictive practices on the arts. But actors, like writers, must eat and pay rent—otherwise they would not be available as and when we want them to act for us. Those definitions all relate to labour time. An actor in a teleplay will be required to attend rehearsals every day for a week or more. But a walk-on may only be called in for the last two days of the rehearsal period, because he has so little to learn. Extras are usually only called in for the day of the recording, and therefore their earnings are comparatively small.

The number of sets and the number of characters are not the only restrictions to consider. There are also 'special talents', babies and small children, and animals. 'Special talents' can mean an actor's ability to swim, sing, play the piano, speak a foreign language fluently, use a typewriter properly, and so on. If it is essential that a character should have a certain special talent, the director will of course find someone who can do what is required. But don't expect too much, and never casually throw into your 'stage directions' that your leading lady is found doing a Yoga exercise which involves standing on her head, or that your leading man is entertaining waifs at the annual Christmas party with his sword swallowing act. ('Stage directions': your scripted description of the set, and the actors' moves and business).

Don't expect babies to act. On the advertising commercials you may have seen a baby react to a particular baby food by giving a beautiful smile. But the director and his crew, and the patient actress playing the mother role, may have had to wait days for that smile. It is good business if the smile sells a million cans of mush, but the cost is enormous. The economics of commercials production are entirely different from those for television drama. Small children are a little easier than babies, in that they can understand what is expected of them. Whether they can do it or not is another matter. Child actors often give excellent performances on the stage; but there it doesn't matter too much if they deliver their lines from a slightly different position from one performance to another. In a television production, where each line must be picked up both by the camera and the microphone above, it is critical that the actor be within three inches of where the technicians expect him to be.

Animals are a problem. Dogs can be trained to perform simple feats, but cats never. The best you can hope for is to have a cat held in the arms of one of the human characters, or for the dog to be stretched out asleep in front of an electrical imitation coal fire. (Never a real coal fire, please. Where will the smoke go in the television studio?) In both instances, the animals would first be sedated by a veterinary surgeon specially called in. All these represent extra cost as well as additional problems for an already harrassed director.

Every art medium has its limitations, and television has its fair share. The only sensible psychological approach is surely to accept the limitations, and then to make the very best of them. These are far fewer than the limitations set on the stage playwright, and people have been successfully writing for the stage for hundreds of years. In fact, first-rate drama can sometimes spring from the limitations themselves. Many years ago that eminent writer Willis Hall was asked by the Oxford University Theatre Group to write a play for them. As soon as he had agreed, they broke the news to him that since they had no ladies in their group, all his characters would have to be male. Being a good writer, he saw no problem in that. They then went on to tell him that owing to the shape and size of their stage, once the actors had made their entrances, it would be awkward for them to make any exits before the final curtain. And finally, of course, there could only be one set, and that should be as simple as possible. Faced with all that, Willis Hall promptly sat down and wrote a full-length stage play about a group of soldiers trapped in a jungle hut during the war with the Japanese. He called it *The Long, And the Short, And the Tall*. Deservedly he must have made a fortune from the many professional theatrical productions of that play all over the world, and the film that eventually followed.

Chapter 4

TAKING THE CAMERAS OUTSIDE

Having discussed studio limitations, let us now look at the reverse side of the coin. In the early days of television, everything was produced in the studios: street scenes, back gardens, scenes on flat roofs, even supposed open countryside. The results were usually terrible, but the audiences accepted them. Then came the use of film, OB, and telecine. Cameras could be taken outside.

When an 'OB sequence' (outside broadcast sequence) is to be made, an 'OB unit' (camera, crew, etc) is sent to the desired 'location' (venue). The OB unit will consist of three or four television cameras plus a 'mobile scanner', which is a pint-sized director's control room (see page 15) on wheels. You may have seen them lurking in an elephantine way behind the stands at television football matches—a vehicle about the size of a furniture van with 'BBC' or 'Yorkshire Television' printed along both sides. The unit's television cameras are all linked to the mobile scanner by very long cables; monitor screens inside the scanner show the director exactly what the cameras are looking at. As in the studio control room, he can select the sequence of visuals he wishes to go on output. The output signal is transmitted from the scanner back to the home-base television station; from there, in the case of a horse race or other live programme, it is fed into the domestic network and transmitted to viewers, or in the case of drama it is recorded onto video tape. Later, back at the studio the drama director will select the shots to be interpolated into the studio production of the play. The advantage of an OB unit is that with three or four cameras all looking at the scene from different angles, the director can do all his cuts from one visual image to another (two shot, close up, long shot, or what-have-you) in one go. The disadvantage is that television cameras can be awkward and heavy to move around, those cables are vulnerable, and a lot of technical things can go wrong.

Film on location can be simpler. A 16mm cine camera can sit comfortably on the camerman's shoulder, and the sound unit is little more than a tape-recorder on a shoulder strap. But there are some disadvantages. If only one camera is used (and that is usual with film) each scene must be played out again and again so that it may be shot from different angles. The OB director makes up his interesting sequence of visuals by selecting from his four monitor screens; the film director makes his selection from hundreds of feet of film back in the studio's cutting room. Whereas the OB director can see on his output screen exactly what is being recorded on the video tape, the film director does not know exactly what he has got until the film has been processed at the laboratories. For this reason film directors will always shoot and double shoot from the same 'set up' (positioning of the camera) before moving on to shoot the scene again from the next set up.

No matter how good the filming, one can always detect a film insert in a tape production because the picture quality is different. However, the Monoculus OB unit is on the way—one very lightweight television camera working from a small van. This gives almost the same flexibility as film, and the outdoor inserts are then of compatible texture and quality with the studio taped material.

Fortunately none of these technical problems directly concerns you, although this glimpse into location problems may make you more understanding when your script editor asks if you can cut down on the exterior scenes. What does concern you is how to make the best use of the exterior scenes that you are allowed to have.

Dialogue can be a problem. If the scene depicts Abraham Lincoln delivering his Gettysburg address and the location is a bit of waste land, the camera (film) or cameras (OB) can be so angled as to avoid including in the shot the near by electricity pylon and the signs pointing the way to the car park. But if, on opening his mouth, Mr Lincoln's immortal words are drowned by the roar of a 747 passing overhead, the scene will be ruined. One solution is to 'post-sync' (post-synchronise), which means the scene is played out regardless of jets, traffic, and Toni Bell the ice cream man; then later, when the film is assembled, the actors go into a special studio and say their lines again, trying to match their own lip movements. This is done a good deal in great-outdoors cinema epics, but it all takes additional costly time for both actors and technicians. So, try to keep down the amount of dialogue to be spoken on location.

There can be special problems with period plays on location. You can find stretches of countryside which haven't changed in appearance since Henry VIII. In some towns, you may still find complete Georgian and Victorian streets of houses. But you will also find the parked car. Even if you can persuade a whole street of motorists to park somewhere else for a day, you are left with parking meters, yellow lines, white lines, and 'Give Way' signs. True, you may know of a gem of a little side street innocent of all modern street furniture or road surface doodles, in Fort William or Penzance. But can a television budget afford sending an entire OB unit or film crew plus actors to the Highlands or Land's End for a few minutes of playing time? To be reasonable, restrict your urban exteriors to the present day as much as possible. If the play is period, set your exteriors in the countryside, with a minimum of dialogue.

In this country, the six-part serial remains popular on television. A serial will have at least one, but more probably three or four, characters who appear in every episode, and these will be the leads. Additionally, there may be twenty or thirty minor actors, walk-ons and extras, most of them appearing in only some of the episodes. For organisational reasons, to do with pressures on studio time available, all the location inserts will be shot some weeks before the serial goes into rehearsals and recordings. For thirty minute episodes, when the home base work starts they will usually rehearse in rehearsal rooms for five days, go into a studio for technical rehearsals and the actual VTR on the sixth day, rest on the seventh, and the next day return to the rehearsal rooms for the next episode, taking in all six weeks to put the six episodes 'in the can' (recorded). If, therefore, the script for Episode 6 requires that a new character, whom we are only seeing for the first time in this episode, should run along a street and go into a house (location), and then must be seen entering a room in that house (studio), the producer will have to pay the actor a retainer fee for all the weeks between the location work and the commencement of rehearsals, and for the five weeks during which Episodes 1 to 5 are rehearsed and recorded. The same principle would apply albeit not so expensively, if there is a character only seen in Episode 1 and Episode 6: they must be paid a retainer to cover Episodes 2 to 5. It is up to you, as the writer, to think of ways round this problem. For instance, let us say that in Episode 1 your hero has to call on his solicitor's office, where he is greeted by his solicitor's secretary.

During the following four episodes the solicitor may feature in the story but always away from his office (seeing the hero in his home, or in his own home, or at the local pub). However, in Episode 6 the plot requires the hero to return to the solicitor's office. If the same secretary is there to greet him, the actress will have to be paid a retainer for Episodes 2 to 5 when she did not appear. So this time, the hero finds a different secretary, and he asks "What happened to Miss Brown?" The new girl says, "She's on holiday. I'm a temporary." Those few golden words can save your producer a great deal of money, which he can spend in other ways that will enhance the production of your serial.

A word in defence of the actor's retainer. If our running man has to be on location in early May, but won't do his studio preformance until the end of June, he may have to turn down other work in order to keep himself available. The retainer is by no means a full performance fee, but week after week it may just keep him in bread until the moment when, hot and panting, he is seen in studio running into that room.

Two ways have evolved for denoting OB tape or film in television scripts, one favoured by the BBC, the other more usual among the ITV Contractors. Picking up from the last few lines of our example script, this is what would happen in ITV script layout when John and Marshall leave the despatch office.

```
               THEY GET UP TO GO.

               JOHN:          With you out of here,
               what happens if that phone rings?

               MARSHALL:      There's an extension to
               a girl in the next office.  You'd know if
               you dropped down here sometimes.  Okey?

               JOHN:          Yes.  Okey.

               MARSHALL:      After you, then, squire.

               THEY EXIT.


               5.  EXT.  WORKS YARD.  (FILM).      DAY.


               PACKING CASES, MAYBE A FORK LIFT, NOISE.
               JOHN AND MARSHALL COME OUT OF THE DESPATCH
               OFFICE HUT.
```

MARSHALL: Where do you want to
start?

JOHN: Where do you do the
loading?

MARSHALL: We've hardly got anything
to load.

JOHN: If you had anything to
load, where would you do it from?

MARSHALL: This way —

MARSHALL STARTS TO LEAD OFF, BUT DAWSON,
A WORKER, COMES UP TO HIM.

DAWSON: You seen this?

DAWSON SHOWS MARSHALL SOME DESPATCH NOTES.
MARSHALL LOOKS.

MARSHALL: Well?

DAWSON: It lists all these things.
But we haven't got any. Clean out.

MARSHALL: I'll talk to you later.

MARSHALL WALKS OFF. JOHN FOLLOWS. HOLD
ON DAWSON AS HE SHRUGS, THEN WALKS OFF
BACK THE WAY HE CAME.

6. EXT. WORKS YARD: LOADING AREA. (FILM).
    DAY.

A LORRY, BACK END OPEN. ONE OR TWO
PACKING CASES. MARSHALL AND JOHN COME
ALONG. MARSHALL STOPS.

MARSHALL: Loading bay.

JOHN LOOKS ROUND, THEN TO MARSHALL.

JOHN: You've lost heart,
haven't you?

MARSHALL: There's nothing for me
to show you here, Mr Morgan. Why don't
you just take a look round for yourself,
then toddle off back to head office?
Okey?

WITHOUT WAITING FOR AN ANSWER, MARSHALL
WALKS OFF. JOHN SIGHS, THEN TAKES A
CURSORY LOOK ROUND.

7. INT. DESPATCH OFFICE.   DAY.

```
SANDRA IS MAKING TEA.  A PACKET OF
SANDWICHES ON MARSHALL'S DESK.  MARSHALL
ENTERS.

SANDRA:          I got your sandwiches.

MARSHALL:        Thanks.

SANDRA:          Who was that fellow, then?

MARSHALL SLUMPS INTO HIS CHAIR.

MARSHALL:        Head office.

SANDRA:          Oh, them.  Cheer up.

MARSHALL:        Yeh.  Cheer up.
```

As you see, ITV's general script layout style is fairly simple. All the scenes, be they for studio or film, are numbered consecutively. The BBC's script layout is much more complex.

```
                 (THEY GET UP TO GO)

JOHN:            With you out of here,
what happens if that phone rings?

MARSHALL:        There's an extension to
a girl in the next office.  You'd know if
you dropped down here sometimes.  Okey?

JOHN:            Yes.  Okey.

MARSHALL:        After you, then, squire.

                 (THEY EXIT)

TELECINE 1

Works Yard.  Day.

Packing cases, maybe a fork
lift.  JOHN and MARSHALL come
out of the despatch office
hut.
                              SOUND:           Works yard noises.

                              MARSHALL:        Where do you want to
                              start?

                              JOHN:            Where do you do the
                              loading?

                              MARSHALL:        We've hardly got anything
                              to load.

                              JOHN:            If you had anything to
                              load, where would you do it from?
```

	MARSHALL:	This way –

MARSHALL starts to lead off,
but DAWSON, a worker, comes
up to him.

DAWSON: You seen this?

DAWSON shows MARSHALL some
despatch notes. MARSHALL looks.

MARSHALL: Well?

DAWSON: It lists all these things.
But we haven't got any. Clean out.

MARSHALL: I'll talk to you later.

MARSHALL walks off. JOHN
follows. HOLD on DAWSON as he
shrugs, then walks off back the
way he came.

Works Yard: Loading Area. Day.

A lorry, back end open. One or
two packing cases. MARSHALL and
JOHN come along. MARSHALL stops.

MARSHALL: Loading bay.

JOHN looks round, then turns
to MARSHALL.

JOHN: You've lost heart,
haven't you?

MARSHALL: There's nothing for me
to show you here, Mr Morgan. Why don't
you just take a look round for yourself,
then toddle off back to head office?
Okey?

Without waiting for an answer,
MARSHALL walks off. JOHN sighs,
then takes a cursory look round.

5. INT. DESPATCH OFFICE.   DAY.

(SANDRA IS MAKING TEA. A
PACKET OF SANDWICHES ON
MARSHALL'S DESK. MARSHALL
ENTERS.)

SANDRA: I got your sandwiches.

MARSHALL: Thanks.

SANDRA: Who was that fellow, then?

36

```
                    (MARSHALL SLUMPS INTO HIS
                    CHAIR.)

        MARSHALL:        Head office.

        SANDRA:          Oh, them.  Cheer up.

        MARSHALL:        Yeh.  Cheer up.
```

First we must understand the meaning of 'telecine' (abbreviated to T/C or sometimes, rather quaintly, to T/K). Telecine refers to the department which is responsible for running through the OB tape or celluloid film which was shot on location prior to the studio production. If one clip is immediately followed by another, as happened in our example (*Works Yard* was followed by *Works Yard: Loading Area*) the two will be joined together, and the combined clip will be given one telecine number. The number is so that the telecine technicians will know in which order to run their clips during the production. So any number of telecine scenes can come under the same T/C number provided they are running consecutively. The studio scenes retain their own independent numbering. Also note how once you go into telecine with a BBC script all the stage directions go to the left, but the dialogue and sounds effects (SOUND, SFX, or FX) go on the right.

Much of this chapter may seem to discourage you from including open air scenes in your play. Well, it's not a bad thing to remember that basically electronic television is an indoor sport. But outside shooting there can be, and the question is—how much? All the producing organisations have made immense financial investments in building and equipping electronic studios, so obviously they are going to want their money's worth. But they also know that some outside shooting, where appropriate, will enliven the finished product. The thing to do for you as a writer is always to ask how much outside work you can include in your script.

Whenever you write exterior sequences, keep them simple. If you want one car to shunt into another, write in a 'cut away' (quick shot to something else) to an 'angle character' (see page 63) who happens to be watching, and let the sound of impact be heard on sound effects. Then cut back to the two cars with fenders entwined, which could be faked by technicians without actually damaging the cars. If you want a helicopter to explode in flight, first let it disappear behind a hill or high trees, then let the audience hear the explosion and see the smoke and flames (easily faked: see page 48).

There can be problems about characters moving and talking. Say you want two characters to be cycling home from work and chatting. A film camera would have to be mounted on the top of a car or van which would drive slowly along just ahead of the cyclists. Perhaps for technical, insurance, or trade union reasons, a special vehicle will have to be hired with its own driver. All that might work, but how is the dialogue to be picked up? Microphones have to be quite close to pick up the actors' speech and *not* to pick up too much of everything else (traffic, jets, wind). Well, we already know that the director would have to post-sync the sound: it's all additional time and money. The simple way is to have your cyclists stop for their discussion. Open the scene with a few moments of their cycling along. Then they come to an intersection where they both go their different ways. It is natural now for them to pause to say goodbye, and here they can play out their scene. With the two actors stationary, the director can set up his camera and get his microphone in close.

Artistically what is the justification for withholding your characters' important lines of dialogue until it is technically convenient for them to be delivered? This is where your craft ingenuity comes into play. You must cover the technical-limitation problem with something that seems germane to the plot and/or the characters. In this example, you might get round the problem along these lines:

TELECINE 1

Country Road. Day.

MARK and ROY are cycling home
from work.

Country crossroads. Day.

MARK and ROY come along on their
bicycles. Both stop. From the
way they stop, we gather this is
an everyday parting point.

MARK:	Well, see you tomorrow.
ROY:	Yes.

MARK is about to cycle off in
his particular direction. ROY
doesn't move.

ROY:	Hold on.
MARK:	What is it?
ROY:	Something I've been
meaning to ask you.	

38

And so we go into the scene. There is another way of doing dialogue in motion, and that is known as 'voice over'. You have your characters in long shot, but their voices in close up. The script would read like this:

```
TELECINE 1

Country Road.  Day.

Long shot of MARK and ROY
cycling home from work.
                              ROY:          (CLOSE ON MIKE)  There's
                              something I've been meaning to ask you.

                              MARK:         (CLOSE ON MIKE)  What's
                              that?

                              ROY:              It's something Jane said
                              the other night, about you and Dorothy.
```

For this, the director would make sure that the two actors were too far away from the camera for anyone to see clearly whether or not their lips were moving. The dialogue would be 'dubbed on' to the film sometime later, but that is no problem if the actors don't have to match their lip movements. This convention can be very effective and has been accepted by audiences. But don't introduce new characters like this. The audience must meet them first in a normal scene, so that they get to know their voices and the things they talk about. If this were the first time Mark and Roy had appeared in the play, the audience would be confused.

Night location shooting can be extraordinarily expensive. The director has to take along huge arc lights, plus mobile generators to make the electricity for them. All the technicians will be working at overtime pay rates. Sequences are sometimes shot at night, but it is a good plan to get agreement to this from your script editor and producer before you go ahead and write them. There is a cheap way round the problem, known as 'day-for-night' shooting. They fix the camera so that it takes a dull picture. If there is a car involved, it always has its lights on to further the illusion. If the director does it well, the audience may be fooled into believing that the scene is taking place in brilliant moonlight, but sometimes even that takes a stretch of the imagination.

One tends to think of film and OB as the only ways to take a story outside the confines of studio interiors—the living-rooms, offices, hospital wards, pubs, and prison cells that give so much of television drama its often claustrophobic effect. But there are other ways of taking the story outside without ever leaving the studio. We shall now take a look at them.

Chapter 5

TRICKS

A British television director visiting a German television control room would feel very much at home. There are the four or more monitor screens, and the big screen for Output. There is the console with its clusters of switches and push buttons. Unless he understands German, he may find the labels a little confusing. Instead of 'Camera 1' the label next to the appropriate switch will read 'Kanal 1'. But one word he will certainly understand. In place of our rather technical term 'Inlay' he will see one set of controls simply labelled 'Tricks'.

There is a great deal of trickery in television production, almost all of it conceived to overcome the inherent restrictions of the medium and to bring down costs. It isn't really essential for the writer to know every technical device that can be used, and it can even be rather irritating to a director to find in the writer's script advice on how this or that scene can and should be shot. But since we have dealt so much on the limitations, it is only fair to tell you about some of the things that *can* be done.

Let us start by understanding what 'Inlay' means. It is the electronic equivalent of a 'matte mask' in films, so we shall take one step further back and begin there. As you already know, taking the camera and cast out on location can be very expensive. Additionally, we British have an unreliable climate and a number of months every year that are likely to be atrocious. So there are many reasons why a film director might choose to shoot a supposedly open-air scene in the studio. This is quite simple if the scene is to be played out against a background of buildings: the fronts of buildings can be erected in the studio, and a wind machine to ruffle the actors' hair a little, plus a 'wild track' of background open-air sounds, can complete the illusion. Most of the scenes can be shot in close shot, so that there is no need to see the

Fig 1

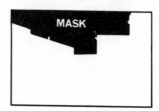

Fig 2

Fig 3

Fig 4

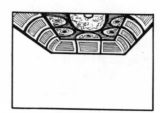

Fig 5

Fig 6

Fig 7

Fig 8

non-existent sky and moving clouds. But in order thoroughly to deceive the audience, there must be at least one establishing shot at the beginning of the scene which does show the sky and moving clouds in relation to the studio sets. How is this done?

In Fig. 1 you see the set as built in the studio. Over the roofs of the buildings (all studio sets) you can see the studio walls, lights and so on. The director takes his establishing shot of this, making sure that the actor walking across the set does not poke his head above the upper limit of the studio set. The film is then developed, but the print is not made yet. Working with one frame from the negative, the matting expert now cuts a little mask which exactly follows the contour of the skyline (see Fig. 2). So as not to make his job impossible, the set was designed with a skyline composed of fairly straight lines, not 'woolly' tree tops. This little mask is then put into the optical printer, so that when the developed film is printed only the unmasked part will come out onto the print, leaving the masked part virgin. Meantime the director has some 'stock film' of a beautiful blue sky with moving clouds. (Special film libraries, which service the whole industry, have clips of 'stock shots' of open country, planes taking off and landing, traffic in busy streets, castles on the Rhine, or almost anything else a producer may need). Now the matting expert makes a mask which is complementary to his first one (see Fig. 3). The incompleted positive (i.e. showing the buildings) is then run through the optical printer, with the buildings masked over by the complementary mask, while at the same time the negative of the blue sky is run through; the result is that the blue sky is now printed onto the original positive in the unmasked area. As we see in Fig. 4 the two pictures have been butted together onto the same film print.

The electronic equivalent is what we call inlay, and it is intrinsic to the difference between the two media of film and electronic TV that all the processes of inlay are done at the same time. There is no pause while film goes to the laboratories for part processing and little masks are cut: in television, all the trickery has to be simultaneous. For our television example, let's say that the television director is going to shoot the ball in that embassy main reception room, the one with the draped curtains and marble mantelpiece. To get a shot of all the couples dancing, the director must pull his camera a long way back, and that means that the camera is also going to shoot over the top of the studio set walls revealing where the ceiling should be and showing us the studio gantries, lights, etc (Fig. 5). They cannot build a real

43

ceiling over the set, because that would stop the studio lights from shining down onto the actors. So the director must cheat-in a ceiling. For this he has an artist prepare a painting of the ceiling as it would be seen from the point of view of the No. 1 camera (see Fig. 6). This painting can be quite small compared with the size of the actual set, but when it is looked at by Camera 2 in close shot it will appear to be in proportion to the set. The intention now is to combine the electronic picture outputs from Cameras 1 and 2, *without* including the studio wall and lights in the top part of the picture coming from Camera 1 (see again Fig. 5). To do this the television director uses the 'portable inlay desk'. This is a gadget which includes a small television camera that looks at a white screen. Onto this screen can be placed black masks—in our case, a mask as shown in Fig. 7. The output of the inlay camera controls an electronic switch. Where the inlay camera sees white, it will switch in the output of Camera 1 (the set), and where the inlay camera sees black it will switch in the output of Camera 2 (the close shot of the small painting of the ceiling), thus producing the combined picture in Fig. 8.

Inlay is an extremely useful device for certain circumstances, such as the ceiling that must be seen but cannot really exist. The one snag with inlay is that if an actor gets into the masked area he will disappear. However, there are times when this can be used to advantage. Say that we have that well-known science fiction theme where the mad professor miniaturises some unfortunate people. In our case as an added refinement the professor keeps his midget victims in a dolls house. We would certainly have a scene in the professor's laboratory where we would see the dolls house standing on a shelf. This shot could be improved enormously if we could see a real little man or woman opening a window and peering out. This could easily be done by cutting a mask exactly to the outline of the dolls house window and inlaying into it a real window plus actor. When he turned away in despair he would disappear behind the dolls house wall, because he had in fact disappeared behind the mask.

Time after time a director wants to place actors against a background which is impracticable in studio terms. One way to do this is with 'back projection' (BP). For back projection the director sets up a film projector on the studio floor, and this throws its film onto a transluscent screen. The actors play out their scene on the other side of the screen, and beyond them are the television cameras seeing both the actors and the moving film. This works very well, but it takes up a considerable amount of studio space and the area of action is extremely limited. An attempt was made to overcome this by the development of 'overlay', which like inlay uses the principle of electronic switching between black and white. A figure dressed in light clothes, positioned against a black back drop, could be transposed to the background of the director's choice. The snag of this is that any deep shadow on the foreground figure 'reads' to the electronic switch as black and brings in the chosen background. So if you had a ballerina dancing, the shadow of her skirt would be enough for the background to be switched in at that point. Result: legs not connected to the body.

Since the advent of colour, this problem with overlay has disappeared completely. This is through the development of Colour Separation Overlay (CSO) as it is known in BBC circles, or Chroma Key as it is known throughout commercial television. It is perhaps the biggest technical development in television in recent years. In general terms, instead of the electronic switch being actuated by the separation between light and dark, which elements appear in every picture, it responds to a particular colour. Taking our ballerina for instance, instead of dancing against a black back drop she would now dance against a back drop of rich deep blue. This blue produces a very strong signal, and the strength of that signal actuates the electronic switch to bring in the background which is being seen by another camera. Of course she must not wear a blue dress, for if she did her dress would disappear (No, it wouldn't be like strip-tease: none of the dress part of her would appear at all—she would be just head, arms, and legs). Any very strong colour can be used instead of blue, but blue is normally chosen because it is a colour not often in the foreground and is not in the flesh tones.

Although CSO can be used for faking-in backgrounds, it seems to work best when you want to have a framed view *through* something such as a window, the mouth of a cave (looking from inside the cave outwards), or an open doorway. What's more, the secondary or overlayed picture does not necessarily have to come from a studio camera. It may come from a telecine machine and is therefore a film or a strip of pre-recorded video tape. Thus you could get a view of Niagara Falls (film) seen from a bedroom window in a London suburb. CSO would be used when the director wanted to show us inside that dolls house. We would see 'inside' by having a camera looking into a normal size three wall set. Behind the window, however, there would be a blue back drop. Meanwhile, another camera would be looking into the laboratory set from the 'POV' (point of view) of the dolls house. This arrangement would give the effect of a normal size room with normal size people, yet through the window beyond a giant professor wandering about his enormous laboratory.

CSO or BP (studio space permitting) are used when the director wants to shoot a scene between two characters sitting in the back of a supposedly moving motor car. Studios are usually equipped with a fine selection of the backs of cars which have been cut into two for this purpose. By cutting away the whole of the front of the car, leaving only the rear end of the cabin with its seat, the television cameras are unimpeded in their view of the occupants. To achieve naturalism, something must be seen through the rear window of the car, so stock film of city streets or country roads is used. Since the film will indicate that the car is turning corners or halting in traffic, the conscientious director will rehearse his two actors to joggle about when the car is supposedly turning a corner, and to sit still when the car is supposedly stopped at traffic lights. Bearing in mind that the two actors cannot see the moving images behind their heads, their reactions to the supposed movements of the car must be cued to them by hand signals from the floor manager.

Mirrors are often used to give the impression of an up-to-down or a down-to-up POV, and their use can save the expense of actually constructing, say, a first-floor room in a studio. Take a scene in a supposed first-floor bedroom, which is actually a normal three-walled set on the studio floor. The girl in the room reacts on hearing from Off the front door bell ring. Instead of leaving the room to go to answer the front door, she goes to a window, opens it, and looks out and down. We cut now to another camera, which sees her poke her head out of the window and look down—all of three feet down to the blank studio floor just below her. Now we cut to the exterior of the front door, which will be in some other part of the studio, where a man is standing. However, we see him not from normal eye level, but from her POV. This is done by hanging a large mirror from the studio ceiling grid, and by having a floor level camera which looks up at the mirror: thus we get the impression of looking down on the unexpected caller. Reversing the process, we might have another mirror propped at an angle on the floor just below the bedroom window: if a camera looks down into that, we shall get the impression of the man's POV looking upwards at the girl. Some studios are equipped with an additional camera on a crane, so that both camera and cameramen can be raised to a considerable height at the same time being manoeuvred around the studio. But if there is no crane, a lot can be done with the traditional conjuror's device of a mirror.

From his place at the director's console in the control room, the inlay operator can produce a number of remarkable effects just by the touch of a button. He has a selection of 'wipes' from which to choose, some of them very fancy. He can make the screen ripple, useful as a lead-in to a dream sequence or flashback. He can cut from one scene to another by way of an iris, so that the next scene appears in a little disc in centre of the picture of the previous scene and then grows outwards, or by a vertical or a diagonal wipe. He can create a split screen effect, so that the right-hand side of the screen shows one set while the left-hand side shows another (you will have seen that done sometimes in two-way telephone conversations).

However, despite all the wonders of CSO, BP, mirrors, and inlay devices, the true knights of television trickery are those enthusiasts you will find in the special effects department of any sizeable studio. These are the people called in when the director needs to show bank robbers blowing up a safe, a submarine underwater, or a space ship in flight. These are the model-makers, who pride themselves on being able to bend, bash, or crush, and finally paint almost any material to make it look like something else. This is how they would create the illusion of a submarine deep down in the sea:

First, no water is used. An exact replica of a real submarine (to match in with existing film of a surfacing or diving submarine) will be made, and suspended on very fine wires in a perfectly dry studio. Now smoke will be introduced into the studio, and a super-fine powder will be thrown into the smoke to look like the texture of floating plankton. Instead of normal studio arc lights, lights giving a continuous rippling effect will be shone onto the submarine, smoke and so-called floating plankton. To round off, the camera to be used will be fitted with a soft focus so that nothing (particularly those tell-tale suspension wires) will stand out too sharply.

Looking now into Outer Space, how would you show a medium long shot of Venus with its swirling, all-enveloping clouds? It would be simple work for any special effects department to make a model of a planet with virtually no atmosphere, but Venus presumably has a 'living' cloak of clouds. This was once done, most successfully, by double filming. A large ball was covered in glue, then cotton wool was stuck all over it. The ball was then slowly gyrated clockwise and

47

filmed. Then the film was rolled back, and used again while the model Venus was slowly gyrated anti-clockwise. This gave a remarkable impression of swirling mist and clouds.

However, if you want to bring real joy into the heart of any special effects specialist, ask him to make an explosion. Probably the best explosion on British television in recent times was when in the BBC's series *Doctor Who*, in a serial called *The Dæmons*, they blew up a little country church. The church upon which the doomed model was based had been well featured in location filming in the story. At the end, however, it had to be blown sky high. So, with meticulous care, the BBC's Special Effects Department built a model which was an exact replica. Much of the story in the sixth episode of the serial depicted action just around the real church. Then, when the moment came, there was a close up of a character as he looked in horror, then a quick cut to his POV—and now we saw not the actual location church, but for a brief moment a film clip of the model church as an explosive charge totally destroyed it. This was so effective that the British Broadcasting Corporation received a number of letters from viewers angered by the destruction of this fine old country church!

Television special effects require the combined skills and patience of model makers, explosives experts, technicians, actors, and cameramen alike. Above all, there has to be split-second co-ordination between all concerned. There is the show-business story about the big film producer who intended to show ancient Rome go up in flames. At enormous expense, he had a wonderful model of Rome built on a hill. To make triple sure that not a lick of flame or wisp of smoke would be missed, he had three film cameras in position, one at the bottom of the hill, one half way up, and the other at the top. Then, sitting back comfortably in his producer's chair, he called over his megaphone the magic words "Roll 'em!" And then he had his beautiful model of ancient Rome put to flame. The models of the buildings burnt furiously. Finally, when the last embers had blackened to ash, the producer got up and strode over to his first cameraman. "Joey," he said, "you got everything in the can?" Joey mopped his brow: "Boss, something terrible happened. Just as the flames got under way, my camera broke. I couldn't fix it." Without a word, the producer stomped up the hill to his second cameraman: "Mike, you got the burning of Rome okey?" Mike looked terrified: "Boss, you're going to hate me, but I didn't get a single frame. My assistant cameraman forgot to reload the camera." Speechless, the producer climbed on up the hill until he had his third cameraman in view. Then he raised his megaphone and in a voice touched with controlled hysteria he called: "Hymie! O Hymie! This is your producer." And the third cameraman called back down the hill: "Ready when you are, boss!"

For that fabulous moment of destruction of the bridge on the River Kwai, legend has it that the producer had six film cameras taken on location to roll simultaneously. Television cannot afford that level of expense. Instead, everyone in television has to think, work, and co-ordinate just that little bit harder.

Chapter 6

DIALOGUE

Of all forms of fiction writing, television dialogue is the nearest thing to talking directly, face to face, with an individual member of the audience. Radio dialogue is deliberately non-naturalistic, because the radio writer must overcome the fact that the audience cannot see anything. Stage dialogue is structured to allow the actor to develop a rapport with his audience. The cinema can effect the intimacy of television, but the epic designed to play to huge groups of people at a time can afford to have John Wayne looking across a stretch of the Old West and making a long prophetic speech about how one day, after he has shot all the bad men, this land will be settled by decent folks with decent kids who will go to a decent church on Sundays.

As we have all seen from documentaries, good television can simply consist of one person in close up talking about themselves directly into the camera. In a cinema, the audience would be embarrassed. But television is almost a one-to-one relationship: most viewers are watching alone, or with two or three intimate relations or friends. Generally, therefore, of the four drama media—cinema, radio, television, theatre—dialogue for television should be the most naturalistic.

Or so it seems. In fact, if you tape record and then transcribe how people really talk you will find their dialogue is peppered with repetition, very long pauses, tautology, circumlocution, and probably occasional burps. The television writer's task is to write dialogue that *seems* natural, but which doesn't really waste a word. W. S. Gilbert once told an actor, "Sir, I have worked all night to reduce that line to its absolute minimum number of words. Treat each one with care. They are precious." Only a professional would work all night to *delete* what he had already written.

Before writing a word of dialogue, always ask yourself whether any dialogue is necessary at all. Ballet and the theatre of mime both tell stories without words. Often more can be said by a look or a gesture than by a line of a dozen words.

Dialogue should not only state plot facts, but also convey character. While economy is the key to good television dialogue, avoid writing a series of telegrams. Here is a man recounting an incident in the briefest possible way:

```
MAN:          I went into the pub
on the corner of Chaucer Street, as
we'd arranged, at eight o'clock. But
Ronnie didn't arrive until eight
thirty.
```

Here he recounts the same incident, and at the same time tells us something about his attitudes:

```
MAN:          I went into that pub
on the corner of Chaucer Street, the
one they've done up and ruined, sharp
on eight, as we'd arranged. But of
course young Ronnie, just like all
his generation, didn't bother to
show his face until eight thirty.
```

Now we know that the speaker is opposed to modernisation, has a respect for punctuality, is aware of his age, doesn't altogether approve of young people, and through the colloquialism 'didn't bother to show his face' is working class.

Avoid using dialogue for special pleading. If you want to make political or other points, which you have every right to do, let them emerge from the play as a whole. Sam Goldwyn is supposed to have told his writers, "If you want to write messages, use Western Union.' Today's television producers want plays that *say* something, but they don't want it spelt out in one solid wodge of dialogue.

All your characters should have their own distinctive speech patterns and lines of dialogue in your play should not be interchangeable between them. Speech patterns can easily be distinctive if you are playing a middle class character against someone with a working class background. But if all your characters have similar backgrounds, speech mannerisms will help to distinguish them. You might have a character who injects into his speech the term 'By the by', which has colour because most people say 'By the way'; or there are such mannerisms as ending sentences with 'Do you get my drift?' and 'Are you with me?' These are very mechanical approaches, but they can be useful.

Don't add to production problems with awkward dialogue. Avoid lines such as 'A silly sort of situation', or any other systematically sustained sequence of several similar-sounding sibilants. Lines like that can be very difficult for an actor to deliver convincingly. Try not to end two speeches in the same scene with the same or similar words:

```
TED:          We called on every
house on the estate, but we couldn't
sell none of the stuff.

MANAGER:      You really went to
every house?

TED:          Honest.  But there's no
money around.  If you want to know what
I think, we're not going to get rid of
any of the stuff.

MANAGER:      Thank you, but I don't
want to know what you think.
```

Part of the actor's memorising technique is to be motivated by cues. The manager's cue to say 'You really went to every house?' was motivated by Ted's '. . . . none of the stuff'. When Ted then ends a speech with '. . . any of the stuff' it would be only too easy for the manager to be 'thrown' (put off balance, or temporarily mentally deranged) and to forget which of his lines is to follow. Television actors work under a considerable strain, so the fewer problems you create for them the more they can concentrate on giving a good performance.

Let's now extend the manager's last speech and find another possible problem:

```
MANAGER:      I don't want to know
what you think, thank you very much.
But I'll bear it in mind.
```

Try saying '—think, thank—' very quickly and see what happens. In its extended form, that speech could be improved:

```
MANAGER:      I don't want to know
what you think, if you don't mind.
But I'll remember it.
```

52

Most directors and actors prefer the cut and thrust of an exchange of short, sharp sentences between characters. In some series drama, you may even find a rule that no speech shall exceed four lines of typing. But there is a case for the occassional very long speech. Here is a long speech, from the play *The Big Client* by Eric Paice and myself produced some years ago for *Armchair Theatre*. The speaker, an American pharmaceutical tycoon called J. G. Henderson, had already been established in the play by way of third-person reference. By the time we arrived at the big speech, the audience was eager to hear everything that Henderson had to say about himself. The scene took place in a London hotel suite where Henderson had summoned representatives from most of London's biggest advertising agencies. Having handed round the drinks, to show his hail-fellow-well-met face, Henderson mounted a rostrum, put on his sincerity face, and talked:

HENDERSON: Gentlemen, as you know, I have to return to New York tonight. That means I have to decide on my advertising agency within the next few hours.

HE PAUSES AND MAKES AN ALMOST IMPERCEPTIBLE SIGNAL. GRETA HEFFNER, HIS PRIVATE SECRETARY, COMES OVER TO HIM WITH A SILVER TRAY ON WHICH IS A DISPLAY. IN THE MIDDLE OF THE TRAY IS A PACKET MARKED 'ZYGOTEN'. HENDERSON PICKS UP THE PACKET, SHAKES OUT A PILL, AND HOLDS IT BETWEEN HIS THUMB AND INDEX FINGER, AND CONTINUES.

HENDERSON: This item is worth half a million pounds to one of you gentlemen or ladies here. I want you to prepare for me an idea — no details — you haven't got time for that; an idea for advertising this product. You know your public, and that's why I want a British advertising agency to handle this. I want your ideas by four o'clock this afternoon. Are there any questions?

THERE IS ABSOLUTE SILENCE.

HENDERSON: (CONTINUING) Well, gentlemen, may I presume the question you'd all like to ask me? Why did I quit my previous agency so suddenly? I'll tell you because there's a lesson

(MORE)

HENDERSON: (CONTINUED) we can all
learn from this. I spent a whole month
with this agency, actually sitting in
with them from eight o'clock every
morning working out the copy platform.
But last night we had a party. One of
the executives got drunk, very drunk.
He started calling me a lot of bad
names. That I didn't mind at all because
I am used to taking hard knocks. But
then he said something about what I might
do with this product.

HE HOLDS UP THE SMALL PILL BETWEEN
THUMB AND INDEX FINGER AND LOOKS ROUND
AT THE ADVERTISING PEOPLE BEFORE HIM.

HENDERSON: (CONTINUING) I don't
have to tell you what he said.

HE LOOKS AT THE PILL AGAIN, THEN
CAREFULLY, ALMOST REVERENTLY, REPLACES
IT IN THE PACKET.

HENDERSON: (CONTINUING) As
successful men and women I think you
will agree with me that if you are
selling a product you must have
confidence in that product. Because
if you don't believe in it yourself,
how can you expect millions of ordinary
people to believe in it. (SUDDENLY
TURNING TO FRY) Don't you agree with
that, Mr Fry?

THE YOUNG ADVERTISING EXECUTIVE, FRY,
IS ASTONISHED TO FIND HIMSELF PICKED
OUT AND SPOKEN TO DIRECTLY BY NAME.

FRY: Oh, good gracious, yes,
definitely. Obviously one must believe
in one's product.

HENDERSON: Deeper than that, Mr
Fry. You see, belief is a necessity
for living. It's like food, it's like
friends. The problem with our society
is that there's a belief vacuum. And
we have to fill it! (THEN WITH A
TWISTED SMILE) You know, only the
other day I was toying with the idea
of setting up belief clinics all over
the United States for those deprived
faithwise.

This was an extraordinarily long speech for a one hour television
play, but there were some justifications for it. First, it was entertaining.
In Henderson we had a larger-than-life character, and everything he
said and did was entertaining. Second, the speech was full of suspense.

Between Henderson and his trapped audience of advertising people there existed a tension relationship. The slightest wrong move by any of them, and they knew they would never get that golden account. Third, and possibly most important, this scene and Henderson's explanation had been *prepared for*. All the earlier scenes of the play had been about Henderson, about his advertising account, above all about his pill. (Incidentally, the construction of *The Big Client* contravened a rule favoured by many script editors and producers, which is that it is generally inadvisable to have characters talk about a third character who has not yet been seen, albeit fleetingly, on the screen. The belief is that audiences never really listen to names mentioned unless they have met the people concerned, although they may absorb descriptions of characters not-yet-seen, e.g. 'father', 'the boss', 'my son'. In *The Big Client* we were able to disregard that rule, because in those earlier scenes people *only* talked about Henderson; so, by the time he finally appeared, it was like the Second Coming, and the audience felt they were seeing someone whom they already knew very well).

Generally, however, it is advisable to avoid long speeches, unless you have big characters to deliver them. You might hold an audience for some minutes with Napoleon explaining to his generals how he intends to conquer Russia (something big that is going to happen), but they would quickly get bored by a witness conveying a lot of plotty information about a small-time crime (something that has happened). If it is necessary for a minor character to relate the details of a past event it is advisable to break up the speech with interjections from another character. The cliché interjection to avoid is "And then?" or anything similar. Here is a witness giving evidence to a policeman:

```
WITNESS:        I'd just left my office,
you see, when I saw these two fellows
sort of lurking about by the shop. One
of them was a negro and the other was
white, so I thought to myself "Well,
that's funny".  So I decided to keep
an eye on them.

POLICEMAN:      What was funny about it?

WITNESS:        Black and white, together.
They don't mix much down our way, see.
I know they should.  But they don't.

POLICEMAN:      All right. Go on.
```

55

```
WITNESS:        Then this big car
pulled up.  They were waiting for it,
see.

POLICEMAN:      You get the number?

WITNESS:        No, I told your sergeant.
I didn't have anything to write it down
with.

POLICEMAN:      Okey.

WITNESS:        Well, all hell let loose
then.  The man in the car handed the
black fellow a brick, and he threw it
through the shop window, and the white
layabout started pulling these furs
out of the shop window and bundling them
into the car.
```

A two handed scene is not difficult to write if you have an ear for dialogue. Three, four, and five handers may present more problems. Still, provided you are sure why all your characters are in the scene, it should not be too difficult to find something for them to say. If it is a scene with some conflict (and *every* scene should contain some conflict, albeit a comedy or a love story) all your characters should be bursting to say something. If they are not, something is wrong with the construction. Even so, you may find yourself with a multi hander in which only two characters are doing most of the talking. Your other actors, particularly leading ones, won't like it if they are left 'stooging' (standing about with nothing to say and no business) for too long. The solution may have to be mechanical. As you write your way through the scene, check back that everyone present has had at least one line to deliver per page. Incidentally, never avoid writing multi handed scenes because they seem difficult. A play consisting of one two hander after another could be very dull.

Directors and actors loathe a proliferation of speech directions. *Don't* do this:

```
EDGAR:          (HOPEFULLY) I think
you once really loved me, Priscilla.

PRISCILLA:      (TENDERLY) I'm still
very fond of you, Edgar.

EDGAR:          (WITH YEARNING) And
could fondness turn into love again?

PRISCILLA:      (ANGUISH) Don't ask
me that, Edgar.
```

```
EDGAR:          (STOICALLY)  It's all
right, Priscilla, you don't have to be
kind.

PRISCILLA:      (EXPLAINING)  I'm not
being kind.  It's just that...

EDGAR:          (HELPFULLY)  Just that
what, Priscilla?

PRISCILLA:      (PAINFULLY)  Just that...
that I don't actually love you, Edgar.

EDGAR:          (FULLY AWARE NOW THAT
WHAT WAS ONCE IS NO MORE, YET STILL
HOPING, AND AT THE SAME TIME KNOWING
IN HIS HEART THAT THERE IS NO HOPE)
Oh.
```

However, there are certain technical speech directions which can be helpful. In a multi handed scene, it may be useful to make clear to whom a remark is being addressed:

```
MICHAEL:        (TO FRANK)  Why don't
you ever speak the truth?  (TO BETTY)
He's always lying to me.  Always.

BETTY:          I think you're
imagining this.  If only you'd be more
reasonable -
```

Two other useful technical directions are (CUTTING IN) and (CONTINUING). So to conclude our example:

```
MICHAEL:        (CUTTING IN)  I am
always reasonable!

BETTY:          (CONTINUING) - and
listen to what he's trying to tell you.
```

When an important move comes in the middle of a speech it is advisable to revert to stage directions, then to pick up the speech again with (CONTINUING). This happened in the Henderson example. It is because the move may involve the director in cutting from one camera to another for the move. In the facsimile on page 61 you will see how the director uses the left side of the script to plot his camera moves (which also explains why in electronic television we always write on the right side). But if the action is very small, and relates only to the speaker and no other characters, it can be included within the speech itself:

```
LANCE:          It's been all go today,
you know.  Haven't had a moment to
myself.  (CHECK HIS WATCH)  And look at
the time now!  It's gone five o'clock.
```

57

Don't write in phonetics to indicate a regional or foreign accent. It insults your actors' intelligence. If it is not clear from the characters themselves that a particular accent should be used, indicate it once in their first speech in the play:

```
ROBINSON:     (FRENCH ACCENT)  I'm
very pleased to meet you, Mr Smith.
```

However, do invest your regional or foreign characters' dialogue with fitting phraseology and use of words. In the north they say "Can you not?" in the south "Can't you?" If you are offered a late night 'drink' in the Midlands it means a beverage, in London it means alcohol. A civilian might say that a sailor is *on* HMS So-and-So; navy personnel will say *in*. Terminology often betrays political attitudes. Left-wingers say 'the Soviet Union', 'a Chinese', 'Mrs Joan Smith', and 'Britain'; those on the right say 'Russia', 'a Chinaman', 'Mrs John Smith', and 'Great Britain'. (These are extreme generalisations. They are here more to prompt you to listen to how people talk than for you to copy).

Never be without a notebook, so that you can jot down colourful phrases that you may hear. Listen to the tipsy lady barrister at the cocktail party who says, "Some of my divorce briefs make *Lady Chatterly's Lover* sound like a Bible reading", or the man in the pub who tells his friend, "Everton were knocking on the door last season", meaning that Everton almost moved up to the First Division.

Avoid hackneyed clichés. They persist, particularly in thrillers, because the dramatic situations which gave birth to them remain with us. Until some new situations can be invented (and people have been trying for years), the temptation to use clichés lies before us like a minefield. Here are some typical cliché situations with cliché phrases:

Situation 1 The hero is searching a room. Another man quietly enters and asks—
Cliché 1 "Looking for something?"
Situation 2 Up until now, the speaker has been the hero's seeming ally. But now he is holding a gun at our hero and reveals he is really on The Other Side. The hero says—
Cliché 2 "I should have known."
Situation 3 But the hero didn't. The traitor escapes. Now the hero learns that the heroine is held prisoner in the villain's fortified country mansion. He tells the heroine's young brother, who happens to be a promising concert violinist, that he (the hero)

intends to rescue her. To heighten the audience's expectancy for blood, the young brother enumerates the terrors to be faced— alligators in the moat, mad dogs, machine guns at every window. All our hero can say is—

Cliché 3 "That's a risk I'll have to take."

Situation 4 Which he does—and gets caught! He is now chained to a dungeon wall, a laser beam pointing his way. The villain, his hand on the switch, says—

Cliché 4 "Before I kill you, tell me what you have told your associates."

Situation 5 Naturally our hero tells him nothing, but says with a touch of gay defiance—

Cliché 5 "You'll never get away with this."

Situation 6 Which, of course, the villain doesn't, because the young brother tricks his way into the mansion, finds the hero and releases him. The hero asks the young brother how he slipped by the alligators, mad dogs, and machine guns. The young brother answers—

Cliché 6 "There's no time to explain."

Situation 7 Just as well, since we the audience saw how he did it. And anyway, the villain is now returning to kill his prisoner. In the fight the young brother is wounded. But by an act of tremendous courage, the hero defeats the villain. The heroine is released, and the young brother is tended by a helpfully handy doctor who just happened to be in one of the other dungeons. The hero has a brief word with the doctor, then goes to report to the heroine—

Cliché 7 "He's going to be all right. Your brother will play the violin again."

The challenge in thriller writing is that you cannot avoid the situations, but you must try to think of original replacements for "That's a risk I'll have to take" and all the others. Writers in other fields have similar problems, because certain genres of drama lend themselves to certain trains of thought. For instance:

Period play	"These are changing times, Victoria."
War story	"One day this damned war will be over. Poppies will grow."
Love story	"We can't go on meeting like this."
Social drama	"There's trouble at mill."
Science fiction	"Take me to your leader."
Daily serial	"I'm worried about Jim."

If you are writing for series drama, make sure that the series leads get most of the good lines. If you are writing for situation comedy give *all* the funny lines to the star, even if this means not using potentially funny lines because—for plot reasons—they could only be delivered by a minor character in the episode.

If your play is set entirely in a foreign country and all the characters are nationals of that country, write the dialogue in normal English and hope to goodness that the actors won't use funny accents. Your real problem is when your play is set in this country but has a two handed scene between two people of the same non-English language group. Why should they speak English when they are alone together? If you were writing for the cinema with its present-day emphasis on total realism, chances are your producer would want that scene in the characters' own language with English sub-titles; the distributors would then show a clip from that scene in their publicity trailer for the country whose language it was, to con local cinemagoers into believing that the whole film was in their language. But sub-titles are rarely used on British television: the exception is some old foreign films on BBC2. Maybe it's believed that their middle class audience has superior eyesight.

So, what to do? It is best to forget the problem, and have your foreign characters talk in normal English throughout the play, whether they are with the English characters or with each other. If you are going to do this, avoid drawing attention to language difficulties. When your foreigners are with your Britishers, don't interpolate their dialogue with those clichés, "I am, *how you say*, hungry," or "This is, *as you English call it*, not a pretty sight"; if you do, how can you logically justify their fluency in English when they play the scene between each other? Of course if your foreigners never have a scene alone together, you can if you wish demonstrate their difficulties with speaking English, if it helps your story. Note that in *Doctor Who* and *Star Trek* all the monsters and extraterrestrial humanoids talk English. No-one has ever complained!

If dialogue troubles you, try writing it freely with little thought of anything said in this chapter, then edit it later. Eventually all these rules and conventions will become second nature, but don't let any of them inhibit you if you are a beginner. There are a lot of mechanics to good dialogue writing, but the real key lies in your understanding of your characters. If you create in your mind real characters, they will write their own dialogue for you.

BOOM A.

46	CAM 1. GROUP SHOT OF AUDIENCE OVER HENDERSON'S R. SHOULDER	HENDERSON: Gentlemen, as you know, I have to return to New York tonight./ That means I have to decide on my advertising agency within the next few hours.
47	CAM 2 M.C.U. HENDERSON	

HE PAUSES AND MAKES AN ALMOST

48	CAM 1 GROUP SHOT A.BF SECRETARY MOVES FORWARD TO HENDERSON	IMPERCEPTIBLE SIGNAL./ GRETA HEFFNER, HIS PRIVATE SECRETARY, COMES OVER TO HIM WITH A SILVER TRAY ON WHICH IS A DISPLAY. / IN THE MIDDLE OF THE TRAY
49	CAM 2 M.S. HENDERSON	IS A PACKET MARKED 'ZYGOTEN'. HENDERSON PICKS UP THE PACKET, SHAKES OUT A PILL, /
50	CAM 3 C/U HENDERSON'S HAND HOLDING PILL	AND HOLDS IT BETWEEN HIS THUMB AND INDEX FINGER, AND CONTINUES. /
51	CAM 2 M.S. HENDERSON, A.BF	HENDERSON: This item is worth half a million points to one of you gentlemen or ladies here./ I want you (OOV)
52	CAM 1 GROUP SHOT OF AUDIENCE (REACTION)	to prepare for me an idea - no details - you haven't time for that; an idea for advertising this product./ You
53	CAM 2 M.S. HENDERSON A.BF	know your public, and that's why I want a British advertising agency to handle (OOV) this. / I want your ideas by four
54	CAM 1 GROUP SHOT A.BF	o'clock this afternoon. Are there any questions?

THERE IS ABSOLUTE SILENCE. /

55	CAM 2 OBLIQUE M.S. OF HENDERSON/CLIP HEADS OF AUDIENCE F/G.	HENDERSON: (CONTINUING) Well, gentlemen, may I presume the question you'd all like to ask me? Why did I quit my previous agency so suddenly? I'll tell you because there's a lesson we can all learn from this. I spent a whole month with this agency, actually sitting with them from eight o'clock every morning working out the copy platform. / But last night we had a
56	CAM 3 M.C.U. HENDERSON	party. One of the executives got drunk, very drunk. He started calling me a lot of bad names. That I didn't mind at all because I am used to taking hard knocks. But then he said something about what I might do with this product.

HE HOLDS UP THE SMALL PILL BETWEEN
THUMB AND INDEX FINGER AND LOOKS ROUND
AT THE ADVERTISING PEOPLE BEFORE HIM. /

57	CAM 2. OBLIQUE M.S. HENDERSON A.BF.	HENDERSON: (CONTINUING) I don't have to tell you what he said.

HE LOOKS AT THE PILL AGAIN, THEN
CAREFULLY, ALMOST REVERENTLY, REPLACES
IT IN THE PACKET.

HENDERSON: (CONTINUING) As
successful men and women I think you
will agree with me that if you are

(MORE)

A page of 'camera script'. This version of a script is only distributed to the
cameramen and other technicians.

Chapter 7

CHARACTERISATION

Characterisation in television is the same as in any other fiction writing, except that it is expressed quicker and more concisely. There was the famous case when Terence Frisby asked the High Court to stop the BBC from transmitting his play *And Some Have Greatness Thrust Upon Them* because they had deleted one line of dialogue during the production. According to his script, his pregnant-girl character was to say, "My friend Sylve told me it was safe standing up". The BBC pleaded good taste. Frisby argued that this one line summed up the girl's entire character and was structural. He won.

With the novel there is a device whereby the writer holds up the action and dips back into the life story of a particular character, perhaps each in turn in the course of a book. The pace of television is too fast for that. However, this doesn't mean that television drama characterisation is shallow. Some television writers compose whole life stories for each character, and write it all down on paper, before starting to write a play. Doing this, they are trying to find the nut of the character, which in the play may be expressed in one line. Lack of character depth will be more quickly revealed in television than in almost any other fiction medium. As with dialogue, the playwright is in direct competition with the reality of the documentary.

Character may be expressed not only in dialogue but also in props, sets, and silent action. If a man opens his tool box and for a moment the camera draws attention to the half-full bottle of whisky in among the hammers and screwdrivers, we know that man leans on liquor. If a businessman has a little bust of Napoleon on top of his filing cabinet, we have some idea about his ambitions. Whether a woman's home is tidy or in a mess tells us a lot about her. Every television picture tells a story.

An excellent example of action portraying character was in the film *Three Into One Won't Go*. It opened with a middle aged man driving his car. A pretty girl with a rucksack thumbed for a lift. He slowed, and stopped some yards beyond her, leant over to unlock the nearside door, and looked back as though expecting her to run up to the car. Instead, she remained where she was, hand on hip, waiting for him to back up to her. Not once had he smiled at the prospect of young female companionship, yet he did back up, just as she wanted. Without a word, we knew about his pent up middle-aged emotions, and about her self-assurance and knowledge of the power she had over a man of his age.

Because television is so revealing, never write about the type of people that you have never met. If you want to write about a Catholic priest, a militant shop steward, or a duke, don't base them on characters you saw in another television play last week. You must make direct, personal observation. If that isn't possible, restrict your writing to the kind of people you know.

Invest even the smallest role with character. In the Graham Greene film *The End of the Affair* the hero hired a seedy private detective to acquire the heroine's personal diary. In due course, the detective delivered the diary. Suddenly apprehensive, the hero asked if the detective had read any part of this very personal document. With dignity the detective replied, "Good gracious no, sir. I don't pry into other people's private affairs." Even if the story fades from memory, the detective never will.

It helps to sort out your ideas if you know who your 'angle character' is. In prose, it is almost always obvious:

> The au pair girl showed Shirley into the room and said Mrs Hally wouldn't be long. Then she left, and Shirley heard her footsteps going away down the hall. She looked about herself. So this is where Norman spent his childhood.

Most prose writing sees the story from the mind of one character. The short story usually remains with the same angle character throughout; the novel often switches angle characters from one chapter to another. Knowing exactly which is your angle character, who may change from scene to scene, will give you more self assurance when you embark on a scene.

Unlike prose, drama often needs the 'confidant'. In the above example of prose, the writer could have continued for pages with Shirley's memories of Norman, while she waited for Mrs Hally. Not so in drama. Characters need other characters to talk and reminisce to. In the thriller both hero and villain need someone to whom to say, "This is my plan. . . ." In constructing your play, beware the pitfall of having no confidant for the moment when one will be needed.

The need for the confidant means many plays are constructed on a two-a-side basis: the hero and his side kick versus Mr Big and his Number Two (to use thriller writer terminology); or the unfaithful husband and the mistress versus the wife and her brother. If your play follows that pattern, be sure to get maximum value out of the confidant by introducing internal conflict. Don't use the confidant simply as a sounding board. If the hero is careful and calculating, let his side kick be rash. Mr Big may be ruthless and cunning, but his Number Two can be a psycopath. Internal conflicts will give you more 'mileage' (additional twists and turns of story).

Be sure you understand the 'binding factor' between your characters. If two characters stick together despite their internal conflicts, there must be some good reason. The binding factor is probably most important in situation comedy. What keeps together Harold and his father in *Steptoe and Son* or Eli and Nellie in *Nearest and Dearest* (see page 222)? Why don't they go their separate ways and find happiness? The truth is they would be very unhappy, because they would miss the love-hate relationship. If any two of your characters live under the same roof, or run the same business, yet squabble, you must know why they stay together. If *you* don't know, the television audience won't believe in the situation.

It is your characters who will convey the message, or root idea, of your play. They are worthy of your every care and attention.

Chapter 8

THE TELEVISION SCRIPT

In earlier chapters you have seen a few snippets of television scripts. Here is a much longer sequence, including a title page and a characters-and-sets page, just as you should submit a play. This script has been specially written for us by that extraordinarily bad television writer who prefers to be known as John Smith. It includes every possible mistake that even he could fit into so few scenes. Later you will see a revised version, totally re-written by that extraordinarily good script editor, Malcolm Hulke. The introductory pages have some bracketed letters which indicate mistakes that, at this stage, you may not even realise are mistakes. The script itself has bracketed numbers, and by now you should be able to recognise most of the mistakes to which they relate. So, as you read the script you can play a guessing game. From page 78, you will be able to check your score.

This is a run-of-the-mill cops and robbers play. It starts with a 'teaser', which means an attention holding device. Theatre and cinema audiences are trapped; television audiences can switch channels the moment they are bored. The teaser opening is essential in television series drama, and it is also pretty important in straight plays as well. Probably the best teaser ever written in a straight play for television was Harold Pinter's prize-winning *The Lover*. It started by showing the husband leaving for work. As he opened the front door to go he paused, turned to his wife and said, "Is your lover coming today?"

After the impact of a good 'hook' opening, it is possible to drop the tension a little, slow the action, then build again to further climaxes.

<u>ANYBODY HERE SEEN KELLY?</u>

A television play

by

John Smith

A

B

CHARACTERS

BOB PRICE [C]

DETECTIVE SERGEANT MILLER [C]

DETECTIVE CONSTABLE RAWLINGS [C]

MIKE BYRD [C]

SPENCER [C]

SERGEANT FISHER

INSPECTOR HILLER

VANESSA [C]

FIONA [C]

CAPTAIN MADISON

JOYCE KELLY

Small and non-speaking

KELLY [C]

POLICE CONSTABLE [C]

WOMAN POLICE CONSTABLE

JUDY

TELEVISION NEWS READER

Extras and crowd

GIRL TYPISTS
[D]

SETS

BOB'S FLAT

MIKE'S FLAT

SPENCER'S OFFICE

SPENCER'S OUTER OFFICE [E]

POLICE STATION

INSPECTOR HILLER'S OFFICE

CAPTAIN MADISON'S STUDY

TELEVISION NEWS STUDIO

JOYCE KELLY'S HOME

FILM

High Rise Block. [F]

Opposite High Rise Block.

Busy High Street.

Country Road.

Madison's House. [F]

68

ANYBODY HERE SEEN KELLY?

by

John Smith

TELECINE 1

High Rise Block. Night.   ☐1

About four storeys up – the
balcony running along the
outside of the building which
leads to the flats. An old
man, BOB PRICE, comes along
the balcony from the lifts,
and lets himself into his
flat.

1. INT. BOB'S FLAT.   NIGHT.

☐2   (WE ARE IN THE SMALL HALLWAY
            OF A FLAT. THE FLAT IS
            MODERN BUT IT IS FILLED WITH
            OLD MAN'S JUNK – BITS OF
            FURNITURE THAT HE HAS
            COLLECTED OVER THE YEARS,
            INCLUDING AN ANCIENT
            GRAMOPHONE WITH A HUGE
☐3   HORN.   THE KITCHEN IS IN
            A MESS AND SO IS THE LIVING
            ROOM. BOB ENTERS, TAKES
            OFF HIS CAP, AND PULLS FROM
            HIS OVERCOAT POCKET A
            NEWSPAPER PACKET OF FISH AND
            CHIPS.   HE EATS A CHIP,
            THEN SELECTS A MORSEL OF
            FISH AND STARTS LOOKING FOR
            HIS CAT, CALLING AS HE GOES
            FROM ROOM TO ROOM.)

☐4   BOB: (CALLING) Puss. Puss.
     Where are you?

☐5   (WHEN HE IS IN THE LIVING
            ROOM THE CAT SUDDENLY
            COMES UP TO HIM FROM THE
            BEDROOM WHICH LEADS OFF,
            RUBS ITSELF AGAINST HIS LEG.)

     BOB: There you are!

            (BOB GIVES THE CAT THE BIT
            OF FISH. THEN HE THINKS.)

☐4   BOB: (CURIOUS) Where were
     you hiding, then?

☐6   (BOB LOOKS UP, REALISES THE
            BEDROOM DOOR IS PARTLY
            OPEN.   HE REACTS AND
            GOES INTO THE BEDROOM. LIKE
            THE REST OF THE FLAT IT IS
            A TERRIBLE MESS. LYING

69

                                    DIAGONALLY ACROSS THE BED
                                    IS A MAN, KELLY, IN HIS
                                    SHIRT SLEEVES. HE IS DEAD.
                                    BOB REACTS.)

TELECINE 2   CREDITS

High Rise Block. Day.

DETECTIVE SERGEANT MILLER,
DETECTIVE CONSTABLE RAWLINGS·
and a uniformed POLICE CONSTABLE
come along the balcony and stop
at Bob's door. MILLER knocks.

TELECINE 3   7

Opposite High Rise Block. Day.

Close shot on MIKE BYRD at his
window looking out, using
binoculars.

TELECINE 4   7

High Rise Block. Day.

BOB opens the door.   8

                    MILLER: Mr Price?

                    BOB: Yes.

                    MILLER: We want to talk to you.

                    BOB: What about?

                    MILLER: Let's go inside, shall we?

2. INT. BOB'S FLAT.   DAY.

                    (BOB HOLDS THE DOOR OPEN AS
           9   MILLER, RAWLINGS AND THE
                     POLICE CONSTABLE ENTER. BOB
                     IS VERY NERVOUS.)

                    BOB: What do you want to see
                    me for?

                    MILLER: Just to take a look
                    around, that's all.

                    (RAWLINGS AND THE POLICE
                     CONSTABLE START SEARCHING
           2   THE PLACE, AND WE SEE
                     THEM IN DIFFERENT ROOMS
                     TURNING THINGS OVER.)

                    BOB: You got a warrant? If
                    you haven't you're out of order. I'll
                    report you.

                              70

10   MILLER: With your record? You
      must be joking. Anyway, that's a risk
      I'll have to take.

3. INT. MIKE'S FLAT.   DAY.

                    (SIMILAR TO BOB'S FLAT BUT
11   WITH MODERN FURNITURE AND
                     QUITE WELL KEPT. MIKE PICKS
12   UP THE TELEPHONE, DIALS A
                     NUMBER.)

                    MIKE: (INTO PHONE) Hello?
                    Can I speak to Mr Spencer, please?...
                    All right, I'll hold on... Mr
                    Spencer? Mike Byrd here. Listen,
                    there's police calling on old Bob.

4. INT. SPENCER'S OFFICE.   DAY.

                    (NOT A VERY LARGE OFFICE.
                     THERE IS A FILING CABINET
                     AND A GRAPH ON THE WALL,
                     AND A DESK AT WHICH
                     SPENCER IS SEATED AND ON
                     THE PHONE. THROUGH A LARGE
                     WINDOW WE CAN SEE OUT TO
13   THE FORECOURT OF A PETROL
                     FILLING STATION WHERE MEN
                     IN OVERALLS ARE FILLING UP
                     CUSTOMERS' CARS.)

                    SPENCER: (INTO PHONE)(CUTTING IN)
14   I told you never to phone me here. I'll
                    call you back in a few minutes.

                         (SPENCER GETS UP, PUTS ON
                          HIS TOPCOAT, AND EXITS.)

5. INT. SPENCER'S OUTER OFFICE.   DAY.

                    (THIS IS A LARGER OFFICE,
                     WITH ONE OR TWO TYPISTS.
                     AS SPENCER ENTERS FROM HIS
                     OFFICE, HIS SECRETARY, JUDY,
15   IS POUNDING AWAY AT HER
                     TYPEWRITER.)

                    SPENCER: I'm going out for a
                    few minutes.

                         (SPENCER EXITS)

       71

6.   INT.   BOB'S FLAT.   DAY.

|16| (MILLER IS INTERROGATING
        BOB.)

MILLER: What I'm asking is, did
you know him?

BOB: Never hear of him.

MILLER: Look at this.

|17| (MILLER PRODUCES A PHOTO.
        BOB LOOKS. IT SHOWS
        KELLY WEARING A MOUSTACHE.)

MILLER: Well?

BOB: I've never seen anyone
looking like that. What do you want
him for?

MILLER: He's escaped from prison.

    (RAWLINGS ENTERS.)

RAWLINGS: Sarge.

MILLER: Yes?

    (RAWLINGS NODS TO MILLER,
    TO TAKE MILLER TO ONE SIDE,
    OUT OF BOB'S HEARING. HE
    SHOWS MILLER A PRISON
    UNIFORM JACKET.)

RAWLINGS: (WHISPER) Kelly's
|18| prison jacket. I found it under the
bed. It's got his name on it.

|17| (WE SEE THE NAME "KELLY"
    ON A TAG ON THE JACKET.
    MILLER TURNS BACK TO BOB.)

MILLER: We're taking you in.
Come on!

TELECINE 5

High Rise Block. Day. |19|

Bob's door opens, and MILLER,
RAWLINGS, BOB, and the POLICE
CONSTABLE come out and go along
to the lift.

Busy High Street. Day.

SPENCER pushes his way along |20|
through shopping crowds, finds

a telephone box and goes inside. $\boxed{12}$
He dials a number.

SOUND EFFECTS: RINGING TONE. THE
RINGING TONE STOPS AND MIKE ANSWER.

SPENCER pushes in his money.

MIKE: (FILTER) Hello?

$\boxed{21}$ SPENCER: (INTO PHONE) I'm calling
you back.

MIKE: (FILTER) They just took
old Bob away.

SPENCER: (INTO PHONE) That's not
surprising with his record.

MIKE: (FILTER) I know. But why
did they call on him in the first place?

SPENCER: (INTO PHONE) He probably
hasn't paid his television licence. Now
stop panicking!

SPENCER slams down the phone.

7. INT. POLICE STATION.   DAY.

(MILLER AND BOB ENTER FROM
THE STREET. MILLER GOES
UP TO THE DESK SERGEANT,
FISHER, AND INDICATES BOB.)

MILLER: Mr Price has dropped in
to help us with our enquiries. Put him
$\boxed{22}$ in the truth room. I'm going to see
Inspector Hiller.

(MILLER GOES OFF TOWARDS
HILLER'S OFFICE.)

BOB: Who's going to look
$\boxed{23}$ after my pussy cat?

FISHER: Don't worry about her.
We'll send a lady from the Women's
Royal Voluntary Service round to feed
$\boxed{24}$ her if you like to give me your front
door key.

BOB: Thanks.

8. INT. INSPECTOR HILLER'S OFFICE. DAY.

73

(A LARGE OFFICE WITH FILING
CABINETS, A DESK, CHAIRS,
AND OTHER FURNITURE. ONE
WALL IS FILLED WITH A
GLASS PANELLED CASE IN
WHICH THERE ARE SPORTS

25   TROPHIES. THERE IS A PICTURE
OF THE QUEEN UP ON THE WALL.
ALSO ON THE WALL IS A MAP OF
THE DISTRICT, CALENDAR, ETC.
HILLER IS A TACITURN-LOOKING
MAN IN HIS EARLY FIFTIES.

26   HE HAS SHARP PIERCING EYES,
A HOOK NOSE, WAVY HAIR, AND
A CLEFT CHIN. MILLER ENTERS.)

MILLER: Good morning, sir.

27 HILLER: 'Morning, Miller. Take
a seat. Like a cup of tea?

MILLER: Please. I could do with
one.

(HILLER LIFTS HIS PHONE.)

HILLER: (INTO PHONE) Send two
cups of tea in, will you?

(HILLER PUTS DOWN THE PHONE,
OFFERS MILLER A CIGARETTE.)

28 HILLER: Smoke?

29 MILLER: Thanks. I could do with
one.

(THEY LIGHT UP. DOOR OPENS

30 AND A WOMAN POLICE CONSTABLE
ENTERS WITH TWO CUPS OF TEA.)

31

HILLER: Ah, lovely!

(THE W.P.C. PUTS THE TWO
CUPS OF TEA DOWN AND GOES.)

HILLER: Now, how's the hunt for
Kelly going on?

MILLER: We found this.

(MILLER SHOWS HILLER THE
PRISON JACKET.)

HILLER: Where did you find it?

32 MILLER: Bob Price's flat. We
know how he always boasts that he knew
Kelly. So we thought we'd go and see
him. I think Kelly spent the night
there.

HILLER: Have you brought Price
in?

MILLER: Yes, he's here now.

HILLER: All right, then. Let's
go and have a talk to him.

|33| (HILLER AND MILLER EXEUNT.)

TELECINE 6

Country Road. Day.

Two public school girls, |34|
VANESSA and FIONA, are |35|
cycling along, both in |36|
school uniforms.

|37| VANESSA: Are you spending Easter
with your mother or your father?

FIONA: Both of them. They're
speaking to each other for grannie's
sake. A temporary truce.

|38| VANESSA: How terribly amusing. I
say, what's that over there?

They see a man's foot sticking
out from the undergrowth.

FIONA: It's a man's foot.

VANESSA: I know, silly. But what's
he doing there? Let's go and look.

They dismount, go to the undergrowth and look. KELLY is
lying there on his back, his
hand clutched round a shotgun.
The two girls scream, jump
back onto their bicycles and
cycle away. HOLD on the foot.

Madison's House. Day.

VANESSA and FIONA come cycling
past a street sign reading
'Lime Avenue. Cul-de-sac'.
They dismount at the house
of Captain Madison. As they
race by the front gate, we
HOLD on the name of the house
on the gate — 'Mon Cul'. |39|

9. INT. CAPTAIN MADISON'S STUDY. DAY.

(THE RETIRED ARMY CAPTAIN
MADISON IS LOOKING THROUGH
HIS BANK STATEMENTS, AND
|40| WONDERING HOW TO MAKE
END MEET IN THE FACE OF

75

|41| EVER INCREASING PRICES.
(SO, INCIDENTALLY, IS THE
WRITER! - J.S.) VANESSA
AND FIONA BURST IN.)

VANESSA: Oh, Captain Madison!
We've just found a man - he's dead.

|42| FIONA: He's got his weapon
clutched in his hand, and he's as
rigid as anything.

VANESSA: Please call the police!

|43| MADISON: Settle down now, and tell
me all about it from the beginning.

|44| (THE GIRLS QUIETEN DOWN
AND VANESSA EXPLAINS WHAT
THEY SAW. WHEN THEY HAVE
FINISHED MADISON REACHES
FOR THE PHONE.)

10.   INT.   TELEVISION NEWS STUDIO.   DAY.

|45| (A NEWS READER IS LOOKING
DIRECT INTO CAMERA (CAN WE
GET ROBERT DOUGALL OR
RICHARD BAKER? I DO HOPE
SO. - J.S.))

|46| NEWS READER: In the House of Commons
today uproar broke out when the Prime
Minister said there could be no
supplementary benefits for old age
pensioners until early in the New Year.
|47| (PAUSE) The body of William George
Kelly was found today somewhere in the
South East of England, but...

11.   INT.   JOYCE KELLY'S HOME.   DAY.

(WE NOW DRAW BACK FROM THE
TELEVISION NEWS READER AND
REALISE HE WAS ON THE SCREEN
OF THE TV SET IN THIS ROOM.
IT IS A NEATLY KEPT ROOM,
VERY SUBURBAN. THE TV IS
BEING WATCHED BY JOYCE
KELLY AND MIKE BYRD, WHO
SIT ARMS ENTWINED ON A
SETTEE.)

NEWS READER: (FILTER)...the police
have refused to say where. A police
spokesman said there was reason to

(MORE)

76

NEWS READER: (CONTINUED) believe that
Kelly, who escaped from Wandsworth
prison last month, had been murdered,
probably some days ago.

JOYCE: So that's it, then.

48   MIKE: Yeh. Poor old George.
So now you're a widow.

49   JOYCE: Do you think that makes
any difference? From the moment the
judge sentenced him to life imprisonment
I was made into a widow. The way people
go on about longer and longer sentences,
they don't think about the wives. In
some countries, such as Mexico, the
prison authorities permit wives to make
connubial visits to their loved ones.

MIKE: So I heard.

            (THEY HEAR A CAR DRAW UP
             OUTSIDE.)

50   MICHAEL: That sounds like a car
51   drawing up outside. I'll see who it is.

52   (MIKE GOES TO THE WINDOW,
             LOOKS OUT. HE SEES A
             SALOON CAR WHICH HAS JUST
             PARKED. GETTING OUT
             OF IT ARE MILLER AND
             RAWLINGS.)

MIKE: It's the police.

JOYCE: (RESIGNED) They're
bound to call, aren't they.

MIKE: But I mustn't be found
here!

JOYCE: Then you'd better slip
out the back way.

            (MIKE EXITS. JOYCE PREPARES
             TO RECEIVE THE POLICE.)

77

Here are the mistakes:
- (A) No 'running time' (length of play) given.
- (B) Never submit scripts without your address on the cover, and your agent's name and address if you have one. Your *very brief* covering letter may get parted from the script at the receiving end.
- (C) Very helpful if you indicate characters to appear both in studio and on film, or on film only. If no indication is given, studio only is presumed.
- (D) The girl typists in Spencer's outer office get mentioned, but what about the petrol pump attendants and the motorists seen through Spencer's window, and the people in the busy high street? It is very easy to overlook listing minor characters when you are using them only as props and decor.
- (E) If one set runs into another they should be listed as a composite. (If your script editor has limited you to, say, five main sets, don't try to cheat in a sixth by pretending that two sets, although joined and therefore a composite, are one. Script editors are not that stupid.)
- (F) More helpful to have listed—

| High Rise Block. | Night. |
| High Rise Block. | Day. |

Also this would be more helpful—

Madison's House in cul-de-sac

—presuming, of course, that there is any story reason for having the house in a cul-de-sac in the first place.

1. Expensive and unnecessary night filming (See page 39).
2. Lack of scene headings. Every time you follow a character from one room to another you need a separate scene heading. The designer needs to know what sets to design, and the cameramen need to know what set to shoot into.
3. The ancient gramophone with the huge horn could be a very expensive prop to buy. Is it essential to the story?
4. Unnecessary speech direction(s).
5. Cats can't act.
6. Why should Bob react surprised to find the bedroom door partly open? He has no confidant to whom to say, "That's funny, I'm sure I left that door closed." We already know he is untidy. So there is no logic behind this.

7. No need for a new telecine number here (see page 37).

8. If we see Bob appear at his front door on film (i.e. from the outside) it means he must be taken on location. The fewer people in location filming the better. Every one, actors and technicians, must be backed up with equipment—mobile dressing rooms, a mobile canteen, probably mobile lavatories. See how in the re-write Bob is kept inside his flat, which means only in the studio.

9. The reverse of 8 above. By bringing the police constable into Bob's flat we bring him into studio. In the re-write, the constable is left standing on the balcony. The only reason for having the uniformed constable in T/C 2 was so that Mike Byrd would know it was the police, and not perhaps rent collectors, calling on Bob. (In real life, it is most unlikely the uniformed constable would accompany the two plain clothes detectives on this mission: here we are taking dramatic licence).

10. "You must be joking" and "That's a risk I'll have to take" are both outworn clichés.

11. Previously we only saw Mike through a window, and he had binoculars to his face. So how will the audience recognise him now as the same man? To make sure they do, in the re-write the discarded binoculars are featured visually.

12. It takes up to 15 seconds to dial a seven digit telephone number, and that is very boring for the audience. See how it is done in the re-write.

13. How do we see the petrol pumps, the attendants and the cars? It might be done with CSO or BP (see page 44). But is it worth it? In the re-write the nature of Spencer's business is established when he leaves his office. It means going on location, so we must presume at least one other scene will be played out against that location background to make it worth while.

14. This is a cliché situation anyway, so no need to underline it with the old cliché, "I told you never to phone me here." Try to find another expression.

15. Where will the director find an actress who can pound at a typewriter? Better to show her doing some filing, or polishing her nails. And do we really need the other typists?

16. Which room are we in?

17. A good idea to use an INSERT here (you will see how in the

re-write). It would be impossible to get a camera into position to look over Bob's shoulder down onto that photo. So to get this shot the director will have a replica of the photo held in someone else's hand somewhere else in the studio, and a separate camera will be lined up in close shot on the held photo. To the audience, they will get the impression that they are looking down onto the photo through Bob's eyes when he looks.

18. Lack of research. Prison uniforms do not carry prisoners' names.

19. Again Bob is shown on location. Is this scene necessary? In a few moments Mike is going to report what happened to Spencer. So do we need to see it?

20. For artistic reasons the director might fancy showing Spencer among shopping crowds—the juxtaposition of the underworld with the normal world. But it is going to cost money to go on location. In the re-write we have a telephone kiosk in the studio standing against a drop of painted brick wall, plus some wild track of street noises. It is better to script it the inexpensive way: if the director finds he's got the budget, he'll be the first to hire helicopters, wild elephants, and a cast of thousands. If a director throws around money, it's art; if a writer does it, he's a bad writer.

21. There are two telephone conventions. Either is viable, but they must not be mixed in the same script. In one (when Mike phoned Spencer) we could not hear what the person the other end was saying when the camera was on Mike; here we are holding the camera on Spencer but can hear what Mike is saying. Choose which convention is going to serve your story best; but having made the choice, stick to it throughout the script.

22. Confusing to have Miller and Hiller in the same script.

23. Bob's line about his cat was quite a nice 'take out' (something visual or oral that rounds off a scene). Fisher's line is unnecessary, and elevates the character to a speaking part (see page 27). It is also very didactic.

24. And most inaccurate! It would be the PDSA, not the WRVS, who might be asked to care for the pet of a prisoner. What's more, since Bob is *not* a prisoner (he hasn't been arrested or charged) under no circumstances would a police officer ask for or accept his keys. Never make statements about the law,

police procedure, medicine, or other technical matters, without researching the facts thoroughly.

25. Too much description.

26. It is pointless to give physical descriptions of your characters. YOUNG AND BRIGHT-LOOKING or OLD AND TIRED are okay. But your director will ignore your WAVY HAIR AND CLEFT CHIN. He will hire an actor who, in his view, looks the part.

27. All this cosy 'good morning' stuff is irrelevant, slows down the pace. By holding on Bob when he delivers his line about the cat, we could cut straight into Miller showing the prison jacket to Hiller. A hold on a person or on an object at the end of a scene can allow us to jump forward in time and go right to the salient point of the next scene.

28. Not many producers allow cigarette smoking these days.

29. A repeated line ending. (See page 52).

30. Even if the canteen kettle was boiling, the constable had no time to pour two cups of tea and bring them in. You must give time for moves, whether on screen or off. If you are uncertain how long it takes to pour a round of drinks, cups of tea, or to eat a meal, act out these actions yourself and time them.

31. More lack of research. Certainly in London there are no Women Police Constables nowadays, although there are Police Constables who happen to be women. Even before WPC's were abolished, they didn't go around serving tea. That would be canteen staff work.

32. We already know all this! In the re-write this whole scene is out. We don't want re-caps, we want action.

33. 'Exeunt' is technically right; but for us simple people in television, just stick to 'exit' for both singular and plural.

34. Are *two* girls necessary? This scene, which consists of someone finding the body, could be played out in mime by one actress.

35. Are these the only upper-crust names the writer knows? In this context, they are cliché names.

36. School uniforms cost money.

37. Cycling and talking. (See page 38).

38. Do upper-crust young ladies really talk like this, except in certain fiction? Has the writer ever met any?

39. 'Mon Cul' sounds cute for the name of a house in a cul-de-sac.

But what if the tape of this play is sold to France? In French, the term means 'my arse'. Never dream up foreign-sounding names for people or places. Always check and double check.

40. How do we know what Captain Madison is thinking, and does it matter?

41. *Never* include jokey messages in synopses or scripts. The script editor will think you are slightly potty. But wit in stage directions may be very much appreciated (see page 186).

42. Beware lines with sexual double meanings. If your audience is absorbed with the play, the double meaning may not be noticed. The problem is the cast. There are enough hazards with television production without having the cast being 'took' (getting the giggles) by having to say certain lines.

43. "Settle down" is the catch phrase of the comedian Ken Goodwin. The actor playing Captain Madison would have difficulty delivering it with a straight face.

44. Every word in a script must be presented as dialogue, and should never be wrapped up inside a stage direction, and this even applies to such lines as "Good morning" and "How do you do." (There is the exception of lines given to walk-ons, but these are 'written' by the director. See page 27).

45. Never try to do the director's casting for him.

46. You should not show a fictitious news broadcast without visually making it clear that it is fictitious. Someone who has just turned on their television set might believe it is real and act upon it in some way.

47. Previously Vanessa asked Fiona how she would be spending Easter, so presumably this play is set in the early part of the year. Here reference is made to something that will happen ". . . early in the New Year", which suggests we are in the later part of the year. Lack of consistency.

48. Since no-one has turned off the television, there should be covering news reader dialogue for Mike and Joyce to talk over.

49. Joyce's line is full of special pleading. All that she says may be true and heart rending, but has it any place here?

50. The character is known in the script as MIKE, not MICHAEL.

51. Unnecessary line in view of the action and the line which is to follow immediately.

52. How do we see what Mike is looking at through the window? See the re-write.

Now to the re-write. Whether you are re-writing your own first draft, or editing another writer's work, never be afraid of the big surgical operation. That is what is to happen to some parts of this script. Note that the re-write is dated, which will save confusion if there are further complete re-writes later on.

<u>ANYBODY HERE SEEN KELLY?</u>

A television play

by

John Smith

(Re-write of 21/12/73)

<u>Running time: one hour</u>

John Smith,
234 Sandringham Road,
London NW11
(01-200 3456)

Author's agent:
William Baxter (Scripts) Ltd,
1 Dawkins Street,
London WC1
(01-401 7890)

BOB PRICE
DETECTIVE SERGEANT MILLER (Studio and film)
DETECTIVE CONSTABLE RAWLINGS (Studio and film)
MIKE BYRD
SPENCER (Studio and film)
JUDY
DETECTIVE INSPECTOR BROWN
SERGEANT FISHER
MARY (Studio and film)
CAPTAIN MADISON
JOYCE KELLY

Small and non-speaking

KELLY
POLICE CONSTABLE (Film only)
POLICE CONSTABLE
PETROL PUMP ATTENDANT (Film only)
MOTORIST (Film only)

Heard-not-seen

TELEPHONIST
NEWS READER

SETS

INT. BOB'S FLAT: HALLWAY)	
)	COMPOSITE
INT. BOB'S FLAT: BEDROOM)	

INT. MIKE'S FLAT: LIVING ROOM

INT. SPENCER'S OFFICE)	
)	COMPOSITE
INT. SPENCER'S OUTER OFFICE)	

INT/EXT. TELEPHONE KIOSK (CORNERPIECE)
INT. POLICE STATION: MAIN AREA
INT. POLICE STATION: INTERVIEW ROOM
INT. CAPTAIN MADISON'S STUDY
INT. JOYCE KELLY'S HOME: LIVING ROOM

FILM

High Rise Block. Day. (Balcony connecting flats)
Opposite High Rise Block. Day. (Long shot)
Car Showroom. Day. (With petrol pumps in forecourt)
Country Road. Day.
Madison's House. Day. (In a cul-de-sac)
Joyce Kelly's House. Day. (A suburban semi-detached)

ANYBODY HERE SEEN KELLY?

by

John Smith

1. INT. BOB'S FLAT: HALLWAY.   NIGHT

(MODERN COUNCIL FLAT,
FURNISHED WITH THE JUNK-
SHOP POSSESSIONS OF A
POOR OLD MAN. BOB
ENTERS FROM BALCONY,
TAKES OFF CAP, PULLS
FROM TATTERED OVERCOAT
POCKET A PACKET OF FISH
AND CHIPS. HE EATS A
CHIP, THEN SELECTS A
BIT OF FISH.)

BOB: Puss. Puss. Where
are you?

(HE WALKS DOWN THE
HALL, TO THE OPEN
BEDROOM DOOR.)

BOB: Are you in there?

(HE EXITS TO BEDROOM.)

2. INT. BOB'S FLAT: BEDROOM.   NIGHT

(SMALL. UNTIDY. BOB
ENTERS.)

BOB: I got some fish for you –

(HE REACTS. CUT TO THE
BED. LYING ACROSS IT IS
A MAN IN HIS SHIRT SLEEVES,
KELLY. HE IS DEAD.)

BOB: Kelly.

                              CREDITS

TELECINE 1

High Rise Block. Day.

DETECTIVE SERGEANT MILLER,
DETECTIVE CONSTABLE RAWLINGS
and a UNIFORMED POLICE
CONSTABLE come along the
balcony and stop at Bob's
doorway. MILLER knocks.
PAN round to and ZOOM IN
on –

<u>Opposite High Rise Block. Day.</u>

MIKE BYRD is at his window
looking out, using binoculars.

3. INT. BOB'S FLAT: HALLWAY.   DAY

                          (MORE KNOCKING. BOB COMES
                          ALONG, OPENS THE FRONT
                          DOOR. MILLER AND RAWLINGS
                          WALK STRAIGHT IN.)

MILLER: 'Morning.

BOB: Here, who are you? What
do you want?

MILLER: Just taking a look round.
(TO RAWLINGS) Check the bedroom and
kitchen.

BOB: I'll sue you for trespass!

MILLER: With your record? (LOOKING
ROUND) This place is filthy, you know.
It's a wonder the Council don't throw
you out.

BOB: Maybe I got friends in
the right places.

MILLER: I bet you have. That's
what I'm interested in.

4. INT. MIKE'S FLAT: LIVING ROOM.   DAY

                          (MODERN. WELL KEPT. OPEN
                          ON THE BINOCULARS LEFT
                          ON THE WINDOW SILL. CUT
                          TO MIKE, WHO IS JUST
                          FINISHING DIALLING A
                          PHONE NUMBER. RINGING
                          TONE, THEN -)

TELEPHONIST: (FILTER) Spencer's.

MIKE: (INTO PHONE) Can I
speak to Mr Spencer, please?

TELEPHONIST: (FILTER) I'll put you
through to his secretary.

MIKE: (INTO PHONE) No, it's
personal and urgent. I mean, he knows
me. It's Mr Byrd here.

TELEPHONIST: (FILTER) Hold on, please.

                          (HE WAITS, LOOKS ACROSS
                          AT THE WINDOW.)

88

```
                    SPENCER:      (FILTER) Spencer.

                    MIKE:         (INTO PHONE) Mike Byrd
                    here.  Listen, there's police calling
                    on old Bob.


          5.  INT.  SPENCER'S OFFICE.                DAY

                         (BUSINESSLIKE, NOT VERY
                         LUXURIOUS.  SPENCER ON
                         PHONE.  JUDY, HIS SECRETARY,
                         COLLECTING SOME PAPERS
                         FROM HIS DESK.)

                    SPENCER:      (INTO PHONE) (BIG PRETEND
                    SMILE)  Well, how lovely to hear from
                    you.  Look, I've just got to pop out
                    for a few minutes, otherwise I'd love
                    to chat.  But I'll give you a ring,
                    soon.  'Bye.

                         (SPENCER CRADLES THE PHONE.)

                    JUDY:         Can I file all these?

                    SPENCER:      What?  Oh, yes.  Thanks.

                         (JUDY EXITS.  SPENCER RISES,
                         PUTS ON HIS TOPCOAT AND HAT,
                         EXITS TO - )


          6.  INT. SPENCER'S OUTER OFFICE.           DAY

                         (JUDY IS FILING.  SPENCER
                         ENTERS FROM INNER OFFICE.)

                    SPENCER:      I'm going out for a few
                    minutes.

                         (HE EXITS TO CORRIDOR.
                         JUDY GOES ON WITH HER
                         FILING.)
```

TELECINE 2

Car Showroom. Day.

A forecourt with petrol
pumps; the showroom in
the background. An ATTENDANT
is serving petrol to a
MOTORIST. SPENCER comes
out of the showroom, and
hurries down the street.

```
          7.  INT.  BOB'S FLAT: HALLWAY.            DAY

                         (MILLER AND BOB)
```

MILLER: What I'm asking is, did you know him?

BOB: Never heard of him.

MILLER: Look at this.

    (MILLER PRODUCES A PHOTO.
    BOB LOOKS.)

INSERT:

    (BOB'S POV OF THE
    PHOTO. IT IS KELLY,
    WEARING A MOUSTACHE.)

RESUME:

BOB: I've never seen anyone looking like that. What do you want him for?

MILLER: He's escaped from nick.

BOB: I wouldn't have anything to do with people like that. There's just me and my cat here. The vicar calls in sometimes –

    (CUTTING IN ON THIS,
    RAWLINGS ENTERS FROM
    BEDROOM CARRYING A ROLLED
    UP PRISON UNIFORM JACKET.)

RAWLINGS: Sarge?

    (RAWLINGS INDICATES FOR
    MILLER TO CROSS TO HIM.
    MILLER MOVES.)

MILLER: Yes?

RAWLINGS: (QUIETLY) Under the bed. Prison issue.

    (MILLER HOLDS UP THE JACKET
    TO SHOW TO BOB.)

MILLER: You ever sweep out under your bed?

BOB: Eh?

MILLER: Come on. You're going for a ride in a motor car.

8. INT/EXT. TELEPHONE KIOSK.   DAY

    (SPENCER ON PHONE. THE
    PIP-PIP-PIP STOPS, AND
    HE PUSHES IN MONEY.)

SPENCER: (INTO PHONE) I'm calling
you back. What's happened?

9. INT. MIKE'S FLAT: LIVING ROOM.   DAY

        (MIKE ON PHONE)

MIKE: (INTO PHONE) I told you.
Only now they've taken him away. I
just saw them.

10. INT/EXT. TELEPHONE KIOSK.   DAY

        SPENCER: (INTO PHONE) Do you
        know why?

            (NOW INTERCUT AS DESIRED)

        MIKE: (INTO PHONE) Maybe
        he's been nicking stuff again down at
        the market.

        SPENCER: (INTO PHONE) All right.
        Well see what you can find out. I'll
        phone again this evening.

            (SPENCER CRADLES THE PHONE.)

11. INT. POLICE STATION: MAIN AREA.   DAY

                (MILLER AND BOB ENTER FROM
                STREET. MILLER GOES TO
                THE DESK SERGEANT, FISHER,
                AND INDICATES BOB.)

        MILLER: Mr Price has come along
        to help us with our enquiries. Put
        him in the truth room. I'm going to
        get Inspector Brown.

                (MILLER GOES DOWN THE
                CORRIDOR. BOB LOOKS UP
                AT FISHER.)

        BOB: Who's going to look
        after my pussy cat?

12. INT. POLICE STATION: INTERVIEW ROOM. DAY

                (OPEN ON BROWN LOOKING
                DOWN INTO CAMERA, FROM
                BOB'S POV.)

BROWN: How long did he stay
with you?

> (ANOTHER ANGLE TO SHOW
> BOB SEATED, BROWN AND
> MILLER STANDING OVER
> HIM. BROWN IS HOLDING
> THE PRISON JACKET.)

BOB: Who?

MILLER: Kelly.

BOB: I don't know any Kelly.

BROWN: You boast about knowing
Kelly.

MILLER: You tell everyone in
the pubs you know Kelly.

BOB: I boast a lot, see. (TO
MILLER) It's like I said to you, that
I got friends in the right places. (TO
BROWN) But it's boasting, see. It
don't mean nothing.

> (OVER THE TOP OF BOB'S
> HEAD, MILLER AND BROWN
> LOOK AT EACH OTHER.
> BROWN SHAKES HIS HEAD,
> INDICATING 'WE AREN'T
> GOING TO GET ANYTHING
> OUT OF HIM'.)

MILLER: How would you like a
cup of tea?

BOB: That would be very
nice, thank you.   Three sugars, if
that's all right.

> (BROWN OPENS THE DOOR.)

BROWN: Constable, stay with him.

> (A POLICE CONSTABLE ENTERS,
> STANDS BY THE DOOR.)

MILLER: After you've had your
tea, we'll have another talk.

> (MILLER AND BROWN EXIT,
> CLOSING THE DOOR. BOB
> TURNS AND SMILES AT THE
> CONSTABLE LEFT TO WATCH
> HIM.)

BOB: It's like I always say,
they're not a bad lot so long as you
treat them right.

<u>TELECINE 3</u>

<u>Country Road. Day.</u>

MARY DUNE, a village housewife,
is walking along carrying a
shopping basket. In among some
trees or bushes at the side of
the road she sees a mound of
old sacks. There is something
about the shape of the mound
that takes her attention. She
advances, curious, to inspect
them. She lifts the corner of
a sack, looks, reacts in horror.
We don't see what she sees. She
hurries away. We <u>HOLD</u> on the
sacks.

<u>Madison's House. Day.</u>

MARY runs past a street sign
reading 'Lime Avenue. Cul-de-
sac'. She goes to the house of
Captain Madison. As she runs
by the gate, we <u>HOLD</u> on the
name on the garden gate –
'Mafeking'.

13. INT. CAPTAIN MADISON'S STUDY.   DAY

           (NEAT, TIDY. MILITARY
           TOUCHES. DOOR TO HALL
           IS OPEN. MADISON HELPS
           IN MARY, NOW IN DELAYED
           SHOCK.)

<u>MADISON</u>:   Sit down. I'll get
you some brandy.

           (MARY ALLOWS HERSELF TO
           BE SAT IN AN ARMCHAIR.
           MADISON GETS BRANDY
           FROM A LITTLE DRINKS
           LOCKER.)

<u>MARY</u>:   I've never seen anyone
dead before.

<u>MADISON</u>:   Try not to dwell on it.

<u>MARY</u>:   But I can <u>see</u> him.

<u>MADISON</u>:   He may not be dead, you
know. I've seen men stunned by
explosives –

<u>MARY</u>:   (CUTTING IN) He's dead,
Captain Madison. I know it.

93

MADISON: All right. I'll call
the police. Get this into you.

    (HE FINISHES POURING A
    SHOT OF BRANDY, PUTS
    THE TUMBLER INTO MARY'S
    HAND.)

MADISON: Here.

    (STILL SHAKING, SHE TRIES
    TO DRINK. MADISON LIFTS
    HIS PHONE, STARTS TO DIAL
    999.)

14. INT. JOYCE KELLY'S HOME: LIVING ROOM. DAY

    (NEAT, WELL KEPT. WE OPEN
    ON A MANTELPIECE FRAMED
    PHOTOGRAPH OF KELLY WITH
    A MOUSTACHE — THE SAME AS
    THE ONE IN SC. 7.)

NEWS READER: (FILTER)(OOV) In the
House of Commons today uproar broke
out when the Prime Minister said
there could be no supplementary
benefits for old age pensioners until
early in the New Year.

    (ANOTHER ANGLE TO SHOW
    JOYCE KELLY AND MIKE
    SITTING ON THE SETTEE,
    ARMS ENTWINED, WATCHING
    TELEVISION. WE NEED NOT
    SEE THE SCREEN.)

NEWS READER: (FILTER)(OOV) The body
of William George Kelly was found today
somewhere in the South East of England,
but the police have refused to say
where. A police spokesman said there
was reason to believe that Kelly, who
escaped from Wandsworth prison last
month, had been murdered, probably
some days ago.

    (JOYCE TURNS OFF THE
    TELEVISION SET.)

JOYCE: So that's it, then.

MIKE: Yeh. Poor old George.
So now you're a widow.

JOYCE: I've been as good as
for the last five years.

MIKE: You visited regular.

94

JOYCE: You call that a marriage,
sitting looking at a block across a
table? - thirty minutes once a month
and neither of you knowing what to say?

SFX: CAR DRAWS UP OUTSIDE.

          (MIKE GOES TO THE WINDOW,
          LOOKS OUT.)

TELECINE 4

Joyce Kelly's House. Day.

One in a row of suburban semis.
A car is parked. RAWLINGS and
MILLER are walking from it
towards the front door.

15. INT. JOYCE KELLY'S HOME: LIVING ROOM. DAY

          (RESUME SC. 14.)

MIKE: It's the police.

JOYCE: They're bound to call,
aren't they.

MIKE: But I mustn't be found
here!

JOYCE: Then you'd better slip
out the back way.

          (MIKE EXITS. JOYCE
          PREPARES TO RECEIVE
          THE POLICE.)

95

Some explanations about the re-write:

Scene 2 Bob's last speech, when he says the dead man's name, may not be entirely realistic. But it 'spells it out to the audience' that he knew Kelly, which is important to what follows.

T/C 1 The suggestion that the director should 'PAN round to and ZOOM IN on' Mike Byrd looking from an adjacent high rise block is so that the shot of Mike will be visually related to the scene that he is observing. In the previous version it may not have been clear to the audience that Mike at his window was in any way related to the policemen calling on Bob's flat.

Scene 3 By having Miller and Rawlings walk straight into Bob's hallway without being asked, which could well be in the character of two tough detectives dealing with an old rogue like Bob, we were able to avoid ever seeing the uniformed police constable presumably left out on the balcony. It would be up to the studio director to angle his camera so that it did not shoot through the doorway during the few moments when the door was open.

Scene 5 Judy is deliberately in this scene to avoid Spencer saying the cliché line, "I told you never to phone me here". Also, her presence puts Spencer on the spot, makes him sweat, and thus gives us more tension.

Scene 6 By 'JUDY GOES ON WITH HER FILING', which suggests holding on her, we kill the moments it took for Spencer to get down the unseen corridor and to be seen leaving the car showroom the moment T/C 2 starts. This is not a technical bridge, as described in pages 18 to 24, because as we are here switching from studio to a pre-filmed insert no time is needed to get the character from one set to another. But it is a dramatic bridge. In other words, it could look comical to see a man go through a door into a corridor, and immediately be seen coming from another door into, say, an exterior.

T/C 2 We must presume that this location at the car showroom is going to be used again in the story. Otherwise it would be far too expensive to use it only for this five second scene. If it were not to be used again, the nature of Spencer's business must be established some other way. Instead of having Judy in Sc. 5, we could have an overalled petrol pump attendant seeing Spencer about some work matter. A couple of lines of dialogue would be enough to tell us what business Spencer is in. A minor role actor could be much cheaper than setting up the car showroom location shot.

Scene 8 INT/EXT means 'Interior for exterior', i.e. an exterior that can be shot in studio.

Scenes 8–10 In an intercutting telephone conversation, where both parties can be seen on screen, for plot or dramatic reasons you may wish to signify whom should be seen at which part of the conversation. However, if it doesn't really matter, and you wish to leave it to the discretion of the director, having established by three cuts that boths parties can be seen, (NOW INTERCUT AS DESIRED) tells the director that you wish to leave it up to him from then on.

Scenes 11–12 Although Sc. 12 opens close on Brown, but for only one short line, there is no technical bridge to get Bob into the set (as was the case with getting John into Gillick's office in the bridging example on page 20). We are presuming that this play will be produced on edited tape, general nowadays in major drama productions. The director will stop the tape at the end of Sc. 11, set up Bob, Miller, and Brown in the interview room set, and start the tape again.

Scene 12 The police constable who enters at the end of this scene to guard Bob will *not* be the same police constable whom we saw on film in T/C 1. If they were the same non-speaking actor, then the retainer must be paid for the weeks between the location shooting and this studio scene. Hence two police constables, one on film only, are specified in the characters-and-sets list. This is an instance where two of the same thing can be cheaper than one.

T/C 3 Using the device of the mound of sacks, we save on taking Kelly on location (we also save on his retainer fee). By not having a scream from Mary when she 'sees' the body under the sacks, we save taking a sound recording unit on location. The film can be shot mute; later a wild track of general open air sounds can be dubbed on. Note that we also lose the cycling (special talents).

The HOLD on the sacks at the end of the first scene eats up the time it takes Mary to arrive at Lime Avenue—another dramatic, but not technical, bridge. There must be some reason later in the story for this to be a cul-de-sac (perhaps a car chase ends here). Your audience's mind will hook onto the peculiarity of this being a dead-end road, and if nothing materialises from it they will feel cheated. This is in line with the novelist's principle that if you describe a scene where there is a gun on the wall *it must be used*, otherwise don't refer to it. The HOLD on the garden gate name 'Mafeking' helps account for the time Mary took to get to the front door, ring the bell, and for Captain Madison to answer. It keeps up the pace to cut straight to Madison helping Mary into his study. It also saves the studio space and expense of showing the hallway in Madison's house.

Scene 13 Presumably Madison's study set, Madison and Mary, are all going to feature again in the story. Otherwise we could simply see Mary find the body, and run to a telephone kiosk; without a word of dialogue it would be obvious she was phoning the police. Also, this would keep Mary entirely on film, and the actress need only be employed for one day.

Scene 14 Featuring the framed photograph of Kelly is again spelling it out to the audience. They know exactly where they are. In this version, it is suggested that the screen of the television set is not seen at all. This saves the added technical complications of having a real television receiving set in the set; also we don't now need a little studio set for the news reader nor a camera to shoot him. The news reader's lines will be pre-recorded by an actor on ordinary sound tape, and this will be played during the opening of this scene.

TC/3 Again it is presumed that the location will be used more than once in the story. Otherise it might be sufficient for the arrival of the police to be reported to us by Mike as he stands at the window.

Anybody Here Seen Kelly? is a script for electronic, or tape, television, the production method consisting of prefilmed inserts and fairly continuous-flow studio scenes. Most people in the industry still refer to this system as 'live television', this being a carry over from former times (see page 14); however, it would be wrong to perpetuate the misnomer in this book. It is a very different system from TV/film, as you will learn in the next chapter.

Chapter 9

TV/FILM—AN INDUSTRY WITHIN AN INDUSTRY

In the days of the Great Temple there was an inner sanctum known as the Holy of Holies where only the highest priests were allowed to enter. So it is with the tight little world of the TV/film writers. If the number of fully-employed tape television series writers in Britain barely exceeds sixty, the number of established TV/film writers can be counted on two hands, and you've still got some fingers over. They make a big lot of money. What's more, they only have six or seven plots between them, which they churn out with unfailing regularity.

That's how it looks to the writer who is on the outside of this industry within an industry. Objectively, the view is correct. TV/film is written by a tiny clique. "But," said a TV/film series editor to whom I put this point, "there are reasons. Most live television writers won't accept the disciplines we have to work to. It takes ages to brief a writer fully on exactly what we want, technically and economically. Most give up half way."

Despite every economy achieved by a good producer/script-editor team, TV/film costs vastly more per entertainment minute than does taped electronic television. The cost of colour film stock is high, and so are the laboratory charges for developing and making prints. Because of our unpredictable weather, location shooting is limited and studios are very expensive to hire. There is also the vicious circle that because TV/film is primarily for export international stars must be used: their fees are high, and they expect very highly-paid cameramen and designers to be used. So it boils down to gambler's economics. Fast action TV/film series, made on celluloid film, can sell anywhere in the world. Every television station, be it an American network or a single mast mud hut in an African jungle state, has facilities for transmitting film. Videotaped shows can be telerecorded onto film, but some quality is lost in the process, and some overseas buyers have a prejudice against it. Tape productions can only sell where videotape play-back facilities exist, and these are by no means universal. Even where overseas buyers have videotape facilities, there can be lineage problems. The image on a television screen is made up of a number of lines and the systems used vary from one country to another. France uses 850 lines per frame, Britain and most of the rest of Europe uses 625, the United States and Canada 525. Since a videotape recording is geared to one specific lineage, if it is to be transmitted over a different system the electrical impulses must first pass through a converter, a very expensive and rare piece of television gadgetry. But every television station in the world must have telecine facilities to show films. What's more, film is less bulky than tape, costs less in freightage charges—and, when you've supplied all the major outlets with colour copies, you cut physical distribution costs by supplying minor international outputs, in countries which haven't got colour television yet, with 16mm black-and-white versions. So, if you produce your series on film, despite all the costs you may strike lucky and cash in on world wide sales. Without luck, you go bankrupt.

To write for TV/film you must think internationally. To quote a leading TV/film editor: "I've been told by critics, even in print, that I crawl to the Americans. This is not true. I crawl to the Americans. I crawl to the Germans. I crawl to the Japanese. I crawl to the Fiji Islanders."

In recent years the series *The Saint, Department S, The Avengers* (from when Diana Rigg started), *The Champions, Jason King,* and *The Persuaders* have been representative of British TV/film output. You may knock them on artistic grounds, you may criticise their lack of social message. But for sheer professionalism, these series are all first rate. And they do contribute something to our sad old balance of payments. As Brecht's pirate Jenny pointed out, "Erst kommt das Fressen, dann kommt die Moral" ("First food, then morals"). The TV/film industry brings in the dollars, the marks, and the yen: perhaps therefore as a nation we can afford the high moral tone and artistic integrity of BBC2.

As for the sameness of plots, note what Dennis Spooner says on page 101. The complicated social problem, based on an intriguing facet of the contemporary British social scene, may make a great drama for *Play of the Week*. But would it be understood in Nigeria, or Osaka, or Idaho? "Maybe we do have only seven plots," says Spooner, "because there are only seven deadly sins, and all the world understands them." Spooner makes another telling point about the differences between American and British TV/film series: "Our product must never be parochial. Hollywood trained the world for years before television arrived. So the average Thai has been educated to know there's a difference between Brooklyn and Texas, but would he know the difference between Bermondsey and Bradford? I doubt it."

Because TV/film series costs so much money to make, the producer has to secure some overseas markets before he starts. At one time the American market had to be secured before all else: it remains a vital market. But now you find consortia of British, West German, and Australian companies getting together, pooling their resources, at least with the assurance of those three markets as a start. The star system has operated strongly in TV/film. Harry W. Junkin, when script supervisor on *The Saint*, was prone to tell would-be writers: "We sell in 87 territories for four reasons. They are Roger Moore, Roger Moore, Roger Moore, and Roger Moore." Some people say the star system is less important now, except for the United States. When selling to the Americans, if you had Paul Newman or Michael Caine signed up for a 26-episode series, you could show them a copy of London's yellow pages, tell them that is the script, and you'd surely make a sale.

Writing for TV/film is film writing at its most economical. It is not akin to the epic *Zulu* mentioned earlier, because no TV/film budget could afford a thousand black extras; but nor is it the cosy claustrophobic world of the typical electronic studio play. The pace is much faster, the overall production slicker. For instance, in the studio there is no fourth wall. In TV/film you can cut to a reverse shot, so that the audience sees the side of the room from which the last shot was taken. This is done by striking the wall on one side, moving the camera to a set up on that side, and putting in the wall where the camera was previously standing. Techniques such as these give much greater reality.

TV/films are not made in story sequence. The production people analyse the script and check how many times a particular set is to appear. That set is built, and all the scenes for it are shot. The set is then struck, another erected, and the process repeated. But even more economical is the re-dressing of the existing set. When one of the basic series sets (e.g. the hero's home) is currently erected in studio, they may use it to shoot scenes for more than one episode. Equally when the series' 'second unit' (camera and crew that only goes on location; 'first unit' only does studio work) is on location with the star's 'double', they may spend the early morning filming the double as he swims across a river for Episode 3, mid-morning filming him as he leaps from a burning house for Episode 7, and the afternoon shooting him as he leaps from one moving car to another for Episode 14. Doubles are used a lot in TV/films, for three reasons: (one) it would be disasterous for the series were the star to get injured and be unable to work for some time, (two) stunt men have trained themselves to feats of physical action beyond the capabilities of most actors, and (three) in a tight production schedule, making one complete TV/film every ten days, it isn't practical to waste the star's time travelling to outside locations. Most TV/film leading actors have both a double/stand-in plus a stunt-double. Both must have a physical resemblance to the star if seen in a long shot. The double/stand-in is used for normal long shot location work. The stunt-double is used for moments of athletic action, and is also almost certainly hired as the 'fight arranger' for the whole series. (Note: If you have a fight in a story, be it for tape television or TV/film, a direction such as 'THEY FIGHT. JOE WINS' is quite enough. A blow-by-blow description in your script will almost certainly be ignored.) In the instance given above, the leap from one car to another would be done on location with the stunt-double. The close shot inside the car, as the hero scrambles through the open door, would be shot in studio using the star himself.

The film maker's way of making cuts has already been described on page 31: every scene is shot at least twice from two, three, or four different angles. Later the film editor and the producer make up the desired composition from hundreds of feet of film (in big-time cinema films, the director would be involved in this process; in TV film he's probably already busy shooting the next episode). Whereas the tape television writer can be delightfully vague in his telecine stage directions, the TV/film writer is required to write a 'shooting script' which clearly indicates each set up. If a set up is in the script, it is obviously wanted for some plot or dramatic reason. A director, running his schedule close, is often tempted to shoot a scene the quick way, which could mean to omit a set up. By the time it comes to the film editing that essential shot is gone—forever! In TV/film, where the director is simply doing the job assigned to him, the script must be watertight before the first foot of film is shot, and the director must keep to it. A lot of the time, the second unit director may not even know what the story is about: so it is not up to him to cut corners.

A big difference between electronic television production methods and TV/film is that in film television there is no production day comparable with a VTR. Equally, there is no 'read through' (to be described in Chapter 12). In fact, you could contrive an entire film script in which some of the actors never meet at all, as was done by Terence Rattigan when he wrote the screenplay for the star-studded film *The VIPs*. If you remember, Elizabeth Taylor and Richard Burton, Orson Wells, Margaret Rutherford, and Rod Taylor, were never all together in the same scene. They made their scenes for the film as and when they were available from other acting commitments. (With present day videotape editing, this can also happen in tape television. See page 32). In TV/film, the filming of scenes takes place every day. An actor learns his lines overnight. Next morning they rehearse for a 'take' (a scene or a little part of a scene) and film it. A take might only consist of:

CLOSE ON MORIARTY

MORIARTY

Who? Me?

Although a take may only be one line, it needs a lot of takes to shoot the daily average of four to five minutes of film. If those takes relate to three or four different episodes it all becomes very complicated. A leading actor may not only have to change his clothes six times in a day's shooting; he also has to change mood, and try to remember which story he is playing in. It isn't easy.

Here is part of our example script as for TV/film production. We can now presume that our story is one of the episodes in a series which we shall call *The Police*. Miller, Rawlings, and Brown are now our series characters (or stars), which means they appear in every episode; Bob, Mike, Spencer, Joyce and the others are now 'episode characters', appearing in this episode only. Research has shown that the old music hall song *Has Anybody Here Seen Kelly?* is not universally known in the United States, so we start off by changing the title. Also, the American's don't have council flats as we know them, so the council now becomes the landlord. You may notice some other changes.

The script layout used in the following pages is for a *commissioned*

TV/film script, i.e. where through pre-scripting discussions with the script editor, the writer knows what will be filmed on location and what will be filmed in studio or studio lot. If you write an uncommissioned, un-discussed script for cinema film, a different layout style is preferred. For a comparison of feature film and TV/film script layouts, see pages 184 to 187 of *The Writer's Guide 1970*, now out of print but still available in many public reference libraries.

<u>"T H E   P O L I C E"</u>

Episode 14

2nd Series

<u>'Loser Takes All'</u>

by

John Smith

John Smith,
234 Sandringham Road,
London NW11
(01-200 3456)

Author's agent:
William Baxter (Scripts) Ltd,
1 Dawkins Street,
London WC1
(01-401 7890)

CHARACTERS

DETECTIVE SERGEANT MILLER (AND DOUBLE)
DETECTIVE CONSTABLE RAWLINGS (AND DOUBLE)
INSPECTOR BROWN

EPISODE   <u>LEADS</u>
BOB PRICE
MIKE BYRD
SPENCER
JOYCE KELLY

<u>SMALL</u>
JUDY
SERGEANT FISHER
MARY
CAPTAIN MADISON

<u>NON-SPEAKING</u>
KELLY
POLICE CONSTABLE (AND DOUBLE IF NECESSARY)
GAS PUMP ATTENDANT
MOTORIST
POLICE CAR DRIVER

<u>VOICES</u>
TELEPHONIST (GIRL)
TELEVISION NEWS READER

STUDIO

     INT. BOB PRICE'S APARTMENT: HALLWAY

     INT. BOB PRICE'S APARTMENT: BEDROOM

     INT. MIKE BYRD'S APARTMENT: BEDROOM

        (i.e. BOB PRICE'S BEDROOM RE-DRESSED)

     INT. SPENCER'S OFFICE

     INT. SPENCER'S OUTER OFFICE

     INT. POLICE STATION: MAIN AREA

     INT. POLICE STATION: INTERVIEW ROOM

     INT. CAPTAIN MADISON'S STUDY

     INT. JOYCE KELLY'S HOME: LIVING ROOM

     INT. POLICE CAR.

STUDIO REPROS

     INT/EXT. BOB PRICE'S FRONT DOOR

STUDIO LOT

     EXT. TELEPHONE BOOTH

     EXT. JOYCE KELLY'S HOME

LOCATION

     EXT. MODERN APARTMENT BLOCK "A" (WITH OUTSIDE BALCONIES)

     EXT. MODERN APARTMENT BLOCK "B"

     EXT. CAR SHOWROOM (WITH GAS PUMPS)

     EXT. COUNTRY ROAD "A"

     EXT. COUNTRY ROAD "B"

     EXT. MADISON'S HOUSE

"LOSER TAKES ALL"

TEASER.

FADE IN:

1. EXT. MODERN APARTMENT BLOCK "A". NIGHT. LOCATION.   1.

   ESTABLISH. IT IS LATE AT NIGHT AND THERE ARE ONLY A FEW
   LIGHTS SHOWING AT THE WINDOWS. WE HEAR DISTANT CITY SOUNDS.

                                                        CUT TO:

2. INT/EXT. BOB PRICE'S FRONT DOOR. NIGHT. STUDIO (REPRO).   2.

   FEATURE THE FRONT DOOR OF ONE OF THE APARTMENTS ON A SECTION
   OF BALCONY. CARRY OVER THE DISTANT CITY SOUNDS FROM THE
   PREVIOUS SHOT.

   BOB PRICE MOVES INTO FRAME, PRODUCES HIS KEY, FUMBLES AT THE
   LOCK. HE IS IN GOOD SPIRITS.

   BOB PRICE IS IN HIS SIXTIES, A LITTLE FERRET OF A MAN WHO HAS
   BEEN MANY TIMES IN PRISON ON PETTY CHARGES. HE WEARS A
   BATTERED CLOTH CAP AND A TATTERED OLD TOPCOAT.

   AS BOB PRICE OPENS THE DOOR AND MOVES INSIDE, WE:
                                                        CUT TO:

3. INT. BOB PRICE'S APARTMENT: HEALLWAY. NIGHT. STUDIO.   3.

   THE HALLWAY IS MODERN, BUT SQUALID AND FURNISHED WITH JUNK.

   BOB PRICE ENTERS, CLOSES THE DOOR. HE TAKES OFF HIS CAP,
   PULLS FROM HIS TOPCOAT POCKET A NEWSPAPER PACKET OF FISH AND
   CHIPS, UNWRAPS THEM.   HE IS A BIT TIPSY, HAVING BEEN DRINKING
   WITH HIS FRIENDS ALL EVENING.   HE EATS A CHIP, THEN SELECTS
   A BIT OF FISH.

                         BOB
                 (CALLING) Puss. Puss. Where are
                 you?

   HE LOOKS.

   BOB'S POV

   THE DOOR TO THE BEDROOM IS OPEN.

   RESUME ON BOB

                         BOB
                 Are you in there, my little darling?

   HE STARTS TO MOVE FORWARD.

   ANOTHER ANGLE

   BOB CROSSES TO THE BEDROOM DOOR, GOES IN.

                                                        CUT TO:

4. INT. BOB PRICE'S APARTMENT: BEDROOM. NIGHT STUDIO.   4.

   THE BEDROOM, LIKE THE HALLWAY, IS MODERN, WITH GLEAMING NEW
   PAINT. AGAIN THE FURNITURE IS JUNK. RAGGED OLD CURTAINS ARE
   CASUALLY HOOKED UP.

   BOB PRICE ENTERS, HOLDING THE NEWSPAPER PACKET, AND THE BIT OF
   FISH.

4. CONTINUED

                          BOB
          I got some fish for you...

HE STOPS DEAD, REACTS, STARES.

BOB'S POV

KELLY IS ON THE UNMADE BED. HE IS DEAD.

GEORGE KELLY. FORTY. A BIG, TOUGH CRIMINAL, BUT WITH THE
LOOK OF A BORN LOSER. HE IS DRESSED IN SHIRT SLEEVES, ILL-
FITTED PANTS WITH SUSPENDERS, HEAVY BOOTS.

RESUME CLOSE ON BOB

HE STARES.

                          BOB
              Kelly!

END OF TEASER.
                                                  CUT TO:

STANDARD OPENING TITLE SEQUENCE: "THE POLICE"

                    U.S. COMMERCIAL BREAK

                                                  FADE OUT

ACT ONE

FADE IN:

5. EXT. MODERN APARTMENT BLOCK "B". DAY. LOCATION.   5.

    ESTABLISH, ANGLE TO A HIGH WINDOW.

                                                  CUT TO:

6. INT. MIKE BYRD'S APARTMENT: BEDROOM. DAY. STUDIO.   6.

    IDENTICAL TO BOB PRICE'S BEDROOM, BUT WELL FURNISHED AND WELL
    KEPT.

    MIKE BYRD IS AT THE WINDOW. HE HOLDS A PAIR OF BINOCULARS TO
    HIS CHEST.

    MIKE BYRD IS TWENTY EIGHT. HE IS GOOD LOOKING, ATHLETIC, AND
    CRIMINAL. HE IS VERY WELL DRESSED IN CASUAL SLACKS AND
    EXPENSIVE SHIRT. HE WEARS A FANCY RING. HE OBVIOUSLY TAKES A
    LOT OF INTEREST IN HIS PERSONAL APPEARANCE.

    HOLD ON MIKE FOR SEVERAL BEATS, THEN:
                                                  CUT TO:

7. EXT. MODERN APARTMENT BLOCK "A". DAY. LOCATION.   7.

    A POLICE CAR APPEARS, STOPS, OUTSIDE THE MODERN APARTMENT
    BLOCK THAT CONTAINS BOB PRICE'S APARTMENT.
                                                  CUT TO:

8. INT. POLICE CAR. DAY. STUDIO.   8.

    MILLER, RAWLINGS, AND A YOUNG UNIFORMED POLICE CONSTABLE
    ARE IN THE POLICE CAR WITH THE DRIVER.

    THE DRIVER PULLS ON THE HANDBRAKE, SWITCHES OFF THE ENGINE.

    MILLER, RAWLINGS, AND THE YOUNG POLICE CONSTABLE, START TO
    GET OUT.
                                                  CUT TO:

9. <u>EXT. MODERN APARTMENT BLOCK "A". DAY. LOCATION.</u>   9.

    MILLER (DOUBLE), RAWLINGS (DOUBLE), AND THE YOUNG POLICE
    CONSTABLE (DOUBLE) LEAVE THE POLICE CAR AND MOVE TOWARDS THE
    MODERN APARTMENT BLOCK.

    WE SEE THIS IN LONG SHOT. AS THEY MOVE AWAY WE ANGLE TO THE
    HIGH WINDOW IN MODERN APARTMENT BLOCK "B" (MIKE'S BEDROOM).

    OVER THE ABOVE SCENES (5, 6, 7, 8, 9) WE HAVE, AS CONVENIENT,
    SUPERIMPOSED AND FADED THE NECESSARY OPENING CREDITS (WRITER,
    DIRECTOR) AND:

    <u>THE EPISODE TITLE:</u>   "LOSER TAKES ALL"

    AS THE FINAL CAPTION FADES WE TIGHTEN IN ON THE HIGH WINDOW
    WHERE WE ESTABLISHED MIKE BYRD.

                                                          CUT TO:

10. <u>INT. MIKE BYRD'S APARTMENT: BEDROOM. DAY. STUDIO.</u>   10.

    <u>CLOSE ON MIKE BYRD</u>

    HE HAS REGISTERED THE ARRIVAL OF THE POLICE CAR. NOW HE
    LIFTS THE BINOCULARS TO HIS EYES. TIGHTEN ON HIM.

                                                          CUT TO:

11. <u>EXT. MODERN APARTMENT BLOCK "A". DAY. LOCATION.</u>   11.

    <u>MIKE BYRD'S POV</u>

    <u>BINOCULAR MATTE MASK</u>

    MILLER (DOUBLE), RAWLINGS (DOUBLE), AND THE YOUNG UNIFORMED
    POLICE CONSTABLE (DOUBLE) ARE WALKING ALONG A BALCONY ON THE
    MODERN APARTMENT BLOCK, MAKING FOR BOB PRICE'S FRONT DOOR.

                                                          CUT TO:

12. <u>INT. MIKE BYRD'S APARTMENT: BEDROOM. DAY. STUDIO.</u>   12.

    <u>RESUME ON MIKE BYRD</u>

    HE TURNS SLIGHTLY AS HE FOLLOWS THE PROGRESS OF THE PEOPLE HE
    IS WATCHING. THEN HE LOWERS HIS BINOCULARS. HE FROWNS. HOLD
    ON HIM A BEAT.

                                                          CUT TO:

13. <u>INT/EXT. BOB PRICE'S FRONT DOOR. DAY. STUDIO (REPRO).</u>   13.

    MILLER IS KNOCKING REPEATEDLY ON BOB'S FRONT DOOR. RAWLINGS
    AND THE YOUNG POLICE CONSTABLE ARE STANDING BY.

    AFTER A FEW SECONDS BOB FURTIVELY OPENS THE DOOR.

                            <u>MILLER</u>
                  'Morning.

    MILLER PUSHES HIS WAY STRAIGHT IN, FOLLOWED BY RAWLINGS.

                                                          CUT TO:

14. <u>INT. BOB PRICE'S APARTMENT: HALLWAY. DAY. STUDIO.</u>   14.

    MILLER PUSHES PAST BOB PRICE, FOLLOWED BY RAWLINGS.

                            <u>BOB</u>
                  Here, who are you? What do you
                  want?

                          MILLER
                Just taking a look round.

    MILLER INDICATES FOR RAWLINGS TO SEARCH THE PLACE.

                          MILLER
                      (TO RAWLINGS)
                Check the bedroom and kitchen.

    RAWLINGS NODS AND MOVES AWAY, GOES INTO THE BEDROOM.

                          BOB
                I'll sue you for trespass!

                          MILLER
                With your record?

    MILLER IS TAKING A GOOD LOOK AROUND AS HE SPEAKS.

                          MILLER
                This place is filthy. It's a wonder
                the landlord doesn't throw you out.
                                                      CUT TO:

15. EXT. MODERN APARTMENT BLOCK "B". DAY. LOCATION.   15.

    WE ZOOM IN SLOWLY ON MIKE BYRD'S HIGH WINDOW, AND HEAR:

                          MIKE'S VOICE
                I want to speak to Mr Spencer.
                                                      CUT TO:

16. INT. MIKE BYRD'S APARTMENT: BEDROOM. DAY. STUDIO.   16.

    CLOSE ON MIKE BYRD

    HE IS USING THE BEDSIDE PHONE. HE LOOKS WORRIED.

                          MIKE
                (INTO PHONE) It's urgent.

                          TELEPHONIST'S VOICE
                (FILTER) I'll put you through to his
                secretary.

                          MIKE
                (INTO PHONE) I just said it's urgent.
                I'm a personal friend.

                          TELEPHONIST'S VOICE
                (FILTER) Hold on, please.

    MIKE WAITS. AS HE DOES SO HE GLANCES APPREHENSIVELY OVER TO
    THE WINDOW.

    MIKE'S POV

    OF THE WINDOW. THE BINOCULARS REST ON THE SILL.

                          SPENCER'S VOICE
                (FILTER) Spencer. Who's that?

    RESUME CLOSE ON MIKE

    HE SWINGS BACK TO THE TELEPHONE.

                          MIKE
                (INTO PHONE) Mike Byrd here. Listen,
                there's police calling on old Bob.
                                                      CUT TO:

17. INT. SPENCER'S OFFICE. DAY. STUDIO.   17.

    IT IS A BUSINESSLIKE, NOT VERY LUXURIOUS OFFICE. ON THE

WALLS A COUPLE OF FRAMED PICTURES OF VINTAGE MOTOR CARS.
SPENCER IS AT HIS DESK ON THE PHONE.

SPENCER. FORTY-FIVE. THIN, SHARP-LOOKING BUSINESS MAN, HAIR
PLASTERED BACK, FORMAL BUT INEXPENSIVE SUIT. IN APPEARANCE AS
NEAT AND TIDY AS HIS DESK TOP.

HIS SECRETARY, JUDY, IS COLLECTING SOME PAPERS FROM SPENCER'S
"OUT TRAY".

JUDY GLOVER. 27. A PRETTY, SUBURBAN YOUNG MOTHER, DOING THIS
MORNINGS-ONLY JOB NOW THE FIRST KID IS IN NURSERY SCHOOL.
INTELLIGENT.

SPENCER SPEAKS INTO THE PHONE WITH A BIG PRETEND SMILE.

> SPENCER
> (INTO PHONE) Well, how lovely to hear from
> you. Look, I've just got to pop out for a
> few minutes, otherwise I'd love to talk.
> But I'll give you a ring soon. 'Bye.

SPENCER CRADLES THE PHONE. HE IS SWEATING SLIGHTLY.

> JUDY
> Can I file all these?

> SPENCER
> What? Oh, yes. Thanks.

JUDY EXITS WITH THE PAPERS. SPENCER LOOKS AT THE PHONE,
HAS SECOND THOUGHTS, THEN GETS UP, GOES TO WHERE HIS HAT AND
TOP COAT ARE HANGING.

From that short example you will see how much more visually, administratively, and above all precisely, the writer had to think. For the close shots of actors at Bob Price's front door, he suggested the use of a studio reproduction. This means the designer would go and look at the location block of flats, take colour photographs of a typical front door, then have an exact reproduction built in the studio. However, whenever you are going to use a studio reproduction, you should first give a long shot of the actual location.

In his pre-scripting discussions with the script editor, the writer learnt that within the 'studio lot' (the car parks, roadways, and out-buildings in the grounds of the film studio) there existed both a public telephone kiosk and a house (maybe where the studio caretaker lives). So his sets list proposes the use of both of these ready made 'sets'. This would save travelling time to outside locations.

A writer embarking on series work, be it for tape television or TV/film, should always ask for two or three copies of existing accepted scripts, if only to check the layout style used for that particular show. In our example, the scenes are numbered. On a TV/film show I edited in Australia, the American producer wanted every set up to be numbered.

Note the US commercial break. Our own Independent Broadcasting Authority (the IBA) permits two commercials in a series episode, one in plays. American television has seven breaks in one television hour.

Since TV/film is made to sell internationally, avoid the convoluted sentences favoured by some English:

> JOHN
> I was thinking, don't you think it
> wouldn't be a bad idea for us to
> have dinner tonight?

Instead, keep it simple:

> JOHN
> How about dinner tonight?

For non-English language markets, don't complicate the dubber's job with chat about word definitions:

> GREG
> I call this drink fair dinkum.

> MATTHEW
> I've always wondered what you
> Australians really mean by that—
> 'fair dinkum'?

How will your German or Portuguese dubbing or sub-titles expert deal with that exchange?

Note in the example script the stylised use of the voice-over technique in Sc. 15, when we are closing in on the exterior of Mike's flat but can already hear his talking; and again in Sc. 16, when our view of the window through Mike's eyes is interrupted by Spencer's voice on the phone. Pace is all important in TV/film, and this is one of the techniques that helps to maintain it. There are three drama speeds in the mechanical media: radio, electronic television, and film. A reversal of the voice-over technique is visual-over. This is when the same conversation is maintained between characters whom we see in a succession of venues. There is an example on pages 218 to 219.

Chapter 10

PROGRAMME PATTERNS

Television has an established itinerary of production genres. It is as well for you to understand what these are, so that you'll know what people in the industry are talking about.

Adaptations Plays, serials, or even sometimes series, based on books, short stories, or stage plays. If the original work is still in copyright, the adaptor must first get permission from the author or his executors. Often all 'mechanical media' (cinema film, television, radio) rights of best sellers are bought by film producers, who then sit on them and never actually make the movie. Many television adaptations are instigated by the BBC or an ITV Contractor, who sort out the copyright problem: they then invite a writer known to them to write the adaptation.

Anthology A series of plays all supposedly written about the same theme, although the link is sometimes laughably tenuous. Different writers contribute, usually by invitation.

Comedy, Situation Comedy: Series of 6, 13, or 26 half hour episodes, using the same leading characters every week, created and all written by the same writer or writing team. Probably the highest paid form of television writing. In recent years, cinema features based on television situation comedy series have been big box office successes. Writers usually trim their original concept to suit their stars; or conceive their situation comedy with certain stars in mind from the outset. Cannot be sold on 'format' (description of a series idea) alone; only one or more complete episode scripts show whether the idea is going to come across as being funny. *Review:* Such as *Monty Python's Flying Circus*. Compositions of sketches and visual jokes. Usually written by a close knit team who in conference hack out themes for the next show, then individually go and write their contributions.

From: Malcolm Hulke,
         c/o Harvey Unna Ltd,
         14 Beaumont Mews,
         Marylebone High Street,
         London W1N 4HE

"FILL HER UP" - RUNNING GAG

1.   Filling station. A motorist drives up. The
      attendant comes to the car: "Yeh?" Motorist:
      "Fill her up." The attendant puts fingers in
      mouth, whistles towards the sales office.
      Other attendants come running from the sales
      office carrying things - bird cage, old
      cushions, fish in glass case, tailor's dummy,
      any kind of junk, and start filling up the
      motorist's car.

2.   Continue filling up process, maybe now on
      speeded up film. Attendants bring out arm-waving
      girl in bikini, huge sleeping dog, brace of
      pheasants, etc, etc. They fill the car's cabin
      to the roof, hemming in the driver. Important
      that the motorist takes all this as being
      perfectly normal.

3.   Attendants packing things into the boot, sitting
      on the lid to make it close. Cabin completely
      packed out. Motorist hardly able to move. The
      motorist asks: "How much?" Totally serious,
      the first attendant brings out notebook, starts
      totting up: "Bird cage, a quid. Two cushions,
      say twenty five pence the pair..."

4.   Attendant still totting up: "Four pairs of old
      shoes, assorted sizes, fifty pence... Let's see,
      that'll come to three hundred and forty seven
      pounds and ninepence..."

This is how you might submit a gag to a light entertainment show—one sheet
of paper, with your name and address or agent's name and address. Always
give gags, jokes, even one-liners, a title for reference and contractual purposes.

No team space for outsiders, although anyone can try their luck submitting a sketch or two. *Gag:* Certain shows built around star comedians or singers use a lot of verbal and some visual gags. Known one-line gag writers are invited, but anyone else can submit material.

Plays Any length from 30 to 45, 60, or 75 minutes. Of these, 30 has the most limited market, 60 the most internationally saleable. Can be any theme by any writer. Some series writers who have never sold a one off play, either because they have no original ideas or are too busy churning out episodes for top-paying series, firmly believe that plays editors *only* accept plays from vicars in Norfolk, housewives in Glamorganshire, or safecrackers just out of Dartmoor. There may be a scintilla of truth in this; plays editors are always looking for new talent, and some believe that the old series writing hands are too commercial, jaded, and slick to write anything fresh and vital. Plays provide the wide open door for beginners. Playwrights are the most respected writers in the industry.

Serials These come in a great variety. The BBC is prone to occasional six-part thriller serials, each 30 minute episode starting with a re-run of the last moments of the previous episode, and ending with a cliff hanger; but much of its six-part serial output seems to be adaptations of period stories. ITV, which for years shunned all but continuing-story serials, suddenly switched attitudes and produced the 13-part *The Guardians* (about Britain under a fascist government) and the long running *Manhunt* (three people on the run in Nazi-occupied war-time France). But both these serials, whose hour-long episodes were written by a number of writers, were so contrived that many episodes were complete stories in themselves. *Doctor Who* is a genre on its own, in that it is a series of serials. Continuing-story serials include STV's *High Living*, Granada's *Coronation Street*, and ATV's *Crossroads*.

Series Weekly dramas depicting the same leading characters set in different stories. Any number of contributors. Most television writers hanker for a 'series created by' credit because, (a) they will get a small royalty for every episode irrespective of who writes it, (b) they may get the lion's share of the episodes to write, (c) they may be appointed as script editor for the series. Very professional, and not much room for beginners.

The programme planners take decisions annually, six monthly, or quarterly on how much drama and comedy will be produced; further decisions are then taken at a lower level regarding the number of plays, adaptation, anthologies, and series and serials.

Contained within the master-minded plans are 'slots' (programme places) for song-and-dance spectaculars, documentaries, sport, chat shows, quizzes, schools programmes, and the like. None of these provide many opportunities for the non-staff writer, with the possible exception of documentaries (see page 237).

Do not regard any of these programme patterns as unchangeable. It is the wise would-be television writer who reads the *Radio Times* and *TV Times* from cover to cover every week.

Chapter 11

'NATURAL BREAKS'

Writing drama or situation comedy for any ITV Contractor means that you have to cope with the 'natural' or commercial break, which often results in contrived and very unnatural story expositions. The IBA sets down a rule about this; briefly it is that the scene which follows the advertisements must be (a) in a different set, or (b) at least five minutes later in 'play-time' (not real time, but the time scale within a play, e.g. in stage craft, if a character says they are going to leave the room for 'two minutes' you can bring them back twenty seconds later). Therefore, the break must not interrupt a speech. This is what *not* to do:

JOAN:	I don't understand.
What are you trying to tell me:	
DAVID:	All right. Then I shall
now tell you the truth—	

END OF ACT I

COMMERCIAL BREAK

ACT II

---

6. INT. LIVING ROOM.	*DAY.*

JOAN AND DAVID EXACTLY AS WE LEFT THEM.

DAVID:	—I am not really your
father.	

If this scene happened to come at about the point where you need to place your commercial break, you might handle it like this:

> JOAN: I don't understand. What are you trying to tell me?
>
> DAVID: All right. Then I shall now tell you the truth. I'm not really your father.

END OF ACT I

COMMERCIAL BREAK

ACT II

6. *INT. LIVING ROOM.* *DAY.*

JOAN IS NOW STANDING AT THE WINDOW, LOOKING DOWN INTO THE STREET. DAVID IS QUIETLY POURING HIMSELF A DRINK. HE LOOKS TOWARDS JOAN AS THOUGH ABOUT TO OFFER HER A DRINK, THEN THINKS BETTER OF IT. HE GOES AND SITS DOWN AFTER SOME MOMENTS—

> JOAN: You're absolutely sure about this?
>
> DAVID: I told you. I was in hospital—that war wound. I was there for a year (PAUSE) I don't want you to hate your mother for this.

David's "I told you" refers to something that we didn't hear, something that was presumably said in the five minutes or more since we left them at the end of Act I.

A one hour play on ITV has one commercial break, but drama series episodes have two. Half hour situation comedy episodes have one. TV/film series episodes, dealt with in Chapter 9, can have up to seven commercial breaks, but only two of these will be used for the UK transmission, and therefore only those two need conform to the IBA's rules. The full seven breaks will only be used for overseas transmissions, such as in America or Australia and elsewhere.

The BBC has no commercials, but some of its overseas clients may have; so, you may find that your BBC script editor will ask you to build to climaxes suitable for the commercial breaks that will be introduced by foreign networks.

The producer Richard Bates makes the interesting point that you should not have in your Act I a penultimate scene in which characters plan to do something that isn't going to happen until Act II. If the last scene of Act I is exciting (which it ought to be, coming just before the break), the audience's minds will be deflected from whatever was planned in the penultimate scene. It is better to have this planning scene as the Act I break, or early in Act II.

If you are a beginner speculatively writing your first play (and write it in full you must; once established you can sell on synopses), should you indicate the commercial break? Come to that, should you adopt the BBC's layout style, or one of the ITV layout styles? Remember that to make your first sale you may have to submit the play to a number of ITV Contractors as well as to the BBC. It is probably simpler not to include a break in your initial draft. If you make the sale to an ITV Contractor, the position of the break is something that can be discussed later with your script editor or producer. As to layout style, unless a play has been commissioned by the BBC, stick to a neutral ITV layout. If you submit it to the BBC, they will think you are a nice fellow who has done his best but doesn't quite know the Corporation's little ways yet. They will presume you have submitted it to them, and only to them, because in their hearts they don't really recognise that these ITV chappies exist.

Chapter 12

HOW TO BREAK IN

Initially the play is the way into television drama writing. It is no good submitting synopses or even complete scripts for series currently on the screen: by the time a series is transmitted all the episodes will be written or under commission. But original plays are an open market, and anyone can sell one if they can write it. You need no formal education, you don't even need to know how to spell. Certainly you don't have to be young and beautiful, and most definitely you don't need to know anyone who is connected with television. Despair should only set in when your play has been rejected by the BBC and *all* the major ITV companies in turn. Even then, if you submit the same play a year later it may sell, because needs and fashions and script department personnel change rapidly.

You will know you are getting somewhere when, instead of rejecting your play, someone asks you in to their office for a discussion. Most script department executives have a genuine desire to encourage talent. They may not wish to buy the play you have submitted for a variety of reasons; but it may have impressed them with your writing ability, so now they want to have a general chat with you, and arising from this you may be invited to write something that they do want. Or, if you are lucky, they really are interested in your play, and the purpose of the discussion is that they want you to make certain changes, and they want to see your reactions.

Because of the extraordinary technical limitations of electronic television in the early days, a psychology has developed among producers, directors, and script editors that no script is ever right the first time. In the past when there were so many things that could not be done, and when very few writers had any experience of the new medium, there was a basis for this attitude. Only the people on the floor—producers, directors, actors, technicians—knew how difficult it all was. Scripts had to be re-jigged to bridge actors from scene to scene, to give time for costume changes, and to fit all the sets into a cramped studio which last week had been a warehouse. Everyone, from the set builders up, had a legitimate right to call for changes in the script to make the production possible. But often the need to change scripts for technical reasons expanded into a desire to make changes for dramatic reasons. This attitude has stuck, and script tinkering is endemic in television.

If they are interested in your play, but have asked you in to talk about changes, your reaction can be crucial. A playwright who doesn't defend his own work is very unimpressive. On the other hand, if you are totally obdurate and won't change a word, that may be an end of it. So you have to walk a tightrope, and the best thing is to defend your play *basically* as it stands. If they say it is too heavy on outside filming, you can't argue: they know their own economic position. But if your play has a happy ending and they want a downbeat ending, politely tell them to go to hell. They will only respect you for it, and you may win them over.

You may be lucky and find yourself talking to one of the really good plays editors. There are a handful of people in the industry who, although they may never have written a play themselves, have a remarkable ability to help writers improve and further develop their work. These people have a sixth sense for perceiving the true values partly buried under a none-too-well-written play. They will be attentive to what you are trying to say in your play, and they will help you to say it more effectively. What's more, once the job of improvement is done, the good script editor will defend your play against any producer, director, or star, who tries to give it an entirely different interpretation from the one you had in mind.

After you have carried out whatever re-writes have been agreed between you and the editor, a director will be appointed. The director's job is both artistic and technical. For technical reasons he may now ask you for additional re-writes, although if your editor is well versed in these sorts of problems the script by now should not present too many difficulties in this respect. But apart from that, the director will want to have discussions with you about the characters, possibly to hear your views on casting, and about the sets. If you've set your play in the chemical factory where you work, or the Cheshire village where you live, he may want you to take him along there and explain it all to him.

In due course you will be invited to the 'read through'. This is when the cast meet for the first time. The read through will take place in the rehearsal room, which may be within the studio complex, or may be an old church hall some distance from the studios. All the actors will have received their copies of the script some days ago, but naturally they haven't yet learnt their lines by heart. The director will introduce you to the cast as the writer: you'll find that most of the actors already know each other, because they've all worked together before, either in television or at the end of the pier at Cromer. The people playing the leading parts may want to have a chat with you before the read through starts. They want to know about their characters—where they were born, how they feel about certain other characters, what is really going on in their mind in Scene 3 when they make that telephone call. (Some smaller part actors and actresses may also ask you depth questions about their roles, and you can be sure that these will be the stars of the future.) Eventually everyone will be called to order, and they will settle down at a long trestle table. The PA will produce her stop watch to time the script, and the read through will commence. For the first time you will hear your dialogue being acted out by professionals. Don't let it worry you if they make fun of the script and send it up a little. That's one of the traditions of television. They are all nervous, because they know they've got a big job ahead of them. A bit of initial larking about is their way of relieving the tension.

After the read through, the director will take you aside to get your opinion on interpretation. There may be lines which should be delivered in a certain way, and the actors may not have grasped this. You should only make your comments to the director, and to him alone. Never go up to an actor after a read through and make any comment on their delivery. That is the director's job.

A week or more later you will be invited to the 'producer's run'. This is when the entire play is acted out in the rehearsal room, with no scripts and no stops, mainly for the benefit of the producer, although some studio technicians, and the writer, are also usually present. You may find that the director has changed some of your lines, usually only minor ones, for practical reasons such as to help an actor make a more natural-seeming entrance or exit. The point of your being present is for you to check that none of these small alterations has affected the mood or plot in any way. Again, if you have any points to make, only speak to the director, not to the actors. (Naturally it is very much in order after the producer's run if you tell the actors how much you enjoyed their performance. That sort of thing, which to outsiders seems so false in our industry, is most important. Every creative person needs applause.)

A few days after the producer's run you will be invited to the studio to watch the VTR. Very probably your script editor will take you to lunch in the studio canteen, then take you along to the VIP viewing room. For the rest of the afternoon you will sit there watching countless rehearsals of the scenes or parts of scenes. From a loudspeaker you will hear not only your lines being delivered, but also the ceaseless two-way chatter of the director and his cameramen as they try to 'line up the shots' (e.g. make certain that when your heroine delivers the punch line of the play there is a camera focused on her face and not her left shoulder). It could be that during your time in the viewing room, you will find yourself in the company of the producer. The work-approach of producers varies from one producer to another. Some producers virtually breath down the necks of their directors throughout all the time in studio, which must shorten the life expectancy of both the producer and the director. Others, more mature, keep themselves well in the background, only making their presence felt if they see something is very wrong, or if the director appeals to them for help. If you spot something wrong, tell your script editor (or producer, if he's sitting next to you). However, by this stage there isn't much chance of changing anything unless the change is fairly simple. For instance, I once noticed that when a character of mine got a gun from his desk drawer during these final studio rehearsals he didn't first unlock the drawer, and also we could see that the drawer contained nothing except the gun. Both these factors were improbable within the context of the story. The first was my fault, because I should have specified in the script that the man should first unlock the drawer; the second was the director's fault, because obviously there would be other things in a very big desk drawer and he should have told the Props Department to put something else in there (papers, anything). I mentioned this to my script editor, who duly phoned the director, who in turn asked the floor manager to tell the actor to mime unlocking the drawer and asked Props to put a few papers into the drawer. The director appreciated my comment because this was something that improved the production (at least two seconds of it) and was easy to put right. But he would not have appreciated a change more complicated than that.

If you have come along to the VTR on your own, and haven't brought your entire family with you, and if your director agrees, you may be allowed to sit in the director's control room during the actual production. This is much more interesting than having to watch it on the monitor in the viewing room, but if you get this opportunity be prepared to sit absolutely quiet for the full two or three hours. Nerves are stretched to breaking point, and the last thing anyone wants is a chatty writer sitting in the background. However, it is well worth the ordeal, for when the final scene is recorded and the floor manager is able to call out "Clear studio!" the director will turn to you and thank you for a marvellous script, and you will thank him for a marvellous production.

Some months later your play will be transmitted. If it is well-liked, your producing organisation will encourage you to write more plays. But the question is, how many entirely original works of art can you write in a year?—two, three, four? It's a rather terrifying prospect. One very successful two hour stage play, seen by a few tens of thousands of people, might make you enough money to keep you for the rest of your life. You may be forced by your accountant, kicking and protesting, to live on your yacht in the Mediterranean to avoid paying off the National Debt single handed through income tax. But one one-hour television play, seen by an audience of ten millions, is only going to keep you for a few months. The income from occasional television plays can be a very pleasant supplement to the salary from your normal job, but television plays alone are not likely to provide you with a very high standard of living unless you are fantastically successful. So, if you want to become a full-time television writer you will almost certainly have to turn to writing episodes for series drama.

When a new series is to be set up, a producer and script editor are appointed and are given the brief to produce, say, thirteen episodes of the show by a certain date. While the producer sets about organising studio time, casting the lead roles, etc., the script editor will issue copies of the format. He will send the format to writers he knows, and whom he believes right for this particular series; but he will also send copies to most literary agents who handle television writers. In due course he will receive story ideas from a number of writers, and will discuss these with his producer. Some ideas will be rejected straight away, either because they aren't good ideas or because they don't really conform to the basic concept of the series as a whole; in other instances, writers will be invited to the office for discussions, and eventually the thirteen episodes will be commissioned. If the programme organisers have given the producer and script editor really enough time to prepare the series, they may prefer to keep all the writing within a small group of only three or four writers. The advantage of keeping the writing team down in numbers, which means each writer will write two or three episodes, is that the overall result may have better continuity. If the show has to be produced in a hurry, the script editor may have to get thirteen writers all writing simultaneously: the result can be thirteen rather different interpretations of the basic concept, and a lot of work for the script editor who must finally bring all thirteen scripts into line.

To enter this very professional world of television series script writers you really need an agent. Then you will be part of the network and on the receiving end when formats for new series are distributed. Few agents will be interested in you until you have proved yourself. So, the normal sequence of events is that as soon as a producing organisation expresses serious interest in buying your first single shot play, find an agent. You will find them all listed in the *Writers' and Artists' Year Book*, and also in a useful little twice-a-year booklet called *Contacts*. (You can't buy *Contacts* in bookshops; you can only get a copy by writing to *The Spotlight* at 42–43 Cranbourn Street, London, WC2H 7PA. The present price is 35p, post free.) For the one off playwright an agent with good overseas contacts (not all have) can quadruple the earnings of each play by selling the script abroad (generally it is the producing organisations who sell tapes and films abroad, agents who sell scripts). For the series writer, the agent can ensure that he is offered the highest possible going-rate for the job, which may be somewhat higher than the minimum agreed by the Writers' Guild. Some agents prove to be the best friend a writer can have. Writers have a predilection for nervous disorders, divorces, domestic upheavals, and suicide. There isn't much an agent can do about suicides, other than to organise the burial (and that's been known to happen). But for anything less final, a good agent steps in like a guardian angel, playing the role of marriage counsellor, psychoanalyst, investment adviser, house agent, and—if it's vital for the writer to get away from it all—personal travel agent. A few agents are crooks. When fees are paid to them, they will hold on to the money for weeks before passing it on, less their 10% to their clients: all the time the money is in the agent's bank it can be earning him interest. Fortunately the angels outnumber the scoundrels and at long last a professional association—The Association of Dramatists Agents (ADA)—has been formed to set down a code of practice.

It is of course possible to survive without an agent and some writers do. But generally it is more difficult. You are a writer, not a businessman. What's more, good agents will have spent years studying the intricacies of contract and copyright law. Remember, in television you never actually *sell* a script, although we all use that misnomer. You, as the writer, grant to the producing organisation a licence to produce your work within a limited time, and also you may or may not grant them the option to sell the tape within specified territories throughout the world in return for which you will receive certain extra residual fees. So it is all very complicated from the start, and needs expert handling.

Ted Willis has an interesting theory that you should change your agent every seven years: "If you move to a new agent, you will take with you a new stature, and he will try to find you work that fits. If you remain for ever with your old agent, he will go on thinking of you as the kid who came in off the street. But of course there are exceptions to this rule and I know of people who have been happy with the same agent for many years. Personal relationships spring up which are difficult to break. But essentially the relationship between agent and clients is a business one; the agent will not fail to drop you when you fail to deliver the goods and the reverse should apply."

However, none of these points about agents are likely to apply to you until you have made that initial break through and have a producing organisation interested in your work. That means you have to submit your first play or plays yourself. The addresses of BBC Television and all the ITV Contractors are listed at the end of this chapter. Since they may change during the currency of this book, keep up to date by occasionally getting a copy of *Contacts*. Always address drama material to the Script Department of the BBC or the ITV Contractor to whom you are sending it. Never send unsolicited material direct to producers, directors, or script editors, even if they are your second cousin three times removed; they will only pass it on to their script department, or quite probably lose it. Always send two neatly-typed and bound copies, and keep a copy on file. If the organisation is organised, and not all are, you should get an almost immediate printed acknowledgement. Wait at least a month before writing or phoning to know what they think of it. The longer they keep it, the more someone there likes it. Rejected material can be handled very quickly. But possible material may go to more than one reader. If it is rejected, don't argue: that never sold a script. If they explain why they rejected, read and re-read their letter, for it may contain golden advice. If you are submitting comedy material, address it to the Head of Light Entertainment, not the Script Department. In most television organisations, drama and comedy keep very separate.

If you become a successful television writer, will this eventually lead to big-money cinema screen commissions? It depends what sort of television writer you become. If you stick to one off plays, and make a name for yourself in that field, and if your agent has good contacts among the movie makers, you may make the grade. But if you concentrate on series drama, chances are the Wardour Street men will never seek you out. There is no logic to this, since some of the finest writing on television is for drama series. But the movie makers regard series writers as hacks, whereas what they want for the cinema are big bold playwrights with something important to say. Having paid an enormous fee for a big bold film script, they will then hire a number of additional writers to take the guts out of it so that it won't offend anyone.

A particular character to avoid is the independent film producer who is neither independent nor is he really a producer. Once your play has been on television, you may be phoned by some nice-sounding person who tells you how impressed he was with your play, and would you be available to take on a commission to write a film script? This *could* be genuine, so be polite. But if it is less than genuine, you will be invited along for morning coffee or afternoon tea (it's never lunch or dinner) in the main lounge of a big London hotel. This is both to impress you, and to save the 'producer' from having to have a real office. He will then tell you about this film that he definitely intends to make, and how your play on television last night demonstrated to him that you are the right person to write the scenario. What he proposes is that you should write the film script as soon as possible, and that you will receive a large sum of money on 'the first day of shooting'. This is strictly against the agreements between the Writers' Guild and the movie makers. If your 'producer' were genuine, he would offer you a commissioning fee, just as you will get in television. What he is really after is work as a film producer. If he can get a script, which he is incapable of writing himself, he can then show it around to film distributors and other people in the hope of raising finance to make the film. Of course this sometimes comes off. But you may just find that you are dedicating an enormous amount of valuable writing time in order to create a shop window for someone else. If you are approached in this way, the simple rule is always to check with your agent, and do whatever he advises. Another group who may approach you are out-of-work actors, and it is surprising what star names are sometimes unemployed. You will be flattered to hear on the phone a well-known voice calling you, and inviting you to his home. He has an idea for a script, or more possibly a series, that you and he could work on 'together'. This probably means that he has some sort of idea, in which he could star, and that you will do all the speculative scripting work. Here again, check with your agent and take his advice.

Will the television people steal your ideas? No, not intentionally. But an idea submitted now, and rejected for the valid reason that it doesn't fit current requirements, may spring to the mind of the person who read it years later; and they may then think it is their own idea. You cannot guard against this, and neither can they. But generally you will find that people in television are scrupulously honest where ideas are concerned. It is also a question of pride, in that they would rather develop their own ideas than use second hand ones from someone else.

Can you get a commission on the basis of a synopsis or story outline? No, not if you are a beginner. A beginner must write and submit a complete play. Once you have overcome that hurdle, and have proved that you can write for television, you should be able to get commissions to write future plays by submitting story treatments (see page 131), or even outlines (see page 132). Once you have become well-known, people will be commissioning you to write groups of plays, even though you haven't told them what you intend to write about. You will have joined that magical circle of writers who can be relied on always to come up with good original ideas, and who have the technical expertise to translate those ideas into good practical scripts.

To protect television writers and to help them generally there is the Writers' Guild of Great Britain at 430 Edgware Road, London W2 1EH, and the writers' section of the Association of Cinema and Television Technicians at 2, Soho Square, London, W1. ACTT is essentially the trade union for directors, cameramen, and other technicians, but it has a small section of writers, more in films than in

CHÉ WOULD HAVE DONE IT DIFFERENT.

Treatment for a television play

by

Malcolm Hulke.

1. Int. Chairman's Office. Day.

End of the business day. George Rutland, the company's staff accountant, is having a discussion, plus end of day drink, with the company chairman, Mason. We learn the company is in property development and made four million pounds profit last year. There is a personal phone call for George.

2. Int/Ext. Phone Kiosk. Day.

Ann - young, well-spoken, in gear - tells George she knows where his son is, and that the boy is very ill. On crosscuts we see George earnestly ask for more information, and we gather that the boy, Tim, left his father and all that his father represents months ago. Ann will only say that if George does exactly what she tells him, she will take him to his son.

3. Ext. Street - London underground station. Day. (Film).

George stands on a corner, embarrassed, rather foolishly holding a copy of the 'Financial Times' upside down. Ann appears, nods to George, goes into the station. George follows.

4. Int. George's home. Day.

Alice Rutland gets a phone call from George's secretary, Miriam, to say that he will be late home this evening. Alice is put out - they're expecting guests.

5. Ext. Street - Another underground station. Day. (Film).

A shabby part of London. Ann emerges from the station, followed shortly by George. Ann goes along the street to a pet shop, stops to look at puppies in the window. George now comes up to her, angry and humiliated: "Where's my son?" Ann says Tim isn't far from here. George cuts in: "Is he still using that terrible stuff?" She nods: "And he's now very ill." She tells George he must watch which house she goes to, then come to the front door five minutes later. George asks if all this charade is necessary. Ann says: "Well, would _you_ like to be seen walking along the street with _me_?" She goes off, and

First page of an example treatment (or story breakdown) showing scene by scene (and, importantly, set by set) what is going to happen. From this a producer could estimate overall cost.

CHÉ WOULD HAVE DONE IT DIFFERENT.

Outline for a television play

by

Malcolm Hulke.

A group of young people, who live together as a
commune in an old house in London, find the opportunity to
sharpen their battle against the Establishment.   Some other
young people, whom our group doesn't know personally, have
been given long prison sentences for using explosives in
order to make known their political discontent.   Our group
intend to take an important businessman prisoner, and to
hold him until the authorities release the martyrs.   They
reckon if it can work in South America, it can work here.

The opportunity is when a member of our group meets
a young man, Tim Rutland, at an all night party.   Tim lets
it be known to all around him that his father, whom he
regards as a fascist pig, is chief money-counter for a big
property development company that makes millions of pounds
profit every year.   Tim mentions his father's name, and
the name of the company.   He also mentions that he has
left his father never to return, and is now happily lost in
London's underground world.

Ann, one of the girls of the commune, phones George
Rutland at his office, says that his son Tim is very ill,
and offers to take George to see his son if he (George) will
do exactly what he's told.   The trick works all too easily.
George goes to the commune house, where Ann shows him into a
room — and simply locks the door.

None of the members of the commune, including Ann,
believed it would be so easy.   What was talk has become
reality.   What's more, they have a real live human being
locked in the other room.   What if he's taken ill, needs
medicine, has a heart attack?   They decide that the British
Establishment would never release convicted people under
duress — there is no precedent for that sort of thing here.
But George Rutland's company might be persuaded to part with
ransom money.   It is agreed to demand £1,000,000, to be
paid in small notes to poor homeless families.

The initial company reaction is that everything possible
must be done to secure George's release.   Then 'saner' counsel
starts to prevail.   A million pounds is a lot of money.   And

First page of an example play outline. It gives just enough to explain the
general idea or theme. At this stage it is unneccessary to show *how* the story is
going to be told (e.g. what will only be revealed to viewers later in the play to
achieve suspense).

television. The Writers' Guild is solely concerned with writers, with more members in television than in films. Over the years the WGGB has negotiated a network of agreements with the BBC and the ITV Contractors on minimum payments for different categories of scripts, e.g. the one hour play, the half hour situation comedy episode, the TV/film script, and so on. These agreements govern staged payments for a script's first transmission in the United Kingdom, the percentage of the original fee to be paid to the writer in the event of a repeat transmission, and residuals if the tape or TV/film are sold abroad. A typical staged payment means that the writer receives one quarter of the agreed fee on being commissioned (e.g. after he has put up a suitable outline), one quarter when he delivers his first complete draft script, and the remaining half of the fee when he has satisfactorily completed whatever re-writes the script editor and producer may require. An agreement may also lay down guidelines on how much re-writing may be expected from a writer, and the extent to which a producing organisation may alter a writer's work (e.g. they may not make a structural alteration). Also contained within these agreements may be 'cut off' clauses, particularly in the case of drama series. That is to say, if the writer fails to bring his first draft script up to the standard required by the producer and script editor, they are not obliged to pay him the second half of his fee, and they can use this money to hire another writer to complete the job. Obviously this cannot happen with one off plays, where the whole concept and copyright belongs to the original writer. But in series drama the writer is using characters and perhaps a basic setting the copyright of which belongs to the producing organisation: therefore the organisation has certain rights over the script which the writer has written. In these instances, the custom is that the original writer retains his screen credit, and the re-writer usually prefers to remain anonymous. Just occasionally a certain type of script editor may use the cut off clause to his own advantage. He will find that a draft script is quite impossible, and that none of the writer's attempts to re-write the script are acceptable. Finally, expressing great regret, he will use the cut off clause—and then hire himself as the anonymous re-writer. Fortunately this sort of thing is rare.

The Writers' Guild has an Executive Council to deal with main policy matters, and a number of sub-committees that specialise in various aspects of the Guild's work. Members receive the monthly *Writers' News* with its useful market information. At the moment, membership by television writers is not obligatory, but the Guild is seeking Agency Shop Agreements with employers under the Industrial Relations Act: if these Agreements become effective, all television writers will have to join, or pay the same subscription without joining, or appeal to be allowed to pay the equivalent amount to a charity of which the Guild approves.

The WGGB was one of the founder members of the International Writers' Guild, which now has member-Guilds in twenty-three countries, including the Soviet Union and the United States. It has not been possible to find out precisely what practical work the IWG does, although from time to time delegates' meetings are held in different capital cities and no doubt some good comes from that. One thing the IWG has not yet achieved in its eight years of life is international policing. All too often one hears of writers going on holiday abroad and seeing on the hotel television set a dubbed or sub-titled tape of a show which they wrote. If this happens to you, keep your cool. When you return to Britain phone up the producing organisation and congratulate them on the sale of the show abroad. They will thank you for congratulating them and, without the bat of an eyelid, will add: "And by the way, dear boy, we've got lots of lovely money for you. Why, we were just now sending off your cheque when you phoned." That way you save their face, don't make an enemy—and get the money!

When the Writers' Guild started many writers resisted the idea of being unionised. It just didn't sound gentlemanly. James Webb, when President of the Writers' Guild of America (West), put forward the American point of view when speaking in London at an IWG meeting. He said: "We are a group of casual labourers banded together in the inalienable pursuit of money." That was many years ago. Most British writers are nowadays as eager to pursue money as are their American opposite numbers.

The Guild's minimum payments agreements not only help writers; in a sense they also protect viewers from what might otherwise be shoddy goods. Since producers cannot pay less than the agreed minima, they can't cut economic corners by getting scripts written on the cheap. Television writing is considered rather prestigious, and there is always the nut who would write a play for nothing just to have the neighbours see his name on the screen. A continuous flow of high quality product requires a professional cadre, and this can only exist if fees provide enough money to pay the rent. Otherwise we'd all go back to driving buses. It is not really probable that any reputable producing organisation would try to get cheap scripts even if they could, but the agreed minima are the final safeguard. However, does this militate against the beginner? It may in series drama. No producer of a series wants to risk money on a newcomer, for if he rejects the first draft he will have to pay out two thirds or one half of the negotiated fee (depending on the type of programme), and he may have on his hands a script so totally bad that no-one can re-write it to bring it up to standard. Although a professional writer's going-rate may be higher than the Guild minimum, had the producer started in the first place with a 'pro' writer he would have saved both money and head aches. To help overcome this problem, and to give beginners a chance, some employers have special arrangements. For example, the BBC may offer a writer previously untried in television an encouragement fee in return for a 'treatment' (detailed storyline), and ATV has its Option Scheme whereby they can offer a smaller percentage of the fee than the normal 50% or $66\frac{1}{3}\%$ to see a first draft of a commissioned play. In both cases the writer retains all his rights in the event of the script being rejected.

Here are some general points and reminders about submitting your work to television:

1. Use the easy, neutral-looking ITV layout. There is no need to insert the commercial break at the initial stage. That can be worked out in discussion with your script editor.

2. Send two neatly-typed copies, keep at least one on file. If you make mistakes (which we all do) correct them neatly and clearly in ink. Use white foolscap paper ($13'' \times 8''$) or A4 ($11\frac{3}{4}'' \times 8\frac{1}{4}''$), not quarto ($10'' \times 8''$). Bond paper is not expected for the top copy; copy paper may be better for the top copy, because then your carbon copies will be clearer. (In television, where a number of people may have to read a submitted script, the clarity of your carbon copy is as important as that of your top copy.) Don't underline speakers' names, etc., in red.

3. Number all the pages and bind them together in some simple way, perhaps within a folder. Don't use pink binding ribbon with fancy bows.

4. The title sheet should include:
   (a) Your name★ and address, and your home and/or work telephone number.
   (b) The running time.

(* Only use a pen-name if you have some very good personal reason. Television is a down to earth industry, and literary touches such as pen-names are never really appreciated.)

5. Don't include on the title sheet "This is the sole copyright of So-and-so" because obviously it is, and that sort of thing looks so aggressive.

6. Enclose a *very* brief letter saying "Here is my play called So-and-so. I hope you like it." That's enough.

7. Enclose a big stamped addressed envelope in case they don't.

8. Send by ordinary mail. Registered post smacks of the amateur.

9. Wait at least a month before you phone or write to know what they think of it. If they reject it don't argue.

10. The moment you have mailed off your first play, go straight back to your typewriter and start on the next one.

BBC TELEVISION AND ITV CONTRACTORS' ADDRESSES

BRITISH BROADCASTING CORPORATION

LONDON
  Television Centre,
  Wood Lane,
  London W12 7RJ

MIDLANDS
  Pebble Mill Road,
  Birmingham B5 7SD

NORTH
  Box 27 Broadcasting House,
  Piccadilly,
  Manchester M60 1SJ

SOUTH & WEST
  Whiteladies Road,
  Bristol BS8 2LR

NORTHERN IRELAND
  Ormeau Avenue,
  Belfast BT2 8HQ

SCOTLAND
  Queen Margaret Drive,
  Glasgow G12 8DG

INDEPENDENT TELEVISION

Anglia Television Ltd,
Anglia House,
Norwich,
Norfolk NOR 07A

ATV Network Ltd,
P.O. Box 78,
Elstree Studios,
Eldon Avenue,
Boreham Wood, Herts WD16 1JF

Border Television Ltd,
The Television Centre,
Carlisle CA1 4NT

Channel Television,
Television Centre,
Rouge Bouillon,
St. Helier,
Jersey C.I.

Grampian Television Ltd,
Queen's Cross,
Aberdeen AB9 2XJ

Granada TV Network Ltd,
Television Centre,
Quay Street,
Manchester.

HTV Ltd,
Television Centre,
Cardiff

London Weekend Television Ltd,
Kent House,
South Bank Television Centre,
Upper Ground,
London SE1 9PP

Scottish Television Ltd,
Theatre Royal,
Hope Street,
Glasgow G2 3PR

Southern Television Ltd,
Southern Television Centre,
Notham,
Southampton SO9 4YQ

Thames Television Ltd,
Teddington Lock,
Teddington,
Middlesex TW11 9NT

Tyne Tees Television Ltd,
The Television Centre,
City Road,
Newcastle upon Tyne NE1 2AL

Ulster Television
Havelock House,
Ormeau Road,
Belfast BT7 1EB

Westward Television Ltd,
Derry's Cross,
Plymouth PL1 2SP

Yorkshire Television Ltd,
The Television Centre,
Leeds LS3 1JS

Radiotelefis Eireann,
Donnybrook,
Dublin 4, Eire

If you have written a play of general appeal, it is advisable to submit it in turn to the six major play producing centres, which means the BBC in London, or ATV, Granada, London Weekend, Thames, or Yorkshire. These six are the big buyers; but don't overlook Anglia and HTV, who produce a limited number of plays every year. A play with a strong regional flavour might fare better if sent to the local BBC, or ITV, address in the region which it depicts. Any of the BBC's Regions, or any of the minor ITV Contractors, may be interested in material and ideas for children's shows, panel games, quizzes, etc., which do not over-strain their limited production facilities.

Chapter 13

WHAT TO WRITE ABOUT

What advice can I, or anyone else, give on what you should write for television *about?* Fashions change; so do producers and script editors. At one time it was easy to say what *not* to write about—corruption in high places, homosexuals, abortion, or anything else that might remotely offend anyone. In the early 1960's a commercial company which had bought *The Girl In The Market Square* by Eric Paice and myself were told by the Independent Television Authority (forerunner of the IBA) that it could not go on because it had in it a crooked police inspector. The company paid us an additional £100 to turn him into the hero. Nothing could be said in television drama about politics, or trade unions, or God, or motherhood.

All that's gone now. Producers vie with one another to shock their audiences, to startle them out of any complacency that may linger on, to rip naked the pubes of the Establishment so that we can all have a good ogle provided we've paid our television licence fee. The single shot or one off plays prepared the ground for it, ably assisted in reality by Christine Keeler and the Lords' judgement in the case of the Thurso Boy. The north-country was suddenly discovered by Wardour Street and Brian Epstein, and with its violent emergence from woad and fish-and-chips brought to drama a new realism, abrasiveness, and bluntness. In television, possibly the real break-through was *Z Cars*, because this was weekly series drama and that's what the mass audience watches. In its first episode a policeman—yes, one of the boys in blue— was accused of theft by a member of the public. Since the introduction of ITV in 1956, the BBC had suffered bad ratings, the masses having shown a marked preference for Persil and Hughie Green over The Epilogue. Something had to be done: *Z Cars* started to turn the tide. By attacking the very guardians of the Establishment, and thus delighting the public, the BBC made sure of its continued Royal Charter, something that could probably only happen in Britain.

Do these remarks suggest that your future success as a television writer depends on finding whatever icons remain, and having a bash at them? No, it's not as simple as that. In any case, icon-bashing is only a half of it. As long ago as 1956 Ted Willis's play *Woman in a Dressing Gown* introduced to a mass audience the concept of a working class woman with feelings and emotional needs. *The Times* described it as a "television masterpiece" and *The Guardian* said ". . . the first play written recognisably for television . . . a significant break through for television drama in its own right." Up until then, much of stage drama had been very stiff-upper-lip, and television had simply followed suit. This one play had a fantastic effect both on its audience and on the future of television drama. Love became something that could be talked about, family problems something that could be discussed.

The thing to remember is that most of your audience, seventy five per cent at least, have never seen a stage play. Many people do not read books in any habitual way. To them, television drama has opened a window on the world outside their own tiny circle of friends and workmates. It has made people more knowledgeable. It has made them admit to emotional problems in a way that only thirty years ago would have seemed impossible. It has, most obviously, made them much more tolerant. It has certainly made them very much more able to understand complex social and personal problems, if they are put in simple, dramatic form. There is today a sympathetic, tolerant and aware audience waiting for almost any dramatic experience.

But do these observations tell you what to write about? Not really, for there is no simple answer. If you want to write and sell a television play, then go ahead and write about what *you* want to write about. If it is a good play, chances are someone will want to produce it. If you want to write situation comedy, then study the market carefully by watching all the comedy you can on television, and try to think up a new original situation which is funny. If you want to write for drama series, then (with certain notable exceptions) write what your script editor wants you to write.

To try to answer this question—what to write about—I asked a number of good people to let me have scripts which they were proud or happy to write or to produce, and also to let me have their comments on why, apart from the money, they wrote or produced these scripts.

The scripts presented in brief in the following pages cover a wide range of television drama and comedy markets in this country plus one aimed primarily at the global market, and one written by a British writer for a continental market and never seen here. This is included as a reminder that the mainland of Europe starts just 22 miles from Dover and abounds with television markets for writers. The comedy writer, Brad Ashton, is regularly writing for shows in Holland, West Germany, and Norway. He opened up his Dutch outlet as long ago as 1963, and that was ten whole years before the rest of us joined the Common Market.

A word about the excerpts to follow in this chapter. Since they relate more to content than to technical layout, they are typeset and not photographic reproductions of actual typed pages. Nonetheless I have kept as near as possible to the original typed layout because it may interest you to see how many variations there are on an original theme. I show these not to frighten you, but to reassure you that there is no single layout set of rules. If your layout approximates to something like the general pattern, that is good enough. For reasons peculiar to printing, a great amount of underlining has had to be omitted (e.g. speakers' names, and *all* the stage directions in the case of Granada Television). Instead, words which would normally be underlined in a typed script are shown in italics (slanting letters). Also our width of printed column invades the left hand side of the page—but again remember the point of interest is content, not layout. When you type your play imagine a line down the middle of the page and keep strictly to the right of it (with the exception of scene headings if you are working to the BBC's layout style). Where layout is concerned, be it for a novel or a script, the rule of the professional writer is: When in doubt, waste paper.

MAN FRIDAY
by
Adrian Mitchell

Produced by the British Broadcasting
Corporation at the BBC, Television
Centre, London.
Producer: Graeme McDonald
Script editor: Ann Scott

A non-naturalistic play with music about Friday's attempts to
civilise Robinson Crusoe.

Robinson Crusoe, on his island, sees a group of black men about to
eat, as a mark of affection and respect, one of their friends who has
accidentally drowned. Misunderstanding the scene entirely, Crusoe
shoots them all—all except one who makes clear his peaceful intentions
and so is allowed to live. 'Friday' is named and educated, taught
English and a range of English ideas. Crusoe tries to explain to him
notions of God, of work, of property, of sport, though when Friday
tries to reciprocate with some of the ideas and practices of his tribe
Crusoe resents and recoils from them. Occasionally they enjoy each
other's company. More often, since Friday is made to do all the work,
the relationship is one of master and slave. Friday, homesick for his
tribe and his island, finally understands how to make Crusoe plan and
build a raft, but can only do it by force and by threatening him with
his own gun. They return to Friday's island, and Crusoe there asks
to be admitted to the tribe. The play takes place within the framework
of Friday's account to the tribe of all this, and finally they decide to
refuse Crusoe's request since his attitudes are unacceptable. When he
understands this, he puts the gun to his own head and shoots himself.

1. EXT. A LONG SANDY BEACH.   DAY.

> (ROBINSON CRUSOE, IN
> TRADITIONAL RAGGED
> GOATSKIN BREECHES,
> JACKET, POINTED HAT,
> CARRYING A GOATSKIN
> SUNSHADE IS STANDING
> ON THE BEACH STARING
> AT A SINGLE FOOTPRINT.
>
> UNDER ONE ARM HE TOTES
> A MUSKET. IN HIS BELT
> THREE PISTOLS ARE STUCK.
>
> CRUSOE WALKS ALONG THE
> BEACH, WATCHFULLY, FOR
> ABOUT FIVE SECONDS.
>
> CUT TO CRUSOE STANDING
> IN HIS FIRST POSITION,
> STARING AT THE FOOT-
> PRINT. HE WALKS THE
> BEACH, AS BEFORE, BUT
> FOR ABOUT FOUR SECONDS.
>
> CUT TO CRUSOE IN FIRST
> POSITION. WALKS FOR
> TWO SECONDS.
>
> CUT TO CRUSOE IN
> FIRST POSITION.
>
> HE PUTS DOWN HIS
> SUNSHADE AND HIS
> MUSKET.
>
> HE KNEELS ON THE
> SAND.
>
> HE RAISES HIS HANDS
> IN PRAYER)

143

2. INT. TRIBAL HUT.   DAY

(THE HUT IS SPACIOUS
AND CIRCULAR.

WOVEN WALLS AND
CEILING. EARTH FLOOR.
THICK POSTS SUPPORTING
THE ROOF ARE PAINTED
WITH INTRICATE SPIRALS
OF PEOPLE AND ANIMALS
IN MANY COLOURS.
PRIMITIVE DRUMS AND
STRINGED INSTRUMENTS
HANG BY THONGS FROM
PEGS.

A TEENAGE BOY AND GIRL,
WEARING LONG, LIGHT
LOOSE ROBES, DIFFERENT
COLOURS, DIFFERENT
PATTERNS, CARRY IN
BETWEEN THEM A PAINTED
GOURD, HEAVY AND FULL
OF DRINK.

THEY PLACE IT IN THE
CENTRE OF THE FLOOR
CAREFULLY.

THEY BOW THEIR HEADS
TO THE GOURD. THEY
BOW THEIR HEADS TO
EACH OTHER. THEY
SMILE AT EACH OTHER.

BOY AND GIRL TAKE
CUPS FROM A CORNER.

SEVERAL MEN AND WOMEN
—AMONG THEM FRIDAY,

WHO IS IN HIS EARLY
THIRTIES, A VERY OLD
WOMAN AND THE DOCTOR,
WHO WEARS VARIOUS
NECKLACES—ENTER THE
HUT.

THEY BOW TO THE GOURD,
BOW TO EACH OTHER AND
SIT IN A WIDE CIRCLE
AROUND THE GOURD.

THE BOY AND GIRL HAND
ROUND CUPS OF THE DRINK.

ALL THE PEOPLE WEAR
LONG ROBES. THEY MOVE
EASILY.

THEY APPEAR PLEASED
BUT NOT OVER-EXCITED.
THEY SIT LOOKING AT
EACH OTHER, IN SILENCE,
EACH ONE LOOKING FROM
FACE TO FACE. SOME
SMILE. SOME SHAKE
THEIR HEADS SLOWLY.

THE OLD WOMAN, WITH
A HALF SMILE, STRETCHES
HER ARM OUT, PALM UP-
WARDS, TOWARDS FRIDAY.

ALL THE MEMBERS OF
THE TRIBE LOOK AT HIM.

FRIDAY PUTS HIS FACE
IN HIS HANDS, THEN
LOOKS UP.

ANOTHER MAN POINTS IN
THE SAME WAY AT FRIDAY.
THEN THE GIRL POINTS AT
FRIDAY. EVERYONE IS
POINTING TO FRIDAY.

AGAIN FRIDAY PUTS HIS
FACE IN HIS HANDS,
THEN LOOKS UP.

ALL THE HANDS ARE STILL
OUTSTRETCHED TO HIM)

DOCTOR:
Whether it hurts you, or whether it
        pleases you,
Whether it hurts us, or whether it
        pleases us,
It is time for you to tell the story.

FRIDAY:
It is time.

        (FRIDAY SPRINGS TO
        HIS FEET, TAKES A
        DRUM WITH ONE HAND,
        A STRINGED INSTRU-
        MENT WITH THE OTHER,
        HANDS THE STRINGED
        INSTRUMENT TO ANOTHER
        MAN, SLINGS THE DRUM
        OVER HIS SHOULDER AND
        BEGINS TO FINGER IT,
        STEPPING IN A SLOW,
        THINKING DANCE, AS
        HE BEGINS HIS STORY.

        THE MAN WITH THE
        STRINGED INSTRUMENT
        ACCOMPANIES HIM.

        FRIDAY SPEAKS AND
        CHANTS HIS STORY

As we have always been together,
Let us drink together,
As we are together now,
Let us dream together,
Let the wine flow,

146

FRIDAY: (CONT)
Let my words flow,
And I will try to tell my story truly,
As truly as I worship you.
My own people.
Close your eyes and see the story
Close your eyes and see the story
Close your eyes and see the story

(THE TRIBE CLOSE THEIR
EYES.

FRIDAY SEES THAT THEY
HAVE CLOSED THEIR
EYES.

FRIDAY CLOSES HIS EYES)

TELECINE 1:
Storm at Sea. Night.
(Paintings)

Powerful waves.

Rain.

FRIDAY: (V.O.) There were five
of us. The night storm caught us. It
broke the back of our canoe. It
swallowed us all down. And then it
sicked us up on to a beach we'd
never seen before.

3.   EXT. BEACH.   DAY.

(THE SAME BEACH CRUSOE
WALKED ON.

FRIDAY AND FOUR COM-
PANIONS, ONE OF THEM
DEAD, ON THE BEACH.

A BRIGHT DAY)

FRIDAY: (V.O.) Five of us on
the beach. But one of us, Old
Hookloser, who used to tell the
funniest stories of them all, he was

147

so full of water that we couldn't
bring him back to life. We tried the
usual spells and dances, but nothing
worked.

(FRIDAY AND COMPANIONS
BUILD A SKELETON SHELTER
AROUND THE MAN, THEN THEY
BUILD A FIRE)

FRIDAY: (CONT) (V.O.) So we
built a journey house for him. And we
built a fire, so we could cook and eat
old Hookloser, so we could all take
some of the soul of that man, who we
loved, into the future with us.

But we were still sharpening our knives,
when death visited us again.

(CRUSOE STANDS BEHIND
A BUSH, WATCHING.

HE IS AROUND FORTY–
FORTY-FIVE, VERY
TANNED. HE IS ARMED
AS BEFORE.

CRUSOE DOUBLES UP, IS
ALMOST SICK, PREVENTS
HIMSELF FROM BEING
SICK.

HE BEGINS TO WALK
STEALTHILY TOWARDS
FRIDAY AND HIS FRIENDS.
HE WALKS STIFFLY AND
TENSELY, UNSLINGING
HIS MUSKET.

FRIDAY AND HIS FRIENDS
LOOK UP, SURPRISED AT
FIRST, THEN CURIOUS.

148

ONE OF THEM SHRUGS
AND SMILES AT CRUSOE.

THE OTHERS SMILE, BEGIN
TO STAND UP, BECKON TO
CRUSOE.

THE FIRST ONE TO SMILE
WALKS TOWARDS CRUSOE.

CRUSOE LEVELS MUSKET
AT HIM.

THE MAN WALKS ON, PUTS
OUT HIS HAND TO TOUCH
THE MUSKET IN GREETING)

CRUSOE: In the name of God the
Father—

(CRUSOE LETS THE MAN
HAVE IT IN THE STOMACH.

MAN COLLAPSES.

THE OTHERS, EXCEPT
FRIDAY, BEGIN TO RUN)

FRIDAY: (V.O.) He shot Ivory
first. You remember Ivory, who used
to sing so loudly, and badly, and
happily. The others ran. I did not
run. I did not run away from death,
knowing that the faster you run away
from him, the sooner he overtakes you.
It was very bad.

(CRUSOE LETS FLY WITH
HIS MUSKET AGAIN.

A SECOND TRIBESMAN
FALLS. ROLLS IN
AGONY.

CRUSOE DESPATCHES HIM
WITH A PISTOL.

A THIRD ONE RUNS INTO
THE SEA.

CRUSOE FIRES AT MAN
IN THE SEA.

THE MAN FALLS BACK
INTO THE SEA)

FRIDAY: (CONT) (V.O.) Then he
killed Weaver, the most cunning
craftsman of our tribe. Then Bentnose,
who painted the poles of our meeting
hut, ran into the sea. But death
ran after him.

(CRUSOE TURNS.

FRIDAY IS CROUCHING
BY THE FIRE.

CRUSOE WALKS SLOWLY
BACK TO HIM.

THERE ARE VINES
APPARENTLY TIED
ROUND FRIDAY'S WRISTS)

FRIDAY: (CONT) (V.O.) I put
vines around my wrists to show I was
not a warrior.

CRUSOE: What's this? A prisoner?
You poor savage.

(CRUSOE PULLS VINES
FROM FRIDAY'S WRISTS)

I have come to rescue you from the
clutches of these foul cannibals.

150

(CRUSOE PLACES HIS
FOOT ON FRIDAY'S
PROSTRATE HEAD.

FRIDAY LOOKS DUBIOUSLY
UPWARDS.

CRUSOE REMOVES FOOT
FROM HEAD. HE RAISES
FRIDAY TO HIS FEET,
HANDLING HIM GINGERLY)

Here, follow me. I have saved your
life.

(CRUSOE STARTS TO
WALK, TURNS AND
BECKONS TO FRIDAY)

CRUSOE: (CONT) And, what is
more, I shall attempt to save your
benighted soul.

(FRIDAY STARES AT HIM

CRUSOE WALKS BACK,
GETS BEHIND FRIDAY,
PRODS HIM WITH MUSKET)

I have changed my mind. You won't
follow me. You will go first. There
must be no risk. No risk at all.

(FRIDAY BEGINS TO
WALK TOWARDS THE
LAND.

CRUSOE FOLLOWS CLOSE
BEHIND, MUSKET READY)

In Scene 1, note how much the writer 'said' without a word of dialogue. Even if the viewer knew nothing of the Robinson Crusoe story, Crusoe's reaction to the sight of that single footprint told us that here was a man who had been marooned and alone for many years. The repeated shots of Crusoe's walking away from the footprint to search for its owner, done by tape editing, served to emphasis his excitement at the discovery. The play was produced in a non-realistic way; the island's flowers and trees were obvious studio cut-outs and set pieces. Note, too, the writer's use of the technique Voice Over (V.O.), where we see Friday as he was in the 'past' while hearing his voice telling the story in the 'present'.

Comment from the writer, Adrian Mitchell

Re-reading *Robinson Crusoe*, I was struck by Crusoe's background, by his religious fervour, by his interest in material objects and possessions and by his efforts to 'educate' Man Friday. I wanted to tell part of the story from Man Friday's point of view.

So I had to imagine the kind of society from which Friday came. I had been reading a number of books of 'primitive' poetry from various tribal societies. I decided that Friday came from a harmonious tribe—not perfect, but a good tribe as tribes go.

So then I had the representatives of a capitalist white culture and a tribal black culture. And I let them try to educate each other, Crusoe arrogantly, Friday by stealth and a form of magic including singing and dancing.

As a framework, I used a tribal meeting at which Friday had to tell the story of his relationship with Crusoe. (Crusoe and Friday had returned to Friday's island on a raft). At the end of the story the tribe had to decide whether to admit Crusoe—who had shot some of their own tribesmen and who had bound and gagged Friday in the manner of Bobby Seale in the Chicago Conspiracy Trial. The decision to admit or exclude Crusoe was very hard and I didn't know how to settle it. I wondered what Crusoe could possibly contribute to the tribe. And then I had him suggest that he could 'educate' the children of the tribe. This is the suggestion which enrages Friday, and makes Crusoe's exclusion inevitable. For Crusoe had already proved himself treacherous, and since he couldn't be trusted not to twist the minds of the children of the tribe, he must go back to his island alone. And there he shot himself out of loneliness. Which was sad—but worse things would have happened if he had stayed with the tribe.

Crusoe wasn't meant to stand for all white men everywhere. But he was meant to embody some of the crimes of the white races against non-white people throughout the world.

I think the text was served excellently by Ram John Holder as Friday, Colin Blakely as Crusoe, the music of Mike Westbrook, the designs of Roger Andrews, and the direction of James MacTaggart. From the start I'd said that it was not a naturalistic play and that I didn't want any location shooting but a set which reflected the feeling of the script.

I can't sum up what I wanted to achieve. I tried to say at least a hundred things in the course of the play. I consider *Man Friday* a political play, an anti-racialist play. My greatest reward came when a black friend rang up and thanked me for the play and said that his two boys had fallen about with laughter every time Friday made a subversive joke. I hope the play helps them to survive. At the time of writing, many TV comics use racialist gags and the *Black and White Minstral Show*, which is an insult to black people, still runs. *Man Friday* was an attempt to fight back against this trend.

Anthology series: LOVE STORY
      Play: FINDERS, KEEPERS
          by
          Rosemary Anne Sisson
          Produced by ATV Network Ltd,
          at Boreham Wood, Hertfordshire.
          Producer: Henri Safran
          Script editor: Maggie Allen

The anthology series *Love Story* consists of separate plays by different writers all around the same basic theme. There are no running series characters.

The story of *Finders, Keepers* begins not with a meeting, but a parting. Tom is a Flight Lieutenant in the RAF and Anne is an officer in the WAAF. It's 1944, and they've just discovered they are in love. Tom has a wife and two children, and Anne is the daughter of a clergyman. They agree never to see each other again, even if they want to.

Eight years later, Tom's wife dies. He has never forgotten Anne, and he wants to find her. But they have cut themselves off so completely that he doesn't know where she is, or even whether she is married. He does find her at last. She is actually working, like him, in London. She isn't married and has never forgotten Tom, or been able to love anyone else. The only trouble is, they have buried their love so successfully that it looks as though they will never be able to find it again. Their meetings are increasingly disastrous, and Tom is almost ready to give up, when, on a last absurdly romantic impulse, he drags her back to the little Norfolk village where they said goodbye. The airfield is closed, and the village pub is deserted and run by a surly landlord with a disagreeable wife. But there they find their love, safe and sound, where they left it.

SCENE 1. INT. SALOON BAR.   DAY.

THE SALOON BAR OF 'THE REED THATCHER'. IT IS A NORFOLK COUNTRY PUB, WITH A LOW CEILING AND OAK BEAMS. ABOVE THE BAR IS A PIECE OF AIRCRAFT FUSELAGE WITH A SWASTIKA ON IT. THE ROOM IS CROWDED WITH RAF OFFICERS, WITH A SPRINKLING OF WAAFS AND ONE OR TWO GIRLS IN CIVILIAN CLOTHES OF 1944. THE NOISE OF CHEERFUL TALK BURSTS UPON US, BUT WE DON'T HEAR ANY ACTUAL WORDS.

CUT TO:

A SHOT OF THE ROOM TAKEN OVER THE SHOULDERS OF TWO PEOPLE WHO SIT AT A SMALL TABLE IN A RECESS. IT IS A MAN IN RAF UNIFORM AND HAT, AND A WAAF OFFICER, ALSO WEARING A HAT.

AS THE NOISE ROUND THE BAR IS RE-MOVED FROM US TO SOME DISTANCE, WE HEAR THEIR WORDS.

TOM: Sandy's promotion's come through.

ANNE: Oh, good. He must be pleased.

TOM: He says he'll be glad of the extra money.

ANNE: What does his wife say?

MOVE ROUND TO SEE THEM FROM THE FRONT. TOM IS ABOUT 30, A FLIGHT LIEUTENANT BUT NOT WEARING FLYING INSIGNIA. ANNE, SITTING ON HIS RIGHT, IS ABOUT 23. SHE HOLDS A GLASS OF GIN-AND-LIME IN HER RIGHT HAND, AND TOM HAS A BEER WHICH HE HOLDS IN HIS LEFT HAND. BOTH ARE SMILING SLIGHTLY, BUT PERHAPS IT MIGHT OCCUR TO US THAT THEIR SMILES ARE RATHER FIXED.

TOM: She doesn't care about the money. She wanted the extra pips to show off in the Ante-room.

155

ANNE: She's entitled to her simple pleasures.

TOM: You think so? She won't be satisfied till poor old Sandy's got scrambled egg on his cap!

A MIDDLE-AGED SQUADRON LEADER, BENDER, WITH WELL-WORN WINGS ON HIS UNIFORM, COMES IN FROM OUTSIDE BY THE OAK DOOR, AND, BEGINNING TO MAKE HIS WAY TOWARDS THE BAR, SEES THEM AND PAUSES, CALLING BACK.

BENDER: Hallo, Tom. Hear your posting's come through.

TOM: (CALLING BACK) That's right. I'm off today.

BENDER: (HEARTILY) Oh—sorry to lose you! How's Betty?

TOM: She's fine, thanks.

BENDER: Still down in Dorset?

TOM: Yes. They're staying with my parents.

BENDER: Good idea. Hopeless dragging the kids all round the countryside. Bet they like it down there.

TOM: Lucy's taken up riding. Fell off the pony three times the first day. Apparently she said she never enjoyed herself so much in her whole life.

BENDER: Great! Well, must grab a quick snifter. Anne, you coming to the Squadron dance tonight?

ANNE: (WITH THE SAME FIXED SMILE) Oh, I can't, Sir, I'm on duty.

BENDER: Too bad. Well, cheerio, Tom. All the best.

TOM: Good-bye.

BENDER CONTINUES TOWARDS THE BAR. WE HEAR HIS HEARTY GREETINGS OF THE LANDLORD.

BENDER: Hallo, George!

RETURNING TO THE TWO AT THE TABLE
SITTING THERE WITH THEIR FIXED SMILES,
WE MOVE DOWN TO FIND THAT THEY
ARE HOLDING HANDS VERY TIGHTLY
UNDER THE TABLE.

ANNE: It can't be right for anyone to suffer like this. Can it?

TOM: I don't know.

ANNE: Isn't it awful, you find yourself talking in cliches. We'll say, 'This thing's bigger than both of us' in a minute.

HE TURNS HIS HEAD TO SMILE AT HER—A
REAL SMILE INSTEAD OF THE PHONEY ONE.

ANNE: I remember once—at school—I fainted in prayers. And when I came to, do you know what I said? I said, 'Where am I?' I really did. I—

SHE TRIES TO LAUGH AND IS ALMOST IN
TEARS.

TOM: Oh, God!

THEY SIT MOTIONLESS IN THEIR OWN
PRIVATE AGONY. A YOUNG PILOT
OFFICER, ON HIS WAY OUT WITH A
GROUP OF FRIENDS, PAUSES TO FINISH A
STORY.

PILOT OFFICER: So I thought, 'That's funny. Those are supposed to be our guns. What're they firing at me for?' And then a voice came over the intercom. 'You bloody fool, look behind you!' So I looked behind me, and there was this doodle-bug chuntering along, right on me tail! I peeled off so fast, I left me markings behind!

2nd PILOT OFFICER: And the doodle-bug picked them up, so the guns shot him down!

THEY GO OUT LAUGHING. THE DOOR
SLAMS BEHIND THEM.

TOM: Darling.

ANNE: Yes?

157

TOM:	We could write at least.
ANNE:	No.
TOM:	If we could write just one letter a year—

ANNE SITS IN SILENCE FOR A MOMENT.

ANNE:	What good would that do?
TOM:	(WITH SUPPRESSED VIO-LENCE) At least we'd be in touch!
ANNE:	That's just it. In touch. I mean—we'd be—thinking about each other.
TOM:	Don't you think we'd be doing that anyway?
ANNE:	We mustn't. Especially you. If you're thinking about me instead of Betty—
TOM:	Just once a year, I think I might be allowed to think about you.
ANNE:	I'd like that. (SHE LOOKS AT HIM) That's the trouble. I'd like it.
TOM:	Well, Then—(URGENTLY) Let's decide on that. One letter a year. (HE LOOKS AT HER ANXIOUSLY) Yes?
ANNE:	I—(SHE HESITATES, TEMPTED) How would we—?
TOM:	Fix a time now—a date. Today. Every year on this day, you write to me, and I'll answer.
ANNE:	Wouldn't Betty think it rather odd? I mean, this letter coming—from me.
TOM:	She wouldn't have to know.
ANNE:	But if it was always the same time this letter came, and you—I mean, Betty would get to know the handwriting, and say, 'Oh, here's that letter again', and you—
TOM:	(QUICKLY) If I knew when it was coming, I could get there first!
ANNE:	You mean, sneak down and—? That would be awful.
TOM:	Yes.

158

THE LANDLORD, GEORGE, COMES NEAR
TO COLLECT GLASSES AND WIPE A NEAR-
BY TABLE. ANNE AND TOM GLANCE AT
EACH OTHER, AND RELEASE THEIR HANDS
AND TAKE A DRINK. GEORGE WIPES THEIR
TABLE.

LANDLORD: (NORFOLK ACCENT) Can I get
you anything while I'm here, then?

TOM: No, we're all right, thanks.

GEORGE NODS AND GOES OFF.

TOM: (UNDER HIS BREATH) To coin
a phrase.

TOM LOOKS AT ANNE AND SMILES, AND
SHE SMILES BACK. THEY BOTH DRINK,
AND THEN SIT IN SILENCE FOR A MOMENT.

TOM: I wish—

ANNE: What?

TOM: I wish we'd gone to bed together.

ANNE: Yes.

TOM: It is the same for you, isn't it? I mean,
I wouldn't like to think that to you it was just something romantic and charming—

ANNE: *Charming?*

TOM: I want it to hurt you as much as it
hurts me.

ANNE: Then you have your wish.

TOM: I don't really.

ANNE: I know.

TOM: And yet I do.

ANNE: I know. (PAUSE) It's funny.

TOM: Funny?

ANNE: Funny peculiar.

TOM: Oh!

ANNE: Daddy being the sort of person he
is—I mean—

TOM: A clergyman.

159

ANNE: A clergyman *par excellence*. I was always brought up to think of love as something very sedate and respectable. You 'fell in love' with someone frightfully suitable, and you walked in the garden together, and gave each other bunches of flowers—

TOM: You never gave me a bunch of flowers.

ANNE: It isn't like that at all.

TOM: No.

ANNE: It—

TOM: Ties your guts into knots.

ANNE: Not quite that. It makes you feel— Yes, I suppose that is it. Do you remember—? (SHE STOPS)

TOM: Remember?

ANNE: That airman who fell out of a window on to the spiked fence? They kept him alive for a week or two with sips of champagne, and then he died. Sitting here talking is the sips of champagne. And then you'll get up and go. And I'll die.

TOM: We'll both die.

ANNE TURNS HER HEAD TO LOOK AT HIM, AND THEIR EYES MEET AND HOLD. THEY STARE AT EACH OTHER MOTIONLESS.

A FOUR-ENGINED BOMBER TAKES OFF FROM NEARBY, AND PASSES LOW OVERHEAD.

ANNE AND TOM TURN THEIR EYES AWAY. TOM GLANCES OVER HIS SHOULDER OUT OF THE WINDOW.

TOM: That damaged Lanc. going home.

ANNE: Oh yes.

TOM: You don't really think I can walk out of this pub, and never see you again, do you?

ANNE: We've got to do it that way.

TOM: Supposing Betty and I broke up.

ANNE: You won't. I don't want you to. And even if you did, it wouldn't make any difference. I don't think you can turn marriage on and off like mod cons. I think, once you take it on, it's like life: You're committed to it until you die. That's how it would've been for me, and I'm not going to make it less than that for Betty. Or for you. (SHE TURNS TO LOOK AT HIM) I love you too much for that.

TOM: That's ironic. You mean, if we'd loved each other less, there would've been more hope for us?

ANNE: (READILY) Oh yes! We could've written to each other, met again—maybe even gone to bed together. But as it is, we've got to bury it so deep that we can never find it again, even if we want to.

TOM: I don't know if I can do it.

ANNE: We must.

PAUSE.

TOM: Do you want another drink?

ANNE SHAKES HER HEAD.

TOM: (CONT'D) George has probably run out of gin, anyway.

PAUSE.

TOM: (CONT'D) What do you think you'll do after the War?

ANNE: I don't know. Keep house for Daddy, I suppose. He's had a rotten time since Mummy died.

TOM: You realise I could come to Endersby and find you.

ANNE: But you won't.

TOM: I must know if you're alive.

161

ANNE: Don't bother. I won't be. (SUDDENLY TRYING TO LAUGH) I didn't mean to say that! I'll be alive, and well, and you'll be alive and happy with Betty and the children, and we'll know that our love is there, and we never spoiled it by using it to hurt other people. It'll be buried deep, and we'll never find it again, but we'll know it's there.

THEY BOTH CROUCH A LITTLE, LEANING AGAINST EACH OTHER. TOM'S HAND IS ON THE TABLE, AND HE SEES THE WATCH-FACE. HE LOOKS AT IT QUICKLY.

ANNE: (PASSIONATELY) Oh no! It's not time yet! Oh no!

TOM: (GLANCING TOWARDS THE WINDOW) Well, I know Jones drives like a maniac, but it's half-an-hour to the station, and—

THEY STARE AT EACH OTHER, SUDDENLY AGHAST REALISING THAT THE MOMENT HAS COME.

TOM: Why on earth did we say we'd say goodbye here? I can't even kiss you!

UNDER THE TABLE THEIR HANDS CLUTCH EACH OTHER AGAIN. ANNE BRINGS HER OTHER HAND TO JOIN HIS, AND HE CLASPS HERS WITH HIS OTHER HAND, SO THAT THEY CLING TOGETHER DESPERATELY, AS THOUGH THEY WERE DROWNING. LEANING TOWARDS HIM, ANNE MANAGES TO PUT HER CHEEK AGAINST HIS SHOULDER, WITHOUT IT BEING APPARENT TO ANYONE ELSE IN THE ROOM WHERE THE NOISE AND CHATTER ROUND THE BAR BECOMES A LITTLE LOUDER.

ANNE TAKES HER OTHER HAND AWAY AND STRAIGHTENS UP AND LOOKS AT HIM.

ANNE: You must go.

TOM: Yes.

ANNE: I can't bear it. I can't bear it.

THEY SIT MOTIONLESS.

ANNE: (CONT'D) It's all right. You must go.

TOM: I'll let the train go, and—

ANNE: No. It's never going to get any better.

UNDER THE TABLE, SHE BEGINS TO DRAW HER HAND AWAY. TOM CLUTCHES IT.

TOM: Darling.

ANNE: Yes.

HE PRESSES HER HAND, AND RELEASES IT. THEY ARE STILL LOOKING INTO EACH OTHER'S EYES AND HE STANDS UP.

TOM: Well—

ANNE'S FACE IS INCREDULOUS AGAIN.

TOM: (CONT'D) I suppose—

ANNE: Yes.

ANNE TRIES TO SMILE AT HIM, BUT CAN'T MANAGE IT. THEY BOTH LOOK AS IF THEY ARE IN FRIGHTFUL PHYSICAL PAIN, AND CAN'T SPEAK. TOM HESITATES A MOMENT LONGER, AND THEN GOES TO THE DOOR, AND TURNS. THEY STARE AT EACH OTHER DESPERATELY. TOM HESITATES AGAIN, AND THEN GOES OUT.

ANNE TURNS QUICKLY TO THE WINDOW, BUT HE HAS GONE THE OTHER WAY. SHE LISTENS, AND WAITS, AND HEARS A SMALL TRUCK STARTED UP IN THE CAR PARK AT THE BACK. SHE LISTENS, WITH HER HEAD BENT TOWARDS THE WINDOW, AND HEARS IT DRIVE AWAY.

SHE SINKS DOWN IN HER SEAT, AND QUICKLY PICKS THE GLASS UP, AND PRETENDS TO DRINK THE DREGS OF THE GIN-AND-LIME, HOPING TO CONCEAL THE FACT THAT TEARS ARE RUNNING DOWN HER CHEEKS.

Technical comment

Contrary to advice elsewhere in this book, the dialogue of this writer contains a number of speech directions, because (to quote her), ". . . I use speech directions when the delivery is *against* the words. It saves time if the actors know how to say the line." Which only goes to prove that in writing there are no clear cut rules, only advice.

Comment from the writer, Rosemary Anne Sisson

The difficulty with this play was that it was true, and I had to make it believable. I heard the story several years ago, including the happy ending, and it stayed in my mind. When I was asked to write a play for the anthology *Love Story*, this was the one I most wanted to write.

If you write today about people who are uniformly vile and heartless and bring misery on all around them, your work is called "hard-hitting and realistic". But as soon as you write a play in which people care deeply about each other, and try to behave well, and which ends happily, everyone (except the public) says "What sentimental rubbish!" and you feel embarrassed at being so naive as to write unfashionable truth instead of fashionable falsehood.

If this play was to succeed, the audience had to believe absolutely in the feelings of the two principals, and the tricky thing is that people, when they feel most, often say least. By choosing to begin with the parting, I was asking the viewer to enter instantly into their anguish, and to believe that they really would agree to part, rather than hurt anyone else with their love. I tried to catch that most haunting quality of a love-affair, the suffering of private agony in a public place. But at the same time there was a tremendous lot of information to be conveyed—that this was wartime, the nature of their relationship, the fact that he was married and had children, that her father was a clergyman, and that they had agreed to part, and make it impossible to find each other again, even if they wanted to. I tried to convey all this while engaging the viewers' sympathy strongly enough to make them care throughout the rest of the play.

Of course, I say, "I was trying to do this" or "meant to convey that", but when I write a play I feel it, and think about it, and act it in my mind until the dialogue comes, and then I put it down on paper. I'm a storyteller, and if viewers watch, and care, and understand, that's all I ask.

THE GRASS WIDOWS
by
William Trevor
Produced by Anglia Television Ltd,
at Norwich.
Head of Drama: John Jacobs
Script editor: John Rosenberg

The wedding is over. For Jackson Major and his bride, Daphne, the honeymoon begins with a flight to Ireland and the Slieve Gashal Hotel. Jackson tells her she'll love the hotel: "Year after year my headmaster used to talk about it—as though it were Paradise."

Meanwhile the headmaster, Angusthorpe, arrives with his wife for their annual touch of Paradise. But the hotel has changed hands, is now run down. Even the Angusthorpe's favourite room has been partitioned into two. In bed, Mrs Angusthorpe can hear the Jacksons' every word through the thin partition, as Jackson tries to make love according to the book. But there are compensations, at least for the two men. Angusthorpe is pleased to find his one-time head boy following in his footsteps by staying at the hotel. Now he introduces the younger man to the real delights of the area, the trout fishing. While the men fish, the women are thrown together. For them there is only the squalid reality of the hotel. The childless Mrs Angusthorpe, unhappily married for 36 years out of 37, believes Daphne has made the same mistake as her own. She warns Daphne and is as cruel as Angusthorpe has been to her in their married life.

Jauntily, the two husbands return from a morning's fishing each to a wife. They represent order, convention, and making the best of things, a far cry from Mrs Angusthorpe's hysteria. Now all four even share the same table in the dining-room, something Daphne feared would happen. But she is calmed down, and in the manner expected of a new wife she continues to make the bed she has elected to lie on. And once again, Mrs Angusthorpe returns to silent acceptance of her lot. While the two men plan further fishing expeditions, Mrs Angusthorpe proposes to Daphne a little walk in the village. Daphne says, "Yes, a little walk would be very pleasant." Daphne's smile is still there, but determinedly so now. It cracks a little as she speaks the last line. Then the camera freezes, on her forced smile.

30. *INT. BAR. DAY.*

MRS ANGUSTHORPE: People don't speak out. All my married life I haven't spoken out, Daphne. (PAUSE) My dear, you're far too good for Jackson Major.

DAPHNE: Mrs Angusthorpe!

AGAIN MRS ANGUSTHORPE RESTRAINS DAPHNE GOING.

MRS ANGUSTHORPE: (VERY QUIETLY; INTENTLY): Pack a suitcase and go.

DAPHNE CLOSES HERS EYES. HER HANDS ARE CLENCHED IN TENSION. SHE SEEMS ON THE POINT OF BREAKING DOWN. INSTEAD, SHE SUDDENLY RELAXES, RELEASES HER BREATH, AND QUITE CALMLY REACHES FOR HER SHERRY.

DAPHNE: Please do not speak to me like this.

MRS ANGUSTHORPE: You've made a mistake, but even now it's not too late to rectify it. Do not accept it; reject your error, Daphne.

DAPHNE: I love my husband, Mrs Angusthorpe. I don't know why you're talking like this: I don't know what you're talking about.

MRS ANGUSTHORPE: My dear, I've seen the seamy side of Jackson Major. The more I think of him the more I can recall. He forced his way up the school, snatching the chances that weren't his to take, putting himself first, like he did in the half-mile race. There was a cruelty in Jackson Major's eyes, and ruthlessness. Like my husband, he has no sense of humour.

DAPHNE: (QUIETLY; CALMLY)
Mrs Angusthorpe, I cannot listen to all this. You
make no sense to me: what my husband was at
school is one thing, what he is today is another. All I
know, Mrs Angusthorpe, is that I was married
yesterday to a man I'm in love with. It'll be all
right—

MRS ANGUSTHORPE: Why will it be all right?

DAPHNE: (SNAPPISHLY) Be-
cause for one thing I shall ask my husband as soon as
he returns to take me from this horrible hotel. My
marriage does not at all concern you, Mrs Angusthorpe. I cannot be here with you.

MRS ANGUSTHORPE: They walked this morning from your horrible hotel, murmuring about the
past no doubt, of achievements on the sports fields
and marches undertaken by a cadet force. While
you and I are having a very different kind of talk.

DAPHNE: What our husbands have
said to one another may well have made more sense.

MRS ANGUSTHORPE: They have not said
that two women in the bar are unhappy. They've
forgotten about the two women: they're more
relaxed and contented than ever they are with us.

DAPHNE: Please stop, Mrs
Angusthorpe. I must go away if you continue like
this—

MRS ANGUSTHORPE: "This man's a bore",
you'll suddenly say to yourself. You'll look at him
amazed.

DAPHNE: Mrs Angusthorpe—

MRS ANGUSTHORPE: Amazed that you could
ever had let it happen.

DAPHNE: Oh God, please stop.

167

MRS ANGUSTHORPE: (WHISPERING) Don't be a silly girl. (SHE LEANS FORWARD STARING INTO DAPHNE'S EYES) That man's upstairs, the man who drives the hire-car. The car'll take you to Galway and I'll lend you money for a plane flight, Daphne. By nine o'clock tonight you could be sitting in your bed at home, eating from a tray that your mother brought you. A divorce'll come through and one day you'll meet a man who'll love you with a tenderness.

DAPHNE: My husband loves me—

MRS ANGUSTHORPE: Your husband should marry a woman who's keen on horses or golf, a woman who might take a whip to him, being ten years older than himself. My dear, you're like me; you're a delicate person.

DAPHNE: Please let go my arm. You've no right to talk to me like this—

MRS ANGUSTHORPE: He is my husband's creature; my husband moulded him. The best head boy he's ever had.

DAPHNE, CALM AGAIN, STARES AHEAD OF HER AT A ROUND ABSORBENT MAT ON THE TABLE THAT ADVERTISES 'CELEBRATION ALE'. SHE IS THINKING OF HERSELF AS MRS ANGUSTHORPE SUGGESTED: SITTING UP IN BED IN HER OWN BEDROOM, WITH A TRAY OF FOOD AND HER MOTHER SAYING IT WAS ALL RIGHT. SHE IS THINKING, TOO, OF THE WHISKEY PRESSED UPON HER THE NIGHT BEFORE AND OF HOW TIRED SHE HAD FELT AND OF HER HUSBAND'S GOING ON ABOUT WHAT THE BOOK SAID.

MRS ANGUSTHORPE, WATCHING HER, IS EAGER, LIKE A VULTURE. SHE SEES HERSELF TELLING HER HUSBAND AT LUNCHTIME THAT ALREADY THE WIFE OF JACKSON MAJOR HAS LEFT HIM.

MRS ANGUSTHORPE: Drive away, Daphne. Before another half hour passes. The longer you go on the harder it'll ever be.

DAPHNE: You're quite outrageous.

MRS ANGUSTHORPE: (HER VOICE RISING HYSTERICALLY) No. No, I tell the truth. The truth is there, instinctively you know it. You need only the courage.

DAPHNE: Oh, please—

MRS ANGUSTHORPE: (VERY SHRILLY NOW) You've made a mistake. You married the wrong man. I made a mistake, Daphne: I know whan I'm talking about.

DAPHNE: (ALMOST EMOTION-ALLY) Mrs Angusthorpe, will you please stop?

MRS ANGUSTHORPE: You were exhausted and depressed, you said last night. He didn't care. He tried to make you drunk so you'd be unaware of his own inadequacies on your wedding night. Jackson Major's that kind of man, Daphne. He beat a boy too hard and wormed his way out of it. He's cruel and a sycophant.

DAPHNE BEGINS TO INTERRUPT AGAIN BUT MRS ANGUSTHORPE RUSHES ON, THOUGH MORE CALMLY NOW.

MRS ANGUSTHORPE: Listen. I've seen people looking at us. How could she ever have married him? I felt those people thinking. And yet one day, a day like yesterday for you, I stood beside him, believing myself in love. And after that I just went on, stupidly. For thirty-seven stupid years.

DAPHNE: (MORE CALMLY THAN BEFORE) You're confusing my husband with yours. They're two different people, Mrs Angusthorpe. (HER VOICE RISING AGAIN) You seem to forget that. (HYSTERICAL NOW) You seem to take a delight in—(SHE BREAKS OFF, WEEPING)

MRS ANGUSTHORPE: What good was winning the half-mile race if he upsets his wife the first time he found himself in a bedroom with her?

31. *EXT. RIVERSIDE. DAY.*

JACKSON HAS JUST LANDED A LARGE FISH.

ANGUSTHORPE: Well done, Jackson.

32. *INT. HALL. DAY.*

DAPHNE PASSES THROUGH. STILL TEARFUL, THOUGH RECOVERING, SHE GLANCES FOR A MOMENT TOWARDS THE DRIVER, WHO'S READING THE NEWSPAPER IN THE RECEPTION AREA. SHE PAUSES SO SLIGHTLY THAT WE ONLY JUST NOTICE.

33. *EXT. GARDEN. DAY.*

MRS ANGUSTHORPE IS SITTING GAZING AHEAD OF HER, QUIETLY WEEPING.

34. *INT. THE JACKSON'S BEDROOM. DAY.*

DAPHNE, LYING ON HER BED, IS STARING AHEAD OF HER, NOT CRYING NOW BUT SEEMING VERY FRIGHTENED. SHE HEARS A SERIES OF VOICES, WHICH BECOME REPETITIVE, FRAGMENTARY AND JUMBLED.

CLERGYMAN'S VOICE: Wilt thou have this man?

JACKSON'S VOICE: What a beautiful stroke!

MRS ANGUSTHORPE'S VOICE: You've made a mistake.

JACKSON'S VOICE: Now listen to me, Daphne—

Technical comment

In Sc. 30, the fact that Daphne remains quite a time listening to Mrs Angusthorpe conveys, without it ever being said, that despite Daphne's protests she is partly interested in the warning. A playwright often says more by presenting the familiar situation than by the actual words he gives his characters to say. The brief cut away to Sc. 31, a pre-filmed sequence, was not to provide a technical bridge for Daphne to get from the bar to the hall, since tape editing was freely used in this production. It was inserted, no doubt, to make the dramatic comparison of the two husbands with the two wives. Sc. 32, when Daphne sees the driver of the hire-car, and pauses a moment, tells us without a word that possibly some of Mrs Angusthorpe's points have gone home. Through-out the play, the lingering hire-car driver acts as a symbol of possible escape from the new marriage. In Sc. 34, the writer takes us into the tormented mind of Daphne. In other parts of the play, the writer frequently makes use of voices over, and of visual flashbacks. The voice over line "What a beautiful stroke!" comes from a flashback earlier in the play, when Daphne remembers playing tennis and how this young man, Jackson, came up to her and congratulated her—their first meeting.

At the front of the script, the writer gives the usual cast list (see page 86). But on a second page, he elaborates on each character with a thumbnail sketch, e.g.

JACKSON MAJOR   Is dull, unimaginative, worthy,
steady, a higher civil servant. He
has no wish to cause his wife pain:
he is unaware that he is doing so.
He shares with Mr Angusthorpe a
lack of humour and a lack of
sensitivity. Together the men are
much more relaxed and at ease than
they are with their two wives.

On another page, the writer gives a general description of how he sees the Slieve Gashal Hotel.

Comment by the writer, William Trevor

Plays present people and, hopefully, truth. Plot interweaves the two. In *The Grass Widows*, as in all my other plays, I attempt no more than that intricate weaving. It is, when you get down to it, quite enough.

Serial: CROSSROADS
Episode: 1751
by
Peter Ling
Michala Crees
Aubrey Cash
Malcolm Hulke
Ivor Jay
Produced by ATV Network Ltd,
at ATV Centre, Birmingham.
Producer and script editor: Reg Watson
Adviser: Dr Wendy Greengross

The continuing-story of *Crossroads* is produced in four episodes each week. To cope with this output there is a storyliner and four script-writers. The storyliner conceives the interweaving plots, and breaks them down into scenes in synopsis form. These 'weekly breakdowns' are discussed at regular weekly or fortnightly script conferences. The script-writers then write the scenes, filling in the details of plot (note how the script writer handled Scene 6). Most television continuing-story shows are written this way—a storyliner to plot, and script-writers to write scenes. In *Coronation Street* and similar shows, the same script-writer writes complete episodes for his particular week in the rosta. But in *Crossroads* the script-writers are allocated story themes, so one writer may carry a story from beginning to end over a number of weeks. The written scenes, delivered weekly, are collated into episodes, and are knitted together by the script editor to ensure continuity flow. The synopsis which follows is by Peter Ling. You will note the initials by the scene headings, which indicate which script writer is to write the scene. The writers get a block or team credit on every episode, irrespective of their contribution. It will be seen that one writer credited wrote nothing for this episode, but had contributed to other episodes in that week.

SCENE 1. MEG'S SITTING-ROOM. (4.10pm). (M.C.)

Pick up—and recap—cliff hanger: Meg and David. How seriously is Timothy hurt? And what about Mrs Holliday? If *she* was driving, there's no knowing what might have happened—come to think of it, Timothy had been knocking them back himself. They decide they will both go to the Coventry hospital, right away.

David says he'll go and find Chris to explain; Meg says she'll tell Sandy—and Tish, who will be left in charge.

SCENE 2. RECEPTION (4.15pm) (M C.)

The aftermath of the party; Stan is helping Mrs Hope empty ashtrays, etc. Meg comes out and tells them the news. She doesn't know how long she'll be at Coventry; if David has to stay there indefinitely she'll come back, of course. She can't find Sandy; they assume he's taken Liz off somewhere. Anyway, she can't spend any more time looking for him.

SCENE 3. MEG'S SITTING-ROOM. (4.20pm) (M.C.)

David comes back, impatiently, as Jill comes in through the french windows; he can't find Chris anywhere—

She laughs: "Me too! *I'm* looking for Wilf—he seems to have vanished!"

But she stops laughing when David tells her what has happened. She is very concerned: "Don't waste time—*I'll* find Chris, and tell him."

SCENE 4. ANTIQUE SHOP (4.30pm) (I.J.)

Ted is alone when Constance comes in—and he says sharply: "Where have you been? Working out how to split your profits with Mr Hurley?" She is taken aback, then tries to bluff—what does he mean?

He explains. He's been a bit slow on the uptake, but at last he's put two and two together. Her 'friend' Mr Hurley is doing a deal with her; they were in cahoots, to convince young Mrs Redington that the contents of her Aunt's house weren't worth much. *He* does the valuation; she buys the contents and resells them—and they split the very handsome profit between them.

She signs: "You'll never understand, will you, Ted? . . . We're running a business here."

He loses his temper. "No, we're not—*you're* not. . . . Not any more."

SCENE 5. RECEPTION. (4.35pm) (M.C.)

Jill and Stan are talking to Mrs Hope. They can't find Chris—or

Wilf for that matter. Stan suggests Chris might have set off for Lake House on his own. They'll drive over there in the van and keep a look-out for him.

Liz comes in; they grab her—has she seen Chris? No, she hasn't. . . . She's been looking for Sandy. He just sort of disappeared from the party, about an hour and a half ago, and she hasn't seen him since.

COMMERCIAL BREAK

SCENE 6. ANTIQUE SHOP. (4.40pm). (I.J.)
Ted and Constance have their final showdown. She tries to explain—she wasn't double-dealing him—she was doing it for the sake of the business—

He says he's not interested. What she and Hurley were up to is illegal, and she knows it perfectly well. She says: "So what are you going to do about it? Make trouble, I suppose?"

He shakes his head. "No—not unless you force my hand. I'm prepared to overlook it—on two conditions. One—that Mrs Redington gets the real value of that furniture. And two—that you accept the offer I've made to you for your half of the business—and get out."

She knows she can't fight him on this. He's won.

SCENE 7. HOSPITAL WARD (INSIDE AND OUTSIDE).
(5.15pm) (M.C.)
Outside the ward; Meg and David are about to go in, but both are stopped by a doctor, who wants a word with them.

The woman who was driving the car was killed instantly.

David asks about his uncle. He'll be all right—just some stitches in the head—but it's the other passenger in the car they're concerned about. He asks if Meg and David can help identify him.

They say Timothy and Mrs Holliday didn't have anyone with them when they left the Motel—as far as they know. They must have picked him up on the way; probably a hitchhiker. Could they see Timothy first?

The doctor leads the way into the ward, and through a set of screens. Timothy is bandaged, and terribly depressed. He asks about "the other two". David tells him not to worry. Timothy murmurs that he "tried to make her stop speeding, but she wouldn't". . . . He goes off to sleep.

SCENE 8. LAKE HOUSE. (5.20pm) (A.C.)
Jill and Stan arrive, and find Wilf and Chris still deep in their

argument—he has brought the old man home to show him his model planes, and is demonstrating one. Wilf is impressed, despite himself, and admits perhaps it has some advantages over kites. . . .

"But," he adds as an after thought, "it'll never replace racing pigeons!"

SCENE 9. MEG'S SITTING ROOM. (5.25pm). (I.J.)

Mrs Hope with her feet up, exhausted. Ted comes in. She comments that he looks unusually cheerful, at the end of a long hard day. He tells her why. He's got his own way. Constance is packing up and getting out.

How did he manage it? He kisses Tish, smiling. "Don't ask me—I'm ashamed to tell you, but I finally fought her on her own ground—and won!"

SCENE 10. HOSPITAL WARD. (5.30pm). (M.C.)

As before. Meg is sitting with David beside the sleeping Timothy when the doctor comes in and signals to her that she should come outside.

Outside the screens, the doctor tells her they are very worried about the other victim. In case by any chance it was a guest from the party, will she please come and see if she recognises the young man?

They go behind a second set of screens, and she looks down at the patient. . . . She stares at him, her face drained of all expression. The doctor asks if she knows him. She tells him: ". . . It's my son."

Selected scenes

SCENE 6. ANTIQUE SHOP.   DAY.

TED
CONSTANCE
*N/S CUSTOMER

(4.40 pm)

TED WALKS AND OPENS THE DOOR FOR A N/S CUSTOMER.

TED: If we come across another lamp I'll let you know.

THE CUSTOMER EXITS. TED WALKS BACK INSIDE.

(*) N/S = non-speaking.

175

CONSTANCE: You know, Ted, just as it takes two to make a quarrel—it takes two to make peace.

TED: No. It's gone too far. You've gone too far!

CONSTANCE: I've only done what I think's best for the business.

TED: Is that an apology?

CONSTANCE: Certainly not.

TED: Wouldn't make any difference. We're incompatible. I don't like your methods . . . (DERISIVE) Methods? Sharp dealing!

CONSTANCE: It's a horse-trading business.

TED: And that's the basic disagreement between us. I don't think it is and I don't think it has to be. And there's no trust, either— between you and me. Why you didn't even tell me about that damn sideboard! You knew—but you didn't tell me! . . . You were ready to let me make a fool of myself.

CONSTANCE: I was very angry.

TED: No, you were just being clever. If I tripped over that one I might believe that our valuation was reasonable. Well, it isn't! And I'm not in the business of extortion. You are! . . . So sell out and get out, Constance!

CONSTANCE: No.

TED: For heaven's sake! . . . It's an impossible situation!

CONSTANCE: What's the saying? If you can't stand the heat in the kitchen . . .? Well, I can. It's not for me to get out . . .

TED: I want you OUT!

CONSTANCE: Saying it doesn't make it so. This is all very futile, isn't it? We've discussed it before who should go and why—and neither of us can convince the other . . . Stalemate!

176

TED: There's got to be a
solution . . . (BEAT) Would you take a fifty-fifty
chance—you or me?

CONSTANCE: What do you mean?

TED: Draw straws . . . Toss a
coin . . . Cut the cards?

CONSTANCE APPRAISES HIM STEADILY . . .
THOUGHTFULLY. SHE GOES TO WINDOW
DISPLAY, TAKES OUT A PACK OF CARDS
FROM A CRIBBAGE BOARD. SHE RETURNS
TO TED. SHE IS SHUFFLING THE CARDS.

CONSTANCE: Aces low?

TED: Agreed.

SHE PLACES THE PACK ON COUNTER.
TED GESTURES. SHE CUTS. NOW TED.
THEY SHOW EACH OTHER THE CUTS.
THEIR EXPRESSIONS ARE IMPASSIVE. WE
DO NOT SEE WHO HAS WON.

END OF SCENE

SCENE 10. HOSPITAL WARD.   DAY.

                        MEG
                        DAVID
                        TIMOTHY
                        DR RYAN
                        SANDY
                        N/S NURSE

(5.30pm)

MEG AND DAVID ARE CONVERSING IN
WHISPERS. TIMOTHY STILL ASLEEP.

MEG: He doesn't look too bad,
David. Just very shocked.

DAVID: The doctor was right—
he's a lucky man.

MEG: Perhaps they'll let him
come home in a day or two.

DAVID: Home?

177

MEG: The Motel's his home
for as long as he needs it, you know that.

DR RYAN ENTERS.

DR RYAN: Mrs Richardson, I
wonder if you'd mind?

HE BECKONS MEG.

DR RYAN: We're very worried
about the other passenger. It's important that we
find somebody belonging to him. I know it's an
outside chance, but there's just a possibility that he
might have been a guest at the party.

MEG: You want me to take a
look at him?

DR RYAN: If you would.

MEG: Yes, of course; any-
thing I can do to help.

DR RYAN LEADS HER BEHIND SECOND
SET OF SCREENS. A NURSE, WHO HAS
BEEN ADJUSTING A SALINE DRIP AT THE
PATIENT'S HEAD, MOVES ASIDE AND MEG
LOOKS DOWN AT HIM.

DR RYAN: Well? Do you know
him?

PAUSE.

MEG LOOKS UP, NODS, TOO SHOCKED
FOR SPEECH, THEN CONTINUES TO STARE
DOWN AT SANDY.

DR RYAN: Mrs Richardson?

MEG: It's . . . he's my son.

CLOSING CAPTIONS.

F/S SHOT: L/S WARD—
SANDY'S BED
SCREENED OFF.
OR C/U SANDY
UNCONSCIOUS.

END OF EPISODE 1751

178

Technical comment

Although *Crossroads* episodes are recorded in advance of transmission, the recordings are on the continuous-run basis, with no video tape pauses and editing. This is caused not by a money economy, but by the very tight four-times-a-week production schedule. So, characters must be bridged. The second of our selected scenes was a dramatic milestone in the show's eight years—yet the scene 'reads flat'. This is something you have to get used to when dealing with scripts, including your own. What the writer did here was skilfully to use the fewest possible words for the high moment of tragedy; that gave the actress playing Meg, Noele Gordon, a real opportunity *to act*. In production, the scene worked excellently.

Note how each scene starts with its own little cast list. This is peculiar to *Crossroads*. 'F/S SHOT' at the end means 'Full Stop Shot', another *Crossroads* peculiarity: after all the credits at the end, they return to a visual of something that symbolises the episode cliffhanger. Here the writer suggests a long shot of the ward or a close up of Sandy, leaving it to the director's discretion.

Using one episode as an example of a continuing-story show is not entirely fair to the show: it is like showing someone a grain of sand to illustrate a mile of beach. For instance, in episodes following our example the tragedy of Sandy, now paralysed, was contrasted with life going happily on back at the Motel, and eventually the effect such an accident could have on the family and a small community.

Continuing-story serials are essentially plotty. In his home in America, P. G. Wodehouse watches a daily serial every afternoon because, he says, he learns a lot about plotting. Also this type of show is often accused of being trite. Terrance Dicks has a theory about that: "Every now and again somebody starts a new serial which is not going to be like any of the others and is going to be a real examination of social problems. This seems to work for the first few months. But gradually, inexorably, the stock themes of soap opera begin to make their appearance, for the very good reason that the basics of birth, death, and marriage, are really what the audience want from this kind of show. The problem with the daily is, to quote Sam Goldwyn, 'Finding some new clichés'."

Comment from the producer, Reg Watson

Why have I produced *Crossroads* for the past eight years? My usual reply is that I've been too busy to stop. However, the truth is that the programme fascinates me, and the longer it runs the more fascinating it becomes. Also, I'm grateful to it.

The fascination began during the planning stages eight years ago when I realised that we were developing a community of characters with an enormous potential. We had Meg Richardson, a widow with two children. What would she look like? What sort of character was she? Is she honest? What was to become of her? Dozens of questions suddenly required dozens of answers. Then we turned to her daughter, Jill Richardson. Blonde or brunette? Pretty or plain? Should she be a tearaway? Should she respect her mother and hate her brother? What about her brother? Who *is* Sandy Richardson really? What's his background? What's his future? As we analysed the growing list of characters we found we now had hundreds of questions requiring answers.

I remember, in those early days, likening the *Crossroads* cast to birds in a nest, with their beaks wide open, yelling for "More plot, more dialogue, more problems, more solutions, more . . . more . . . more!" And with it, for me, came more knowledge. Experts from every walk of life were consulted as each character developed. We had detailed discussions with marriage guidance counsellors, doctors, clergy, stockbrokers, hoteliers, the army, the navy, the air force, the post office, health department, farmers, solicitors, Lord Mayors, unmarried mothers, designers, bomb disposal experts, social workers, occupational therapists, witches, accountants, pilots, gynaecologists, police, spinsters, old-age pensioners, prison governors, actors, writers, viewers and critics.

The list seems endless. These good people patiently imparted their knowledge to us and read and re-read stories. Over the years, with their help, we tackled subjects like broken marriages, illegitimacy, divorce, malnutrition, mental health, alcoholism, kleptomania, fraud, murder, loneliness, gambling, cruelty, bankruptcy, childless couples, in-laws, big business, vandalism, abortion, anti-smoking, child stealing, religion, education, bigamy, farming, the canals of the Midlands, cookery, travel, fashion, prisons, prostitution, illegal immigrants, teenagers, old age, death, local government, nursing, pollution, manslaughter, drunken driving, paraplegics, romance, respect, humour and happiness.

I am grateful to *Crossroads* because it broadened my horizons and gave me an insight into many social problems I may otherwise have ignored. The fact that 12,000,000 viewers watch each episode four nights a week is a compliment to the many people who work so hard to make it believable and entertaining.

Series: DOCTOR WHO
Serial: CARNIVAL OF MONSTERS
Episode: I
by
Robert Holmes
Produced by the British Broadcasting
Corporation at BBC Television Centre,
London.
Producer: Barry Letts
Script editor: Terrance Dicks

Doctor Who is a series of mainly four- or six-part serials. The Doctor is projected through Time and Space in his TARDIS, a craft that from the outside looks like an old fashioned London police box. He arrives where something is happening, gets involved on the side of the oppressed, then continues on his travels, and that takes the viewer into the next serial. He usually takes along with him one young companion—Jo Grant in this episode. (There is a paperback about the series. See page 256.)

In this first episode of *Carnival of Monsters* two visitors arrive on an alien planet. They are a wandering showman and his girl assistant. They have the Scope, a kind of super-technological peepshow which maintains, in miniature, different life-forms from all over the galaxy, kept in a simulation of their natural environment. The visitors are greeted by members of the planet's ruling class. Meanwhile, the Doctor and Jo emerge from the TARDIS to find themselves apparently on board a cargo steamer in the Indian Ocean in the year 1926. But the Doctor insists things are not what they seem, and his theory is confirmed when a prehistoric monster rears its head from the sea. The Doctor and Jo meet their astonished fellow passengers who treat them as stowaways and lock them up. On the alien planet, the wandering showman struggles to repair his Scope, which seems faulty. He decides some foreign body is lodged in the circuits. On the ship, the Doctor and Jo escape and make their way back to the TARDIS. As they approach, a giant hand (the showman's) reaches from above to take the TARDIS. We realise that the Doctor and Jo, along with all the other 'specimens', are prisoners inside the showman's Scope.

(In Episodes 2, 3, and 4 of this four-part serial, the Doctor and Jo find themselves in another section inhabited by ferocious monsters called Drashigs, which pursue them back to the ship. Eventually the Doctor escapes from the Scope, and returns the captive specimens to their own time and place. Then he and Jo go on their way in the TARDIS).

Selected scenes

1. EXT. CITY. DAY. (CSO)

(WE ARE OUTSIDE THE GATES
OF A MYSTERIOUS METALLICALLY
GLEAMING CITY ON AN ALIEN
PLANET.

ABOVE THE CITY WALL IS A
RAISED AREA, THE TERRITORY
OF THE RULING OFFICIAL CASTE.

BELOW AROUND THE CLOSED
GATES ARE CLUTTERED ARCHWAYS
LEADING TO THE TERRITORY
OF THE LOWLY FUNCTIONARIES
WHO ARE TO BE SEEN MOVING
ABOUT. THEY ARE SQUAT AND
BRUTISH, DRESS IN ROUGH
SERVICEABLE WORKING CLOTHES.

SUDDENLY THERE IS A
THUNDERING RUMBLE.)

TELECINE 2
Model shot
We see a rocket sink slowly
to land behind some nearby
buildings.

2. EXT. CITY. DAY.

(WE CUT TO KALIK AND ORUM
WATCHING FROM THEIR RAISED
AREA.

THEY ARE TALL, THIN, GREY
HUMANOIDS, GREY SKINNED,
GREY HAIRED, DRESSED IN
GREY)

KALIK: The cargo shuttle has
arrived.

182

ORUM:　　One must prepare oneself
to encounter the aliens.

KALIK:　　Reluctantly, one agrees.

(KALIK AND ORUM DESCEND FROM
THEIR PLATFORM TO GROUND
LEVEL.

WE CUT TO ANOTHER PART
OF THE SET WHERE THERE
IS A KIND OF LUGGAGE
CHUTE LEADING FROM SOME
UNSEEN LOADING AREA.
VARIOUS ODDS AND ENDS
OF PARCELS, CRATES, AND
BOXES, BEGIN TO RUMBLE
DOWN THE CHUTE.

AMONGST THEM TUMBLE
VORG AND SHIRNA.

VORG IS A PERSON OF
DRAMATIC PRESENCE, WITH
FIERCE EYEBROWS WAXED
TO POINTS LIKE KITCHENER'S
MOUSTACHE.

HIS COMPANION, SHIRNA,
IS A VERY PRETTY GIRLOID
UNDER HER MULTI-COLOURED
MAKE UP.

ONE GLANCE TELLS US
THEY ARE MEMBERS OF
EQUITY GALACTIC: A
SECOND GLANCE THAT
TIMES ARE HARD, VORG'S
GOLDEN BOOTS ARE DOWN
AT HEEL AND SHIRNA'S
FISH NETS HAVE BEEN
COBBLED SO OFTEN THE
PATTERN IS LOST.

VORG AND SHIRNA PICK
THEMSELVES UP AND DUST
THEMSELVES OFF.)

SHIRNA: (ANGRILY) Top of the
bill, he says! Received like a
Princess, he says.

VORG: (PLACATINGLY) Now,
Shirna . . . Don't be so . . . Oh no—
the Scope!

(VORG RUSHES TO THE
CHUTE AND IS JUST IN TIME
TO GRAB THE SCOPE, A
LARGE GAUDY CYLINDER, A
CROSS BETWEEN A JUKE BOX
AND A SAMOVAR)

VORG: (CONT) Well, come on!
Help me!

(TOGETHER VORG AND SHIRNA
MANAGE TO LOWER THE SCOPE
TO THE GROUND.)

SHIRNA NOTICES KALIK AND
ORUM, WHO ARE NOW APPROACH-
ING.)

SHIRNA: Look out! Here they
come.

(THERE IS A SCUFFLE SOME
LITTLE WAY AWAY.

ONE OF THE FUNCTIONAIRES
HAS OBVIOUSLY GONE BESERK?
AND IS GRAPPLING WILDLY
WITH HIS FELLOWS, THROWING
THEM ASIDE AS THEY TRY
TO RESTRAIN HIM.

HE DASHES OFF AND BEGINS
TO CLIMB TOWARDS THE RAISED

184

AREA. HE REACHES IT AND
BEGINS TO ADDRESS HIS
FELLOW FUNCTIONARIES WITH
A STREAM OF INCOMPREHENSIBLE
BUT OBVIOUSLY REVOLUTIONARY
GOBBLEDEYGOOK.

CUT TO KALIK AND ORUM
WATCHING. KALIK DRAWS
HIS LASER GUN AND AIMS
IT AT THE FUNCTIONARY.
KALIK FIRES. THE
FUNCTIONARY FALLS.)

ORUM: Good. You have eradicated
him.

KALIK: No, no. Merely rendered
him unconscious.

ORUM: But he will be disposed
of?

KALIK: Naturally. But first his
mental and nervous system must be
subjected to analysis.

ORUM: Of course.
  (KALIK AND ORUM TURN
  BACK TOWARDS VORG AND
  SHIRNA.)

Now one must deal with the aliens.

  (VORG AND SHIRNA QUAIL)

3. INT. SHIP'S HOLD.   DAY.

          (SHAFTS OF LIGHT THROUGH
          A GRILL ILLUMINATE THE
          HOLD OF A SMALL CARGO
          SHIP. IT IS FAIRLY FULL
          OF BALES AND CRATES.

          THE TARDIS MATERIALISES.

185

AFTER A MOMENT THE DOOR
OPENS AND DOCTOR WHO
STEPS OUT IN ARGUMENTATIVE
MOOD.)

DOCTOR WHO: I tell you, there's
no need to test, Jo. I've been
here before and the atmosphere is
perfectly—

(DOCTOR WHO BREAKS OFF
SNIFFING IN SOME ALARM.
JO STEPS OUT OF THE
TARDIS.)

JO: It smells.

DOCTOR WHO: That's odd.

JO: Sort of farmy.

DOCTOR WHO: Gaseous sulphides, low
concentration. Nothing to worry
about.

Technical comment

This is a typical opening to a *Doctor Who* serial. Something is
happening, perhaps on Earth or perhaps on an alien planet. Meanwhile,
unseen by the serial principals, the Doctor and Jo arrive in their
TARDIS. The Doctor and Jo can then wander into the existing
conflict situation and become involved. The ingenuity of this particular
opening by Robert Holmes is that the setting in which we first see
the Doctor and Jo seems to be totally unrelated to the world of
Kalik and Orum.

Note the writer's 'in' joke contained in the stage directions about
"EQUITY GALACTIC" (you'll recall that Equity is the actor's
trade union). Most script editors and directors appreciate witty stage
directions, and some writers are renowned for it.

You will see that the first telecine sequence gets the number 2.
This is because in this series, T/C 1 is reserved for the filmed opening
credits.

The stage direction about the "STREAM OF INCOMPRE-
HENSIBLE BUT OBVIOUSLY REVOLUTIONARY GOB-

BLEDEYGOOK" seems to contradict item 44 on page 82, i.e. that *all* dialogue must be written and none should be implied within stage directions. In this case, however, it was impossible for the writer to write the type of sounds which the character was supposed to emit. The string of sounds had to be worked out during rehearsals.

Comment by the producer, Barry Letts

Once our audience gets past the *Andy Pandy* age, the great danger in producing children's television is that we may make it childish.

Nowadays we try to make *Doctor Who* as much for adults as for children. The programme started in 1963 as a children's show undoubtedly, but in the ten years of its life, and especially during the last four years, it has developed to the point where nearly 60% of its viewers are over the age of fifteen.

However, this just means that we follow in the footsteps of all good children's writers in not talking down to the younger members of our audience, although we never forget them.

The first episode of *Carnival of Monsters* by Robert Holmes works very well on both levels. It is exciting for children and at the same time intriguing and amusing for adults. A line such as the one spoken by one of the ruling species about dissatisfied serfs on the feudal planet of Inter Minor, "Give them a hygiene chamber and they'll store fossil fuel in it . . ." will go right over the heads of anybody born since the war, but what a super line it is!

Comment by the writer, Robert Holmes

Over its many years *Doctor Who* has acquired a very devoted and loyal audience. It has also acquired a number of equally devoted writers who will tell you frankly it is their favourite assignment— technically difficult though it usually is.

The reasons why a 'children's show' should inspire such a reaction among blasé professional writers may seem hard to fathom. I know, in my own case, when I am commissioned to write for the programme, the cover comes off my typewriter with little delay. (Normally, I have to wait until guilt over an imminent deadline, and fear of my bank manager, combine to overcome inertia!)

I believe the truth is that *Doctor Who* releases a writer from his normal mental straitjacket. He can, for once, leave the padded cell of reality and fantasise through eternal time and space. It is an enjoyable and refreshing exercise.

187

There is one other way in which this programme is different. *They say* only an average of about ten million people watch it. Well, I've often written for shows rated in the top ten and even my wife hasn't noticed. But when I write for *Doctor Who* everyone, from my milk boy to Aunt Jessie in the Orkneys, seems aware of the fact.

Series: THE EXPERT
Episode: DEATH IN THE RAIN
by
N. J. Crisp
Produced at the BBC Television
Centre, London

The series *The Expert*, devised by N. J. Crisp and its producer Gerard Glaister, is about forensics in criminal investigation. The series characters are a pathologist (Dr Hardy, played by Marius Goring), his wife (Dr Jo Hardy, a general practioner, played by Ann Morrish), and Detective Chief Inspector Fleming (played by Victor Winding).

In this episode, set mainly in a working-class area, a little girl is found lying by the side of a road, dead. There is a hexagonal indentation in her skull. Children tell the police about a man they saw talking to the girl just before she was found. The man, Stephen Trimmer, is found, questioned. He is a self-employed carpenter, a loner, a psychiatric out-patient with a history of deep depressions. From the moment Trimmer goes to the police station to 'help the police with their enquiries', the dead girl's father and neighbours regard Trimmer as the killer. Trimmer's tool box contains an oddly-shaped hammer; but Dr Hardy insists that this hammer could not have caused the fatal injury. In a bus depot, a cleaner finds blood and hair on a wheel nut of a bus. With Dr Hardy's help, the police establish that death was caused by accident. It was raining; the girl's father had put stick-on soles onto his daughter's shoes to save shoe repair costs; a stick-on sole had flapped back as the child ran, and she hurtled head first against the wheel of the passing bus. Trimmer is allowed to go home. But the girl's father cannot accept that his own penny pinching (caused by his own poverty) was the real cause of the girl's death. Neither can the neighbours. As Trimmer goes back home, he is treated by people in the street as a child murderer.

18. INT. C.I.D. OFFICE.   DAY.

(TRIMMER AND FLEMING)

TRIMMER: Am I free to go?

FLEMING: I'd rather you didn't,
Mr Trimmer.

TRIMMER: I've told you all I can.

FLEMING: You haven't been much
help though, have you, Mr Trimmer.

TRIMMER: I've told you again and
again—what more can I say?

FLEMING: As far as we know, you
were the last person to see Lucille
Norton alive. Now that makes you very
important, Mr Trimmer. If we keep on
talking, perhaps you'll remember
something else, something that might
help us.

TRIMMER: What are you trying to
make me say? That I killed her?

FLEMING: Did you?

TRIMMER: No. I talked to her,
that's all.

FLEMING: Sure?

TRIMMER: Why don't you believe me?

FLEMING: I haven't said that I
don't.

TRIMMER: Your whole manner says
you don't. Why? What possible grounds
have you got?   -

FLEMING: You were there. You talked to her. No one saw her alive again. She was killed with a violent blow. Possibly from a hammer, or similar instrument. Do you deny that you were carrying tools at the time?

TRIMMER: No. I told you I was.

FLEMING: I also wonder why you refused to give us permission to search your premises.

TRIMMER: Look, suppose someone comes to you, says they want to pry into your personal belongings for no reason, no . . .

FLEMING: But we did have a reason, Mr Trimmer.

TRIMMER: I had every right to refuse.

FLEMING: Certainly. On the other hand, Mr Trimmer, my experience is that people usually refuse when they've got something to hide.

(ASH OPENS THE DOOR)

ASH: Doctor Hardy, sir.

FLEMING: Right.

(HARDY COMES IN, ASH STAYS OUTSIDE.)

FLEMING: Mr Trimmer, this is Doctor Hardy, the pathologist on the case.

(HARDY SITS FACING TRIMMER)

HARDY: Mr Trimmer, in your desk
was found a letter making an appointment
at the out patients department of the
hospital.

(TRIMMER LOOKS AT FLEMING)

HARDY: Inspector Fleming was
telephoned. He does know. Let me say
that I have talked to your doctor at the hospital,
I explained the position, he has given
me certain details. I simply want to
try and clarify the background. Do you
understand?

TRIMMER: Yes.

HARDY: You have been receiving
treatment as an out patient for mental
illness for some time.

TRIMMER: Yes.

HARDY: Have you ever been an
in patient?

TRIMMER: No. They said it wasn't
necessary.

HARDY: Quite so.

TRIMMER: I've been getting better.
I have.

HARDY: Your original symptoms
were loss of appetite, loss of weight,
a state of anxiety, deep depression.

TRIMMER: Then, yes—

HARDY: And included an attempt
at suicide, which brought the necessity
for treatment to the notice of your
doctor.

TRIMMER: Yes.

HARDY: You are a lonely man,
Mr Trimmer.

TRIMMER: Yes.

HARDY: You felt at odds with
the world.

TRIMMER: Yes.

HARDY: Do you still feel at
odds with the world?

TRIMMER: Is that what
the hospital says?

HARDY: I'm asking you.

TRIMMER: Not so much.

HARDY: But you do.

TRIMMER: Mostly, yes.

HARDY: Still. Despite
extended treatment.

TRIMMER: Doctor, I know I'm not
normal. Getting to live with it, that's
the point, isn't it?

HARDY: In what way are you not
normal?

TRIMMER: It's all written down,
I'm sure.

HARDY: I'd rather hear it in
your own words.

(NO RESPONSE FROM TRIMMER)

193

HARDY: You lead a solitary
life. You live alone, you work alone,
you seem to have no friends. Is that
by preference?

TRIMMER: Yes.

HARDY: Why?

TRIMMER: People don't like me.

HARDY: Why do you feel that?

TRIMMER: I just can't talk.
People talk. They talk all the time.
I listen to them, but I can't seem to
join in. When I was a little boy, I
used to think I was invisible. No one
took any notice of me. No one. So, I
do my work, I'm a craftsman, that's
enough.

HARDY: But you would like friends.

TRIMMER: I manage.

HARDY: Women friends?

TRIMMER: Women. In all my life,
no woman's looked at me, not as if I
was a man like any other man. But then,
I'm not, am I.

HARDY: Why do you go out of
your way to talk to little girls?

    (NO REPLY)

Have you told your doctor at the hospital?

TRIMMER: No.

HARDY: But you do, don't you.

TRIMMER: I like children. That's all.

FLEMING: Is it? Are you sure you . . .

HARDY: Fleming, please. (TO
TRIMMER) You find it hard to talk to
adults, but you can talk to children.

TRIMMER: Children, well they don't
look at me as if I was different.
They just accept that I'm there. That
I'm someone. They listen, they tell me
things, sometimes I can even make them
laugh. That's all. But as for harming
one of them, no, never.

HARDY: Your hospital doctor spoke of
certain fantasies. He also mentioned
lapses of memory. Periods, quite short
periods, when you didn't remember what
you'd done.

TRIMMER: Not lately, doctor. I'm
better, I tell you.

HARDY: Completely?

TRIMMER: Yes.

HARDY: Mr Trimmer, the police
sergeant who searched your house found
a considerable quantity of obscene
photographs. Also a number of books.

(WHICH WAS WHAT TRIMMER
WAS AFRAID OF)

TRIMMER: I swear I haven't looked
at them for months. I swear it.

HARDY: Because of the improvement
in your mental health.

TRIMMER: Yes.

195

HARDY: You didn't need them any
more.

TRIMMER: That's right.

HARDY: Then why didn't you
destroy them, Mr Trimmer? (PAUSE) Why
did you keep them?

TRIMMER: I don't know.

HARDY: (TO FLEMING) All right.

(FLEMING OPENS THE DOOR)

FLEMING: Frank.

(ASH COMES IN)

FLEMING: Take Mr Trimmer to the
canteen and give him a meal. (TO
TRIMMER) Doctor Hardy will need to
examine the clothing you were wearing
last night.

TRIMMER: I've got it on.

ASH: I've brought something
for you to change into.

TRIMMER: (TO FLEMING) I didn't
kill that girl.

ASH: Come on.

(ASH AND TRIMMER GO)

FLEMING: Or perhaps he doesn't
remember killing her. How much better
is he according to the hospital?

HARDY: No as much as he imagines.

FLEMING: Erotic fantasies, memory
lapses, mentally ill, a loner, feels
himself an outcast—just the sort of
nut who usually turns up in cases like
this.

HARDY: The hospital regards
him as mentally ill, not mentally
diseased.

FLEMING: What's the difference?

HARDY: A great deal. Trimmer
is suffering from psycho-neurosis,
which is a milder form of
mental disorder, but he is not psychotic.
There is no history of violence, except
self inflicted violence. Mental
illness is simply an illness like any
other and should be regarded in that
rational light.

FLEMING: All right, but let me ask
you a question. Does it ever happen that
a man receives treatment as an out
patient, and it's later discovered that
it's more serious than they thought?

HARDY: Trimmer is in first class
hands, I very much doubt if any
deterioration would . . .

FLEMING: Never mind your doubts,
doctor. Does it ever happen?

HARDY: It has happened.

(ASH COMES IN)

ASH: We're getting a bit of
a crowd outside, sir. Waiting for a
sight of Trimmer.

FLEMING: Then tell them to clear
off.

ASH: I'm going to, sir.
Thought you'd like to know.

(ASH GOES)

FLEMING: Beats me how they get to
hear about it. They always do, though.

HARDY: What's the position with
Trimmer?

FLEMING: At the moment? He's one
of those men who spend several hours at
the police station helping the police
with their enquiries. You've read about
them.

Technical comment

Note the economy of stage directions, and the total absence of speech directions (see page 56). The writer has left interpretation to the director and the actors.

This particular scene demonstrates well the relationship between Dr Hardy and Detective Chief Inspector Fleming. The expert and the authoritarian are not unique to this series. You find them cropping up time and again in literature: the expert, who is always a civilian (one of Us) finally proves himself right, and the man in authority (one of Them) is made to look a fool. *The Expert* takes a more mature look at the relationship. Neither Hardy nor Fleming are always right, and neither comes across as a fool.

The series ran for 52 episodes.

Comment by the writer, N. J. Crisp

I regard myself as a storyteller, a narrative playwright, so a successful series episode, to me, is one in which I have managed to write my own original play within the framework of the series, without anyone noticing. Or, to be more precise—since producers know perfectly well what I and a number of other writers are up to—in a form in which the 'play' element adds to and does not detract from, the series format.

Often my stories for *The Expert* were built up from some factual occurence from the past, and that is how *Death In The Rain* began. My job was to involve the three leading characters, and—hopefully— to create something for myself as well. Doctor Hardy's role as the pathologist was obvious, and merely depended on research, and his already established character. Jo Hardy, his wife, was a GP. So the father of the girl, unable to face telling his wife that their daughter was dead, went to their family doctor, Jo Hardy, and asked her to do this terrible job for him. This gave us a patient for Jo to look after. Detective Chief Inspector Fleming, as a policeman, needed a suspect, because at first it looked like murder. So there was a man, Trimmer, who had been seen where the child was playing, and had in fact given her some chocolate. So far, this process was mechanical, the mere assembly of the clockwork, which is what it would have remained if characters were not created who came to life—the part of my job which to me matters most. It was because I think that 'my' characters (the suspect, the father, the mother, and other episode characters) were real, and moving, and said something about human nature, that, for me, this script worked better than most.

Trimmer was played by Michael Gwynn, and a beautifully sad and moving performance it was. The child's father, Norton, played with angry conviction by Glyn Houston, had suffered a terrible and unexplicable loss which he could only come to terms with if there was someone to blame.

I have chosen this script because the regular artists were all involved in a way which arose naturally out of their respective jobs in life. Although, to be honest, the apparently fascinating forensic aspect—on the face of it the raison d'etre of *The Expert*—is dealt with briefly, and almost in passing. But Trimmer and Mr and Mrs Norton became real people whose lives were deeply affected in various ways by the tragedy. Finally, I think it was done with economy—another aim of mine.

Series: JASON KING
Episode: AN AUTHOR IN SEARCH OF TWO
CHARACTERS
by
Dennis Spooner
Produced by Scoton Ltd, for ITC at
EMI/MGM Elstree Studios, Boreham Wood.

The series *Jason King* was devised by its producer, Monty Berman, and Dennis Spooner. It is about a rich, famous, and flamboyant, author. The title role was created and portrayed by Peter Wyngarde. The character originally appeared in a previous TV/film series, *Department S*, as one of a team of investigators. That series was also devised and produced by Monty Berman and Dennis Spooner.

In this episode Jason King is hired for an enormous fee that only he could command to re-write a film script. Income tax being what it is, and Jason King being what he is, he does a deal with the film company to be paid in cash. It is his intention to smuggle the money out of the country and to lay it to rest in his deposit box in Switzerland. However, a group at the film studios learn of the deal and decide to relieve King of his fortune. The opening sequence which follows has Reynolds, one of the villains, having second thoughts, and intending to warn King of the plot against him. Ackroyd and Tredgett are equally intent on forestalling Reynolds. The eccentric disguise of their costume is subsequently explained by their connection with the wardrobe department of the film studio.

1.   TEASER.

FADE IN:

1.   *EXT. LONDON. NIGHT. STOCK (0.10)*   1.

IT IS BETWEEN TWO, AND THREE O CLOCK, IN THE MORN-
ING. WE ESTABLISH DESERTED STREETS, AND SEE A LINE OF
STREET LIGHTS ALONG THE EMBANKMENT. WE CAPTURE
THE MOOD OF THE CITY ASLEEP.

CUT TO:

2.   *EXT. LONDON HOTEL. NIGHT. LOCATION. (0.10)*   2.

WE ESTABLISH THE ENTRANCE OF A LONDON HOTEL. (THE
FLOODLIGHTS ARE ON, ILLUMINATING THE FACADE OF
THE BUILDING). A COMMISSIONAIRE STANDS ON DUTY.
HE STIFLES A YAWN.

CLOSE ON A BRASS PLAQUE

IT STATES: 'ROYALTY HOTEL'. HOLD, THEN:

CUT TO:

3.   *INT. KING'S HOTEL ROOM. NIGHT. STUDIO. (0.20)*   3.

JASON KING SITS AT HIS DESK, IN THE LIVING ROOM OF HIS
HOTEL SUITE. HE IS BURNING THE MIDNIGHT OIL, POUND-
ING THE TYPEWRITER. HE HOLDS A CIGARETTE BETWEEN
HIS LIPS, AND SCREWS UP HIS EYES AGAINST THE SMOKE.

AS WE JOIN KING HE FINISHES THE SEQUENCE HE IS WRIT-
ING. HE TAKES HIS CIGARETTE FROM HIS LIPS, AND PUTS
IT OUT IN THE ASH TRAY.

KING STUDIES THE TYPEWRITER, AND THE PAGE IN THE
ROLLER. HE TWISTS THE HANDLE, AS HE READS THE PAGE
TO HIMSELF. HE DOES NOT READ ALOUD, BUT HIS FACE
REGISTERS SEVERAL VARYING, EXAGGERATED, EMOTIONS,
AS HE GIVES HIS LINES MEANING. HE SEEMS SATISFIED.

KING REACHES FOR A BOTTLE OF CHAMPAGNE, IN AN ICE
BUCKET. IT IS PLACED STRATEGICALLY NEAR HIS DESK.
HE 'POURS' OVER HIS EMPTY GLASS, BUT THE BOTTLE IS
DEAD. HE PLACES IT, NECK DOWN, IN THE ICE BUCKET.

KING TAKES THE PAGE FROM HIS TYPEWRITER, AND SLIPS
IT INTO A FILE THEN HE STRETCHES, AND FLEXES HIS BACK.
HE REGISTERS THAT THE ROOM IS HOT, AND HE LOOKS AT
HIS WRIST WATCH.

4. *EXT. LONDON HOTEL. NIGHT. LOCATION. (0.10)*   4.

WE PICK UP A MAN, REYNOLDS, AS HE APPROACHES THE HOTEL ENTRANCE. HE SEEMS NERVOUS, AND TENSE. HE GLANCES AROUND, AND MOVES TO ENTER THE HOTEL. THE COMMISSIONAIRE FORESTALLS HIM. THE TWO MEN HAVE WORDS, OUT OF EARSHOT.

ANOTHER ANGLE

WE SEE A CAR PULL INTO THE SERVICE ROAD OF THE HOTEL. AS IT STOPS, WE:

CUT TO:

5. *INT. ACKROYD'S CAR. NIGHT. STUDIO. (0.05)*   5.

TWO MEN ARE IN THE FRONT SEATS OF THE CAR. ACKROYD AND TREDGETT. ACKROYD IS AT THE WHEEL. AS HE STOPS THE CAR, AND PULLS ON THE HANDBRAKE, BOTH MEN LOOK TO:

CUT TO:

6. *EXT. LONDON HOTEL. NIGHT. LOCATION. (0.05)*   6.

ACKROYD AND TREDGETT'S P.O.V.

THROUGH THE WINDSCREEN. WE SEE REYNOLDS TALKING TO THE COMMISSIONAIRE. AFTER A SECOND OR SO, REYNOLDS GOES INTO THE HOTEL.

CUT TO:

7. *INT. ACKROYD'S CAR. NIGHT. STUDIO. (0.05)*   7.

RESUME ACKROYD AND TREDGETT.

THEY EXCHANGE FROWNING, CONCERNED, GLANCES. NOW:

CUT TO:

8. *INT. KING'S HOTEL ROOM. NIGHT. STUDIO. (0.10)*   8.

KING HAS SLIPPED ON A COAT, AND IS ABOUT TO LEAVE HIS ROOM. TIRED, BUT NOT READY TO SLEEP, HIS WORK STILL ON HIS MIND, HE HAS DECIDED TO TAKE A WALK.

KING GLANCES AROUND TO MAKE SURE HE HAS FOR-GOTTEN NOTHING. HE PICKS UP HIS CIGARETTES, AND LIGHTER, AND HIS ROOM KEY, AND THEN LEAVES THE ROOM. AS HE DOES SO, WE:

CUT TO:

KING COMES OUT OF HIS ROOM, AND CLOSES THE DOOR. HE POCKETS HIS KEY, AND MOVES ALONG TO THE ELEVATOR.

ANOTHER ANGLE

KING REACHES THE ELEVATOR, AND PRESSES THE CALL BUTTON. HE WAITS. AFTER A COUPLE OF BEATS HE GLANCES UP AT THE LIGHT INDICATOR, AND SEES THAT IT IS STILL REGISTERING 'GROUND'.

KING PRESSES THE BUTTON AGAIN. WHEN THE LIGHT STILL DOES NOT CHANGE, HE MOVES IN THE DIRECTION OF THE STAIRS. HIS ROOM IS ON THE FIRST FLOOR.

WE ALLOW KING OUT OF SIGHT, AND THEN ANGLE BACK TO THE LIGHT INDICATOR. WE SEE IT CHANGE FROM THE 'GROUND' FLOOR TO THE 'FIRST'. THE DOORS SLIDE OPEN. REYNOLDS COMES OUT OF THE ELEVATOR. HE LOOKS AROUND TO GET HIS BEARINGS, AND THEN MOVES TOWARDS KING'S ROOM.

CUT TO:

10. INT. ACKROYD'S CAR. NIGHT. STUDIO. (*0.05*)   *10.*

ACKROYD, AND TREDGETT, SIT IN THE CAR. THEY LOOK COMPLETELY LOST AS TO WHAT ACTION TO TAKE. THEN, SUDDENLY, TREDGETT CATCHES SIGHT OF SOMETHING THROUGH THE WINDSCREEN. HE DIRECTS ACKROYD'S ATTENTION TO:

CUT TO:

11. EXT. LONDON HOTEL. NIGHT. LOCATION. (*0.05*)   *11.*

ACKROYD'S AND TREDGETT'S P.O.V.

THROUGH THE WINDSCREEN. KING HAS LEFT THE HOTEL. HE IS EXCHANGING A FEW WORDS WITH THE COMMISSIONAIRE.

CUT TO:

12. INT. ACKROYD'S CAR. NIGHT. STUDIO. (*0.05*)   *12.*

RESUME ACKROYD AND TREDGETT..

THEY EXCHANGE A LOOK THAT SUGGESTS THAT ALL IS NOT YET LOST.

CUT TO:

13. INT. HOTEL CORRIDOR. NIGHT. STUDIO. (0.10)   13.

REYNOLDS IS RAPPING AT KING'S DOOR, OBVIOUSLY NOT FOR THE FIRST TIME. HE WAITS, LISTENS AT THE DOOR, AND THEN, DECIDING THAT KING MUST BE ASLEEP, HE TAKES A PLASTIC CARD, OR AN IMPLEMENT, FROM HIS PERSON, AND UNLOCKS THE DOOR.

CUT TO:

14. INT. KING'S HOTEL ROOM. NIGHT. STUDIO. (0.20)   14.

REYNOLDS MOVES INTO KING'S ROOM, AND CLOSES THE DOOR BEHIND HIM. HE LOOKS AROUND THE ROOM.

ANOTHER ANGLE

REYNOLDS MOVES ACROSS THE LIVING ROOM, PART OF THE SUITE, AND OPENS A DOOR THAT LEADS INTO THE BEDROOM.

ON REYNOLDS

AS HE LOOKS INTO THE (UNSEEN) BEDROOM, AND NOTES THAT KING IS NOT THERE. HE CLOSES THE DOOR, AND TURNS AWAY.

ANOTHER ANGLE.

REYNOLDS CROSSES TO THE DESK, LOOKING FOR A CLUE AS TO WHERE KING HAS GONE. AT THE DESK, WHICH IS BY THE WINDOW, HE HEARS THE MURMUR OF VOICES BELOW. REYNOLDS TURNS TO THE WINDOW. WE ARE ON HIM AS HE LOOKS OUT.

CUT TO:

15. EXT. LONDON HOTEL. NIGHT. LOCATION. (0.05)   15.

REYNOLD'S P.O.V.

WE SEE KING BELOW, MOVING AWAY, AND GIVING A SALUTORY WAVE TO THE COMMISSIONAIRE, WE HEAR, IN MUFFLED TONES:

> KING:
>
> . . . A walk round the Park might help me sleep . . .

AND KING TURNS, AND MOVES AWAY.

CUT TO:

16. *INT. KING'S HOTEL ROOM. NIGHT. STUDIO. (0.05)*   **16.**

RESUME REYNOLDS.

IT LOOKS FOR A MOMENT AS THOUGH HE IS GOING TO CALL OUT, BUT, REALISING KING WILL NOT HEAR HIM, AND THAT KING IS ALREADY MOVING AWAY, HE TURNS.

ANOTHER ANGLE.

REYNOLDS CROSSES THE ROOM, AND EXITS. AS THE DOOR CLOSES:

CUT TO:

17. *INT. ACKROYD'S CAR. NIGHT. STUDIO. (0.05)*   **17.**

ACKROYD, AND TREDGETT, IN THE CAR, STARE THROUGH THE WINDSCREEN AND WAIT. AFTER A COUPLE OF BEATS, WE SEE A REACTION ON THEIR FACES.

CUT TO:

18. *EXT. LONDON HOTEL. NIGHT. LOCATION. (0.05)*   **18.**

ACKROYD AND TREDGETT'S P.O.V.

THROUGH THE WINDSCREEN. WE SEE REYNOLDS LEAVE THE HOTEL. HE HAS A FEW WORDS WITH THE COMMISSION-AIRE, WHO POINTS OFF, IN THE DIRECTION TAKEN BY KING. REYNOLDS MOVES OFF, TAKING THE SAME ROUTE.

CUT TO:

19. *INT. ACKROYD'S CAR. NIGHT. STUDIO. (0.10)*   **19.**

RESUME ACKROYD AND TREDGETT.

THEY EXCHANGE A GLANCE. ACKROYD GESTURES, WITH HIS HEAD, TO A HOLD-ALL IN THE BACK SEAT OF THE CAR. TREDGETT NODS, AND REACHES FOR IT, AS ACKROYD STARTS THE CAR, AND RELEASES THE HANDBRAKE.

TREDGETT PULLS THE HOLD-ALL ONTO HIS LAP, AND OPENS IT.

ON THE HOLD-ALL.

TREDGETT'S HAND PULLS OUT ITEMS FROM THE HOLD-ALL. AT FIRST IT APPEARS TO BE CLOTHING, THEN WE SEE, AND HOLD, A FRANKENSTEIN'S MONSTER MASK. NOW:

CUT TO:

ESTABLISHING SHOTS OF A PARK, AT NIGHT. POSSIBLY HYDE PARK, SHOWING A BANDSTAND, AND A BRIDGE OVER THE SERPENTINE. AFTER A COUPLE OF BEATS:

CUT TO:

21. *EXT. STRETCH OF WATER. NIGHT. STUDIO LOT.* (*1.00*)   21.

WE ALLOW KING TO MOVE INTO FRAME. HE STANDS, PERHAPS BY A LIGHTED STREET LAMP, AND LOOKS OUT ACROSS THE STRETCH OF WATER.

KING TAKES OUT A CIGARETTE, AND LIGHTS IT, BREATHING OUT THE SMOKE. HE TAKES IN THE AIR, AND THE NIGHT SKY.

AFTER A WHILE, WE HEAR:

> *REYNOLD'S VOICE:*
> (CALLING)   King . . . *King* . . . !

KING REGISTERS THE CALL, AND TURNS.

ANOTHER ANGLE.

REYNOLDS IS SOME DISTANCE AWAY FROM US. A STRETCH OF GRASS BETWEEN HIM AND THE CAMERA.

ON KING.

FROWNING. PUZZLED.

ANOTHER ANGLE.

REYNOLDS, HAVING SEEN KING, IS MOVING TOWARDS HIM. HE GETS REASONABLY NEAR, THEN STOPS, AND REACTS, SCARED.

ON KING.

EVEN MORE PUZZLED AS IT LOOKS AS THOUGH REYNOLDS, WHO IS OBVIOUSLY FRIGHTENED, HAS REACTED TO HIM. KING GOES TO CALL OUT TO REYNOLDS, AS WE TAKE:

ANOTHER ANGLE.

TO SHOW REYNOLDS TURNING, AND RUNNING AWAY.

RESUME KING.

CONVINCED THAT REYNOLDS IS NOT SCARED OF HIM, HE TURNS, AND HIS EYES WIDEN.

KING'S P.O.V.

ACKROYD, UNRECOGNISABLE, WEARS FULL COWBOY GEAR. A SCARF MASK IS PULLED UP OVER HIS FACE. HE PULLS A GUN FROM HIS HOLSTER, IN TRUE WESTERN FASHION, AND FIRES.

RESUME KING.

FROM THE DIRECTION THE GUN IS AIMED, AND KING'S REACTION, WE COULD THINK FOR A SPLIT SECOND THAT KING HAS BEEN SHOT. THEN HE TURNS, AND SEES:

KING'S P.O.V.

REYNOLDS, RUNNING, HAS BEEN HIT IN THE BACK. HE FALLS TO THE GROUND. WE REALISE THAT REYNOLDS WAS THE INTENDED VICTIM.

RESUME KING.

NOW OPEN MOUTHED, AS WELL AS WIDE EYED, HE REGISTERS THE SHOOTING. HE IS ABOUT TO TURN BACK TO THE GUNMAN WHEN HE IS AWARE OF SOMETHING ON HIS OTHER SIDE. HE TURNS SHARPLY.

CLOSE ON THE FRANKENSTEIN MONSTER.

LOOMING OVER KING. HIS FIST SMASHES DOWN ONTO CAMERA. THE MONSTER IS, IN FACT, TREDGETT.

ANOTHER ANGLE.

KING FALLS TO THE GROUND, UNCONSCIOUS.

ON THE FRANKENSTEIN MONSTER.

HE LUMBERS FORWARD, AND PEERS DOWN AT US, THE CAMERA. HE IS, SUPPOSEDLY, STARING DOWN AT KING. HOLD.

END OF TEASER.

CUT TO:

THE OPENING TITLE SEQUENCE: 'JASON KING'

Technical comment

In item 40 on page 82 the example script is criticised for telling us in stage directions what Captain Madison is thinking about; here, in Scene 8, we see 'TIRED, BUT NOT READY TO SLEEP, HIS WORK STILL ON HIS MIND, HE DECIDES TO TAKE A WALK'. The difference is that the actor playing Captain Madison could not possibly *act out* his thoughts. How can you look into a camera and convey that you are 'WONDERING HOW TO MAKE ENDS MEET IN THE FACE OF AN EVER INCREASING COST OF LIVING'?! But Dennis Spooner's direction asks for a very simple thought process to be conveyed, something familiar to us all, something that any competent actor could do. A yawn, a stretch, a glance at the topcoat hung by the door; then standing up, clearly fully awake.

Note that for this show the writer is required to give the time length of each scene in minutes and seconds, e.g. (0.10).

In some scenes we see the use of a night location, outside the London hotel, with the star on location. As you already know, this can be very expensive. No doubt there was good justification for it. Elsewhere the writer suggests the use of stock film. A lot of use can be made of stock, and with the matching of stock to studio takes.

Comment by the writer, Dennis Spooner.

Jason King grew up from one of those meaningless specks of information one acquires. Apparently—and I do not even know for certain if it is true—the Cabinet, during World War Two, put together a lot of adventure, and thriller writers, and said, more or less, "All right, you're supposed to be geniuses, how do we win the war?" Outlandish suggestions from this group were mixed with several ideas that proved practical.

Jason King, in the *Department S* series, filled this role. The team were supposed to solve an insoluble mystery each week, and, from his fertile, author's mind, sprang many improbable explanations for the inexplicable. The actor, Peter Wyngarde, supplied and worked on many facets of the character, who (in my opinion) he brilliantly portrayed. Eventually, due to the popularity, a 'spin off' occurred and *Jason King* became a series in its own right.

I think the script I have chosen is typical of the series. It is somewhat outrageous, with a story unfolding as a sequence of events, rather than a detailed, twisting plot. This approach allowed time to develop Jason King and his attitudes. The character was not devised to be a question and answer detective subservient to his surroundings.

As to the story, the expense of this method of production means that the UK cannot, in any way, be self-supporting. Therefore the economic necessity for international appeal results in the writer having to devise his story in a much more pictorial form. Sub-titles, or dubbing into a foreign language, is only satisfactory when it can be kept to a minimum. So story content tends to rest on broader issues. A parochial subject, relying on, say, knowledge of the society, and culture, of the North of England is very hard to get across in the Far East. Whereas a robbery, with a group of peoply trying to steal a million pounds, is all things to all men. Write about the robbery.

I enjoyed making the series. Perhaps Jason King, with his silk dressing gown, champagne, and be-ringed fingers flicking idly over a silent electric typewriter is what I think writing should be about.

The restrictions and rules of film television suit me as a writer. Give me a £5,000,000 budget and say write what you like, and I stare at a piece of blank paper for a long time. If someone wants a script tomorrow that can be filmed in forty minutes with two actors and three sets that have already been built, and, somehow, the juices start to flow.

Most writers say it is perspiration, not inspiration. Me? I like desperation.

Series: GESTERN GELESEN . . .
(Read Yesterday . . .)
Episode: EINE RECHNUNG ZUWIEL
(One Bill Too Many)
by
Malcolm Hulke
Produced by Profil-Film in
Cologne for transmission by
Westdeutsches Werbefernsehen GmbH
Producer: Frank Tietz
Editor: Lisa Scheu

Synopsis

Gestern Gelesen is a weekly half hour series featuring an attorney, Dr Fuhrmann, and his assistant, Dr Ursula Balke. Most episodes are strong drama. This was comedy.

Franz Schläger and Joseph Lemmer are jointly accused of a confidence trick. Their 'business' has been to check the obituary columns daily, then send to the recently dead invoices for the repair of non-existent umbrellas. They never charged more than a few Marks. The bereaved executors usually paid up without question. The story opens with Schläger being talked into joining the racket by Lemmer. Then we realise this is only Schläger's story, because now we see how Schläger talked Lemmer into becoming a criminal. Dr Fuhrmann, who defends Schläger, must prove that of the two villains his client is the least guilty. He does so finally by proving that Lemmer was busily sending out phoney umbrella repair invoices years ago when his client, Schläger, was safely behind bars in a Bolivian jail for a different confidence trick.

12. SCENE
LEMMER'S OFFICE
INT. DAY.

Lemmer stops typing. Quickly he puts away the typed invoices and covers the "Deaths" newspaper with another newspaper. He goes to the door, opens it. Schläger is there.

Schläger: (diffident)   Good morning.

Lemmer: (not inviting Schläger in)   Good morning.

Schläger: I have a small account that I want to pay. May I come in?

Lemmer: Yes, of course.

Lemmer steps aside to allow Schläger to enter. Schläger looks around as he talks. He produces an invoice.

Schläger: You repaired an umbrella for my sister—

Schläger looks at the invoice, gets out his wallet, produces money.   —twelve Marks.

Lemmer: That's very kind of you. I'll get you a receipt.

Lemmer gets a receipt book from a desk drawer, prepares the receipt.

Schläger: Yes, I suppose I'll need that. I have to settle all her affairs.

Lemmer, looking up: Settle her affairs?

Schläger, with a sigh: She died last week.

Lemmer, flourishing invoice: I'm terribly sorry to hear that. Really, you needn't have bothered about this. Such a small amount.

Schläger: I was passing. In any case, "the smaller the debt, the greater the honour."

Lemmer looks quizzically at Schläger because he's never heard that quotation before (true: Schläger just made it up):   Yes, yes, I suppose you're right.

Lemmer busies himself completing the receipt.

Schläger:

As a matter of fact, it's rather a coincidence. When my brother died two years ago, he also had just had an umbrella repaired by you.

Lemmer reacts. He is worried. But he turns to Schläger with a smile, offering the receipt:

Really? What a strange coincidence.

Schläger, continuing:

But the coincidence isn't that you sent them both invoices *after* they were dead. The coincidence was that neither of them ever had an umbrella!

Lemmer:

I don't think I quite understand—

Schläger:

You understand perfectly. And the police are going to understand, too! I've found out your little trick! Every day you send invoices for umbrella repairs to everyone who has just died. And honest people like me, settling the affairs of their loved ones, are fools enough to pay you!

Lemmer:

You've no proof of this!

Schläger whips away the newspaper covering the newspaper with the ticked 'Deaths' announcements:

What's this, then?

Lemmer:

Mr . . . (He looks at the invoice) Mr Schläger, could you find it in your heart *not* to tell the police?

Schläger:

Let a scroundrel like you go free? A vulture, living off the dead!

Lemmer:

Mr Schläger, I implore you, don't send me to prison. For years I was an honest man—I worked in a factory. But what chance has an honest man of ever enjoying the good things of life? Every year my boss went on holiday to Bermuda for a month, while I went to the Black Forest for a week.

213

Schläger:	What's wrong with the Black Forest?
Lemmer, continuing:	He rode in a motor-car. I could not even afford a bicycle.
Schläger:	Walking's more healthy than riding.
Lemmer, continuing:	He enjoyed high-living, the company of beautiful women!
Schläger:	None of this gives you an excuse for being a criminal!
Lemmer:	Mr Schläger, a criminal steals people's life savings. At least I wait until they're gone. I take a few Marks here, a few Marks there. Why, I don't take as much as the taxes.
Schläger:	It's still robbery!
Lemmer:	Mr Schläger, how much do you earn where you work?
Schläger:	That has nothing to do with it.
Lemmer:	Are you one of the exploiters, or are you an ordinary worker as I was?
Schläger pauses before answering:	As a matter of fact, I haven't worked for anyone for two years. I've been looking after my sister. She was ill. No-one else in the family would help her.
Lemmer:	That was truly noble of you. I hope that you have been justly rewarded now that she has gone.
Schläger:	Only by her love and respect. She had no money; and the house she's left to our sister in America.
Lemmer:	After all you've done?
Schläger:	Yes, it came as a surprise to me. I phoned my sister last night—the one in America. She said to sell the house and send her all the money.
Lemmer, very sympathetic:	So after all you've done, you've got no job, no money and no home?
Schläger:	That's none of your business.

Lemmer:	Then let me make it my business! Mr Schläger, I'm going to put a proposition to you. I need a man like you to become my partner. I want to expand my business, and with you I could do it.
Schläger:	You know nothing of my qualifications.
Lemmer:	But I do, Mr Schläger. I do. Look at the way you paid your brother's bill for umbrella repairs, and the way you've come in here today to pay this (flourishing receipted invoice). You have the most valuable asset that any man could have for a business partnership. Honesty.
Schläger:	What would I have to do?
Lemmer:	Can you use a typewriter?
Schläger:	Not very well.
Lemmer:	I shall teach you. (Indicating newspapers) Do you realise how many people die every day?
Schläger:	No . . .
Lemmer:	I can't cope with the number, even working here till ten o'clock at night. Why, if there was an influenza epidemic I'd be losing business because I couldn't keep up with it.
Schläger:	That would be terrible.
Lemmer, indicating newspapers again:	These relate to only one corner of Germany. There's Hamburg, Frankfürt, Berlin—
Schläger:	No-one's going to believe their loved one came all the way from Berlin to have an umbrella repaired!
Lemmer:	We can have different invoices printed—Lemmer and Schläger, book publishers! We can say we have just supplied the deceased with a valuable book, by post.

Schläger:	I suppose people would fall for that . . .
Lemmer opens his safe and brings out whisky and two glasses:	Mr Schläger, I am going to propose a toast. From now on, 'Hans Schmidt, Umbrella Repairs' will be run by
Lemmer fills glasses, hands one to Schläger.	Lemmer and Schläger. Whatever we do, and wherever life takes us, from now on we shall be together!
They raises their glasses.	
	CRASH CUT

13. SCENE
COURTROOM
INT. DAY

Schläger and Lemmer are standing together in the 'dock'. They are not looking at each other. Schläger has just finished telling his version to the Court. The Judge looks up.

Judge:	Have you anything else to say in mitigation?
Schläger:	No, sir.
Judge:	Anything you wish to raise, Dr Fuhrmann?
Fuhrmann:	Only to put a question to my client. (To Schläger): When you entered Lemmer's office on that day, what was in your mind?
Schläger:	To catch this scoundrel, and report him to the police!
Fuhrmann:	Thank you.
Judge:	Dr Lücke?
Lücke:	No questions at this stage, sir.
Judge:	Then I shall hear from the accused Joseph Lemmer.

They all look at Lemmer. He gives Schläger a 'look', then starts.

Lemmer:	What you have heard, sir, is a total distortion of the truth. It is true, I regret, that I am guilty of fraud. But it was this man standing beside me who induced me into the racket! (Pause for his melodramatic effect) For many years I worked as assistant to a financier in this city. His name will mean nothing to you, because all his dealings were through his many representatives. You see what a position I am in, unable to prove anything of my previous character!
Judge, with edge:	A very sad situation. (Checking his watch) Would you continue, please?
Lemmer:	One day I went to my usual place of work—my employer's penthouse. He had gone—vanished—disappeared —flown—as though he had never been there. No forwarding address, not a stick of furniture, nothing ...

Lemmer pauses again for effect, and looks around the Court. We pan with his P.O.V.—rows of faces quite uninterested in his theatrical performance. He decides he'd better get on with his story more quickly.

Lemmer:	My job was over, finished. I daren't go home to tell my loving wife. I needed time to think what to do next. There was a bar in a street nearby; a place I had never been to, of course— not very respectable, but I was depressed and at my wits end. I went along there, to think things over ...

217

14. SCENE
AMERICAN BAR
INT. DAY

Soft lights, a piano tinkling. Lemmer
at the bar, looking very worried. He
is very soberly dressed. One small
drink in front of him, untouched. A
hostess comes up to him. The V of her
dress is cut down to her waist.

Hostess:

Hello. Lonely?

Lemmer, in one breath:

I'm-a-happily-married-man-with
two-children-and-I'm-not-lonely-
thank-you.

Hostess, amused:

Sorry I spoke.

She goes away. Camera follows her,
and so comes to the street doorway
where steps lead up. Schläger, just
arrived, stands there. He is in a sharp
Italian suit, black shirt, white tie, like
a 'Rififi' gangster. He is lighting a fat
cigar. He flicks the match away,
strides to the bar.

Barman, big smile:

'Morning, Mr Schläger. The usual?

Schläger nods. He looks at Lemmer
and the untouched drink.

Schläger:

What is it? Money or women?

Lemmer:

I've lost my job.

Schläger:

That's tough.

The Barman, who had started pouring
Schläger's usual on sight, now serves
it. Schläger produces an enormous
bundle of 100 DM notes, throws one
to the Barman.

Schläger:

Keep the change.

Barman:

Thank you, Mr Schläger.

Schläger:

Lost your job, eh? What type of
work were you doing?

218

15. SCENE
EXPENSIVE RESTAURANT
INT. DAY

Lemmer and Schläger, dressed as in
Sc. 14, at a corner table. Waiters are
taking away their hors d'oeuvres
plates.

Lemmer: I was working for a financier.

The waiter offers Schläger the menu,
but Schläger ignores it.

Schläger: Venison?

Lemmer: Surely it's out of season.

Schläger: Only for some. (To the waiter)
Venison.

Technical comment

The scene continues with Schläger inducing Lemmer into crime. Or, more accurately, the conversation continues uninterrupted over a number of scenes, which is a stylised but acceptable technique; Scene 16 is in a strip club, with them still talking, and in Scene 17 Schläger pauses for a second to pay cash for a vastly expensive American car because he can't find a taxi to take them both back to his office. The important thing to notice in this example is that with the brief exception of the Courtroom, everything else is subjective. Fantasy rarely works well on television, but it can sometimes work if it is a subjective memory by one of the characters. The show was shot on film, not tape. Note the entirely different style of script layout used in West Germany.

Writer's comment

They wanted to try having occasional comedy episodes in the *Gestern Gelesen* series, but apparently there aren't many comedy writers in Germany. So I was invited—not because I'm known as a comedy writer, but because they think all Englishmen are born wits. It meant finding a German lawyer in London to explain to me West German courtroom procedure. Ours is accusatorial, theirs is in-quisitorial. This means the Judges do most of the talking, great importance is attached to the Accused's character, and the Accused can take all the time in the world to make his "excuses". As to the story, I'd read of this umbrella con trick actually being done. The man was never caught; the nature of his business only became known when he died and his wife, who thought her husband was a small-time insurance agent, found he had left her a fortune. A peculiarity of the Continental inquisitorial legal system is the establishment of the *degree* of guilt. This suggested that two villains should be jointly accused, one defended by the series star, Dr Furhmann, the other by another attorney. This would provide not only pre-arrest mileage, but also good Courtroom conflict. I wrote in English, and they translated. However, the awareness that it was all to be translated into another language had a peculiarly stultifying effect on the flow of my English dialogue, from which I couldn't break myself during the writing. The general comic-dramatic style I adopted, and which they liked very much, wasn't difficult. I had worked with and for Germans before, and have close friends there, so I had some idea what makes them laugh. German life is so hidebound with logic and respect for authority that in humour they like the reverse. After the transmission, two German viewers called Hulke, a name I'd always regarded as positively English, wrote and asked which part of their family I belonged to, and where on earth did I acquire a *dummkopf* first-name like Malcolm.

Series: NEAREST AND DEAREST
Episode: GETTING TO KNOW YOU
by
John Stevenson
Produced by Granada Television
Limited in Manchester.
Producer: Peter Eckersley

Synopsis

The comedy series *Nearest and Dearest* is about a grown up brother
and sister, Eli and Nellie Pledge, who still live together under the
same roof. In this episode, Eli announces his intention to go away for
what he hopes will be a dirty weekend. Nellie, however, wants him
to stay and redecorate their house. He is insistent to go away, but she
persuades him at least to go with her down into the cellar to fix some
fuses. Once they are in the cellar, they become accidentally locked in.
There is no means of escape, and no-one knows they are there. The
scene which follows came after the commercial break, when they
wake up after an uncomfortable night.

5 *INT.   THE CELLAR*

*ELI AND NELLIE ASLEEP, ON A TABLE.
THEY ARE SLEEPING BACK TO BACK
COVERED IN NEWSPAPERS.*

*NELLIE TURNS TO FACE ELI. ELI TURNS
TO FACE HER. THEY ARE NOSE TO NOSE.
VERY SLOWLY ELI WAKES UP AND LOOKS
AT HER. SHE WAKES UP AND LOOKS AT
HIM. PAUSE.*

> *ELI:*

Bloody hell. It's the bride of Frankenstein.

> *NELLIE:*

Look who's talking. I've seen better-looking objects
on top of bonfires.

*THEY LIE THERE, DOG-TIRED AND LOOK
AT EACH OTHER, LACKLUSTRE.*

> *ELI:*

That's the worst night's sleep I've had since V-J
night. I took this A.T.S. girl home and got me
head stuck under the wardrobe.

> *NELLIE:*

I've never heard snoring like that in my life.

> *ELI:*

I should hope you haven't.

> *NELLIE:*

It sounded as though you'd got two hundred-
weight of coke up your nose.

> *ELI:*

Caw. I was freezing. You kept pulling all the
newspapers off me. (*HOLDS UP SCRAP OF
PAPER*) All I had on top of me was bloody
Marjorie Proops.

> *NELLIE:*

What about you? You kept snatching at my late-
night final. Look at the state of you. I always said
you'd end up in the News of the World.

223

ELI:

What was all that you were mumbling in your sleep?

NELLIE:

I don't talk in my sleep.

ELI:

You what? I'm lying here . . . St Saviour's church clock strikes three and you suddenly shout "Mind you don't ladder me stockings . . . they're clean on".

NELLIE:

(*LYING WITH DIGNITY*) I dreamt I were wrestling with Jackie Pallo.

ELI:

Did he get a submission?

NELLIE:

(*WITH DIGNITY*) I was wrestling for charity.

ELI:

So that's why you kept saying "I'm anybody's for five bob".

NELLIE:

What about you? You kept getting hold of me in your sleep and saying: "What are you worried about? He's on the night shift isn't he?"

ELI:

Yes. I dreamt me dad was trapped in a coal mine disaster. (*A BEAT*) By the hell Nellie, this table's hard. I thought I'd never drop off.

NELLIE:

Yes, and when you did I thought you'd never get back on.

ELI:

Chee, you know, Nellie, I'd sell me left clinker for a nice hot cup of tea.

NELLIE:

It's all very well to talk on a Sunday, when all the shops are shut.

ELI OFF THE TABLE.

ELI:

I've got to have a fag.

FAG IN MOUTH HE PUTS THE END TO A NAKED LIGHT BULB, AND SUCKS HARD.

NELLIE:

Look at you. Standing there like a drug-addict.

ELI:

Is it glowing? Is it glowing? I'm sure it's getting warm.

NELLIE GETS OFF THE TABLE. BEGINS TO GROPE ABOUT IN THE CELLAR JUNK.

NELLIE:

There must be something to eat down here.

ELI:

There's nothing in this cellar. Even the mice have emigrated. I saw a spider in the night and that was nothing but skin and bone.

NELLIE:

Hey, Eli, look there's a pair of me Dad's old false teeth here.

ELI:

Oh yes, they'll be lovely with a portion of chips and a few french beans.

NELLIE:

I wasn't talking about cooking them. I was just commenting.

ELI:

If we want any commenting doing, we'll get Kenneth Wolstenholme to join us down here. And God knows I could do with a match of the day.

(HE HOLDS UP CIGARETTE)

NELLIE:

Eli—look what I've found.

ELI:

Don't tell me—it's a fossilised black pudding.

225

NELLIE:

No, Eli, look. It's the bottle of pickles that won me Dad first prize at Cleethorpes in the National Pickling Competition.

ELI:

When was that?

NELLIE:

(*CONSULTING THE LABEL*) 1922.

ELI:

Well they should be about ready now.

NELLIE:

(*OPENING THE BOTTLE*) Oh, Eli. There's only one left. We'll just have to share it. Half for you and half for me.

ELI:

Have you ever tried splitting a pickled onion in half with your bare hands? Especially one that's been standing in malt vinegar for 47 years. I'd better have it. After all, if I flake out from hunger where will you be?

NELLIE:

Going through your pockets. . . . I know what we'll do. We'll dip for it.

ELI:

All right. Dip . . . ickle ockle chocolate bockle, ickle ockle out. You're out. I win.

HE PREPARES TO EAT THE PICKLE.

NELLIE:

Just a minute Clement Freud. You ickled twice when you should have ockled.

ELI:

I never. Two ickles, two ockles, and a chocolate bockle.

NELLIE:

I'll dip. Dip . . . ip dip dash, my blue sash, sailing on water, like a cup and saucer, ip dip dash. Thank you very much.

SHE TAKES THE PICKLE OFF HIM.

ELI:

Aw hey, fair dos. I'm starving too you know. What about me?

NELLIE:

You'll be all right. I'll breathe on you. (*SHE EATS THE PICKLE WITH ELI FOLLOWING EVERY CHEW*) Hm, not bad. You can say what you like about me Dad, but that man could certainly pickle. What an artist. He could take a little runt of a gherkin that nobody else would look at, and when he'd finished with it that gherkin could almost talk. (*A BURP*)

ELI:

Charming. Bloody charming. That's typical of you. If there was ever anything going, you got it. You were rotten to me when I were a little lad, and you're still rotten.

NELLIE:

Don't come it. When you were a little lad I used to get lumbered with you. Me mam made me look after you. Many's the time I've taken you out in your little pushchair and pushed you all the way up that big hill behind the clough.

ELI:

Yes. And then you used to let me roll all the way down to the bottom.

NELLIE:

It were only a bit of fun.

ELI:

Fun? How would you like to be strapped in a pram rolling down a big hill into the park lake? It can warp a child's mind can that sort of thing. What I am today is your fault.

NELLIE:

You were always a little mardy-pants. You were always skriking.

ELI:

That was because I had a lot to skrike about. What about bonfire night that time? You know what I'm talking about. You lit a banger and then you shoved it down my welly. . . .

And so the scene, a very long one, continues with its swapping of insults, long cherished indignation about past misdeeds, and some cruel observations about the other's defects. It ends, or seems about to end, on a note of brotherly/sisterly love with intimate confessions from both. Nellie reveals that she has a tatoo mark which no-one has ever seen, and Eli confides that he has taken to wearing a man's corset. Then, true to good comedy, this harmonious mood is smashed by a final insult from Nellie.

Note the importance of the nostalgia binding factor between Eli and Nellie (see page 64 on binding factors). Note also the emphasis on reminiscence and character observations in comedy writing, compared with the amount of visual action.

Comedy plotting has been summed up by Barry Took as ". . . Just the same as drama plotting, except that nobody gets killed."

Comment from the writer, John Stevenson

Towards the end of the third series of *Nearest and Dearest* the producer asked me to write a show that would cost less to make than usual. We had done a run of scripts that called for expensive sets and rather large casts, he had exceeded his budget for the series, and he wanted a show that would bring the average cost down.

Writers hate being admonished to cut out the elephants and the dancing girls in the background to set the mood for a vital scene. But in this case I didn't mind because it gave me the chance to write an episode I'd had in mind for some time.

To explain this I need to say something about the nature of *Nearest and Dearest*. It is the television equivalent of the seaside comic postcard, which George Orwell defined as a ". . . world where marriage is a dirty joke or a comic disaster, where the rent is always behind and the clothes are always up the spout . . . where the newly-weds make fools of themselves on the hideous beds of seaside lodging houses, and the drunken red-nosed husbands roll home at four in the morning to meet the linen-nightgowned wives who wait for them behind the front door, poker in hand." *Nearest and Dearest* strays from these classic lines only inasmuch as Nellie and Eli Pledge, the principal characters, are brother and sister rather than husband and wife.

Inevitably in this vulgar world the plots and the action take the characters into pubs, doctor's waiting rooms, magistrates' courts and all the other classic backgrounds for this sort of low comedy. Moreover, since the show has five regular characters—besides Nellie and Eli there is droopy cousin Lily, her silent decrepit husband Walter, and Stan the aged pickle works foreman—the typical *Nearest and Dearest* plot has to be fairly complex to bring all these people in.

And yet the more complex the plot, the more free-wheeling the action, the further the show gets away—inevitably—from its most interesting characteristic, the relationship between Eli and Nellie Pledge.

This is why I welcomed the opportunity to write an episode which would go for simplicity—a quality hard to achieve successfully. The episode *Getting to Know You* has no real plot, only the very basic situation of Nellie and Eli locked in their own cellar for the weekend. It requires only two sets, as compared to the show's usual four or five. It uses only one extra character beside the show's regular five.

Locking them in the cellar was simply a device to accentuate the horrors of togetherness, which in the case of Nellie and Eli is the product of habit and economic necessity. It was also an opportunity for deepening the time scale of the relationship, delving back into the fifty-odd years it has existed, by taking Eli and Nellie through boredom and panic back towards a state of childishness.

I always welcome the excuse to reach back into childhood, and of course some of the memories, including the firework down the wellington boot, are my own. The 'dipping' for the solitary pickle was something I particularly wanted to bring in, for these solemn rituals have always fascinated me and I believe that most of us adults, walking about with our paunches and preoccupations, are still children mentally. It is just that we are trapped inside old bodies.

The main problem in the writing was to get a pace and rhythm to compensate for the absence of comedy's handiest props—changes of scene and all the business of exits and entrances. It was even more important than ever to construct the show so that it could be played right through without breaks for costume changes or time lapses—with the unavoidable exception of the half-time commercial break which is one of the conventions of the form in an ITV production.

Having read through the foregoing I am struck by the fatuity of all this. You can analyse as much as you like, and even draw diagrams and construct scale models, but the audience may still decide not to laugh. In the case of this script they did, but it may have been for reasons I haven't even thought of.

Chapter 14

THE IDEAS MARKET

In the beginning there was the one off play. Then the programmers, first in America and later here, discovered that far bigger audiences could be gained by serving up the same characters at the same time every week in basically the same situations. With the one off play, viewers had to grasp the characters, the setting, *and* the story, and that could be hard work. With a series episode, viewers need only acclimatise themselves to a new story, and if the story is simple enough they can watch while making tea or love or playing Monopoly.

Many series are formulated within the production organisations and result from pooled ideas at the regular programming meetings. *The Avengers* started like that, and so did *Doctor Who*. When this happens either a staff script editor works out the details, or a well-known freelance writer is commissioned to prepare the format. But there remains a wide open market for outside writers to submit ideas. Success requires a good idea, but may also result from good luck or a good filing system or a combination of both.

Back in the Fifties the Granada Television programmers wanted to put on a regular comedy show, and careful analysis of cinema box office takings proved that anything about the army drew big audiences. Just at that time Sid Colin submitted to them a pilot script called *The Army Game*. The show ran for years. In the early Sixties I heard the BBC wanted new ideas for children's series, so I submitted a format about a veterinary surgeon based on a suggestion from my agent, Harvey Unna. The BBC almost, but didn't quite, buy it; so it went into my filing cabinet where it was to reside for some years. Then one day Talbot Television Ltd, who are international TV/film distributors, told me that a company in Australia was looking for ideas for a children's series. Within hours I had Australianised my format, and had it rushed by taxi to Paul Talbot's London office. From there it went by airmail to the company in Sydney, where it was the first completely worked out idea to result from their search. A few months later I was in the desert outside Broken Hill, NSW, watching the first episode being filmed.

However, we seem now to have passed the time when a series could be based simply on someone doing a specific job. We've had series about policemen, solicitors, doctors, hospital, vicars, vets, probation officers, military policemen, spies, hoteliers, and detectives. The formula has been to depict a central character whose job gave them authority, and who either went to people in trouble or had troubled people come to them. The police-type series stills pulls the ratings, but more and more audiences demand something extra. Ironside is crippled, Longstreet blind, both effective dramatic gimmicks if you like that sort of thing, which presumably the Americans do. On our side of the Atlantic the tendency is towards deeper characterisation, with more development of character as the series progresses. These days there are fewer watertight compartments as series increasingly overlap with serials (e.g. *The Guardians*, about Britain under a fascist rule) and with anthologies (e.g. *The Villians*, 1972 version, which showed a number of convicted men escaping from a prison coach, then in each episode followed what happened to them as individuals).

If you have a good idea for a series, for goodness' sake try to sell it. But first consider whether it really *is* a good idea. Test this by working out at least half a dozen episode stories based on your theme. If six stories come easily, you may have a winner. But if you get stuck on the third or fourth story, forget it. The primary criterion for any series idea is its potential as a story vehicle. Here is a suggested scheme for your format:

Front cover

Title of the series; state that this is a format; your name and address. The importance of a good series title cannot be overstressed. *Z Cars* and *Doomwatch* instantly conjure up pictures in the mind. When the BBC mounted *Moonbase*, the American network interested in a co-production immediately asked for 26 episodes on hearing the title. Never try to sell a series idea on a 'working title', i.e. a make-do title which writers and editors will sometimes use temporarily because they can't think of anything better at the moment.

Page one

The basic idea in not more than 100 words, fewer if possible. To be written vividly.

Page two

A few lines explaining that this is for a weekly live-television or TV/film production; that each story episode will be a separate story, or that there is a continuing story thread; that each episode is for a half hour or one hour time slot or whatever.

Page three

Some factual background stuff. If, say, it's about airline pilots, give some details about training, working conditions, pay, the staff structure of airlines, etc. Show you've done some homework.

Pages four and five

Depth characterisations of your series leads. *Not* what they look like (see page 81), but their family background, life experience, how they think and feel.

Page six and on

At least half a dozen storylines, from which the reader can see not only that the idea has story potential but also the type of stories which can be created from it.

If it is drama there is no need to write a complete pilot episode to submit with your format. But if it is a comedy idea, a complete pilot episode is essential, and you can almost forget the format. Comedy depends on funny lines more than framework.

Although there is very little legal protection of an idea, the more detail you put into your format, the greater the copyright you create for yourself. On the other hand, a fifty thousand word format is not going to be appreciated by the person who has to wade through it. Make sure yours is well-typed and generally well-presented. Keep copies.

If you make a sale, you'll get a nice 'Created by' credit on the screen every week, plus a per episode royalty whether you write any episodes or not. If you don't make a sale, try another producing organisation. If they tell you that unfortunately they are already mounting a similar series, believe them. They really don't want or need to steal your ideas.

As things are, when your format flops into the In tray of some script department it will be judged basically by whether or not the people there like it. They have plenty of experience in what makes a good show, but inevitably subjectivity will play its part in their thinking. However, this is likely to change. There exists nowadays an organisation called TAPE (Consultancy) Ltd. TAPE (Television Audience Programme Evaluation) advises producing organisations on series audience potential, not only here but anywhere in the world. By considering in a special scientific way all the factors contained within a creative idea, plus the likely competition and the time of transmission, TAPE has predicted ratings with unnerving accuracy. The firm's managing director, Michael Firman, says: "The real use of TAPE is as a slave and not the master." Yet already TAPE has been asked by one worried programme planner to create a series idea to combat unyielding competition from another channel. So what of the future? In a world of ever-increasing rationalisation shall we eventually see on our screens 'Created by IBM System/370'?

Chapter 15

STAFF WRITING

When a person buys a book called *Writing for Television* it seems likely they want to write a work of fiction and sell it as a freelance. Hence the emphasis on freelance drama in this book. In truth, freelance drama is only about one fifth of the total output of British television. The other four fifths is made up of news and news magazines, weather forecasts, commercials, current affairs and documentaries, religious programmes, adult and school education, children's programmes, music, sport, outside broadcasts, and chat shows. Most of these programmes use writers, but these writers are either on the staff or are on very long term contracts. In this chapter we shall take a look into the world of the television writers who have come in from the cold—or, perhaps even more sensibly, have never been out in it.

One way of knowing that you're getting older is when BBC script editors start looking younger. Where do they all come from, these bright young men and women (but mainly men) who throng the corridors of power at the BBC's London Television Centre? If you have submitted interesting and promising material to the BBC, and particularly if something has been accepted, you may be offered an attachment contract. This means that for three months you can be tea boy or girl to an established editor. If you succeed, which may mean if your editor's show succeeds, you may be asked to stay on.

With certain exceptions, the major ITV companies don't employ full time script editors, preferring to bring in a freelance writer for that role for a particular series. However, there are staff jobs as script department executives. Here you may find yourself doing some editing, at the same time negotiating script fees, organising readers, and advising the programme controller on ideas submitted for new series.

This is because none of the ITV companies can match the BBC for size, and therefore work is not so compartmentalised.

Some years ago when the well-meaning Writers' Guild opened its doors to the people who write the commercials, at least one dramatist member was so disgusted he tore up his Guild card and wrote to *The Times* about it. The gesture proved futile. Few if any of the admen and women showed any inclination to become unionised. Labouring directly under their capitalist masters, instead of indirectly as is the unadmitted lot of any dramatist with an ITV contract, most copywriters expressed satisfaction with their pay and conditions by not joining the Guild.

There are about 750 advertising agencies in Britain, 400 of them in London. Of these only about 30 regularly make television commercials. Actual production is farmed out to independent film makers, but the scripts are conceived and written by full time agency copywriters. They have offices and secretaries, but a lot of their creative work is done at home if their minds function better there. Pay is good, holidays regular, and an important binding factor is the sense of team work with other bright, intelligent people. Almost everyone in advertising is nice. They even use nice words. 'Consumer' is a nasty word, invented by *Which?* They prefer to call us 'people'.

A television commercial is preceded by intense research. With a new product this means finding out from the client exactly what the product is physically and who might want to buy it (almost all television advertising is directed at women between the ages of 20 to 40; men rarely buy anything). The manufacturer's boffins will enthusiastically blind the copywriter with scientific formulae, omitting to mention that the factory is guarded by radio-controlled geese. It is little things like this that a bright copywriter may use to drive home the sales message, to make the product seem exciting or cuddly or prestigious. In consultation with one of the agency's art directors, the copywriter now prepares a 'storyboard' (see next page) and this is presented to the client for approval. Copywriting comes under the most intense pressure and criticism. Taking into account the overall cost of a single 30 second commercial at from £4,000 to £20,000, plus £100,000 on buying air time, the client is paying about £1,000 per word. He has a right to quibble.

Because advertising copywriters work strictly to order and their main purpose is to sell their clients' products and services, they tend to be looked down on by other categories of writers. It might be

8.   Robinson filling own glass.

Nobody else can match Robinson's quality.

9.   Cut to C.U. of bottle and glass as water pours in.

Because, you know.

10.   Robinson looks off screen to boy with surprise.

---

there's really only <u>one</u> Robinson.

11.   Cut back to see that boy is drinking from the glass.

Perhaps it's just as well.

Y&R

YOUNG & RUBICAM LTD.

TV Creative Recommendations

Client __Reckitt & Colman__

Product __Robinsons - Barley Waters__

Title _____

Time length __30 seconds__   Word count _____

Job No. __58508__   Date: __1/9/72__   Approval required by:

Copywriter __CP__

Art Director _____

TV Producer _____

Manager - TV _____

Manager - Copy _____

Manager - Art _____

Dep. Creative Dir. _____

Creative Director _____

Client _____

remembered that the writers who sell soap and deoderants are the same people called upon to sell ideas for the public good. Copywriters with the agency Young & Rubicam created the 'Clunk, click' seat belt campaign featuring Jimmy Saville. Masius Wynne-Williams do 'Don't drink and drive', and Saatch & Saatch do some of the anti-smoking commercials. Napper, Stanton & Wolley launched 'Watch out, there's a thief about'.

Roderick Allen of Allen, Brady & Marsh Ltd, has this to say about the technique of writing television advertisements: "Writing good television commercials is as disciplined and demanding as writing a good poem. You have to say what you have to say in about three sentences, show what you want to show in four or five filmed scenes. And out of this create a character for the product, emphasise its attributes and dramatise its ability to fulfill a need. The key-line—the one you want people to remember—must try to say it all. For British Rail we could have said 'Don't-endure-the-nerve-wracking-hell-of-driving-to-work-through-the-jams-and-the-snarl-ups-and-then finding-you-can't-park-the-bloody-car-when-you-get-there.' But 'Let the train take the strain' said it better."

Documentaries make up about 6% of total television output. It is a small market, with almost no room at all for the outside freelance writer *per se*. Most documentaries start with an idea in the mind of a television director, who may be staff, on long term contract, or freelance. Having conceived the idea, he or she then goes to the BBC or an ITV company and tries to 'sell' it. If they like it in principle, the director will be contracted to do some depth research on the subject. If after that the idea still looks good, the director will be commissioned to go out with a camera and crew and make the film. There may never be a script as such. Naturally the director will have an idea of form in his mind, but essentially the modern documentary is written with the camera on the spot, a work system that allows for maximum flexibility. The documentary director-writer must also be his own producer in that it will be up to him and his secretary to organise everything from location hotel accommodation to getting police or other permissions to film in certain places. If a writer is an established authority on a subject, then the production organisations may consider an idea coming from him. The writer Tony Parker, who has made himself an expert on prisons, has put up ideas to the BBC. When they have liked his ideas, which they usually do, he has been put on a short term contract and asked which of their directors he would like to work with. But you have to be very well-known, and very well-trusted, to arrive at that position. If you are unknown and have an idea for a documentary about something *in which you are expert*, then you might try putting it up to the head of a BBC or ITV documentary department (you'll find them listed in *Contacts;* see page 127).

A point of comment by some visitors to this country is the British preoccupation with news. Apparently we buy more newspapers than most other peoples, and 10% of our television time is taken up with newscasts and news magazines. Both the BBC and Independent Television News (ITN) employ a large number of journalists. To prepare *News at Ten* work starts fourteen hours before, when at 8am the editor prepares the day's schedule. Having talked by phone to all the regional ITV company news editors, he lists the stories that he considers will make news for that day. Meantime the foreign news editor is preparing his list, and at a 10.30am conference the framework for the day is fixed. But because their product is news, their best laid plans can be knocked sideways by the unexpected. Television news means showing what's happened, not just talking about it. There is a corps of first-class despatch riders who bring in clips of film from London Airport and from anywhere in Britain for immediate processing by the laboratory. There is a graphics department available to produce diagrams, some of them animated, that will help illustrate certain news items; and there's a library of still pictures that can be drawn on when no film of an event is available. As with newspaper work, a lot of material written at intense speed for television newscasts never reaches the screen because some later momentous news story pushes lesser items into the background. The editor of ITN, Nigel Ryan, says: ". . . we have to select with great care the stories we choose for the programme. We are aware of the important decisions we are making in such areas as Northern Ireland, law and order, political and industrial strife, and in fact anywhere where there is a clash of opinion in an important matter. One of the continual problems is balance in a bulletin. . . ." In January 1971 the Association of Cinema and Television Technicians monitored all television news and news-type programmes for a week. As a result they produced a document, *One Week*, with tables, score marks, and comparison checks, for bias or impartiality in the reporting of trade union and industrial matters. "Television is legally required to be impartial," said the *One Week* editor, Caroline Heller, "and we attempted to find out how far it satisfied this requirement. The results of our careful word-for-word monitoring gave reason for some disquiet." The overall conclusion was that, certainly in industrial reporting, television news was ". . . erratic and superficial . . . with . . . departures from impartiality" to the detriment of the trade unions. Specific criticisms were made of the use of emotive language, and in this the BBC was worse than ITN. (For speed in reporting events, industrial and general, the BBC came off best.) ACTT General Secretary Alan Sapper says: "Auto-censorship is apparent in all fields of television, particularly so in news because there it is more noticeable." If you fancy yourself as a news writer, with auto-censorship or otherwise, the way in is through journalism. Apart from news writers there are also the on-the-spot reporters, those men you see facing camera with microphone clutched in hand against a background of wrecked Belfast pubs or Blackpool beauty queens. The way in to that type of work could possibly be through local radio, which fortunately is on the increase in this country. Local radio is a boon to would-be broadcasters because it provides a real opportunity for the amateur to learn how to be a professional.

Next to the news, we British are obsessed with our weather. We have good reason to be. The people who prepare the BBC weather forecasts at the Meteorological Office have to be both writers and scientists. As writers, they work to very exacting disciplines. Although a few broadcasts are aimed directly at specialist viewers, in general presentations are devised to satisfy the greatest possible number of viewers. Scripts and captions have to be clear, unambiguous and free from too much technical language. The television weathermen know that the first sentence has the major memory-impact, and therefore this must always refer to the most marked weather feature. A colloquial style is used, without lapsing into slang. As with news writing, weather scripts are designed for the spoken word: this means they can use phrases which may be inelegant in print but are acceptable in conversation. Forecasts must never use such subjective words as 'good', 'bad', 'better' or 'worse', for to say that 'the good weather will continue another three days' is likely to enrage the drought-stricken arable farmer whose crops are wilting through lack of rain. Where possible qualitative phrases are used which enable the viewer to relate the information to his own experience, e.g. 'a brighter day than today'. As well as the general forecasts, there are other forecasts specially written for the farming audience. Here the writer who knows his isotopes from his millibars can revel in such technicalities as 'soil moisture deficits' and 'Beaumont periods'. There are two types of presentation, personal and with a pre-prepared script. In the personal presentation, when we see the weatherman standing before his charts and maps, he is literally thinking on his feet, giving one of those few truly live television broadcasts that we ever see nowadays. Because information is still being gathered up to transmission time, there is no opportunity to produce either a script or material for a 'teleprompt' machine (a gadget just under the television camera that carries the script printed in big letters on a roll of paper; it is often the use of a teleprompt that allows the presenters and 'anchor men' of chat shows to make those faultless opening announcements while seemingly looking direct into camera). As well as the personal 'on camera' presentation, there are the pre-prepared weather forecasts which do have a script, and which are either spoken OOV with just a caption on screen, or are read by newscasters at the end of news bulletins. A number of versions of these scripts, each complete within its own right, have to be prepared, all of different lengths; this is because they seem never sure until the last moment exactly how many minutes or seconds will be available for the weather forecast. If you are scientifically inclined as well as wanting to write for television, this may be the right job for you. It could be very exciting. As they say on the Continent about British weather, if you don't like it—wait half an hour.

The producing organisations employ both staff and freelance writers on educational television (ETV). With adult education and schools programmes taking up almost a tenth of total transmitting time, there is a fair amount of work here for the would-be ETV writer. In addition to the BBC and the ITV Contractors as the obvious employers in this field, the educational authorities in Glasgow, Hull, London, and Plymouth run their own schools television services, which are complementary to those transmitted on the networks. The closed-circuit service run by the Inner London Education Authority now reaches over 1,000 schools, plus 400 other educational establishments in the London area. If you want your written word to reach the masses, these figures are not very impressive; but at least you can bank on having a trapped audience.

The BBC regions and many of the ITV companies produce daily and weekly magazine programmes, such as the BBC's *Nationwide*, Thames' *Today*, and Southern's *Day by Day*. They all employ staff writers and researchers. Here again the way into this type of work could be through journalism or through local radio.

Allied to news writing is the world of sport. To cover the 15% of air time dedicated to muscle and adrenalin, television employs an army of sports writers. Again, start with journalism. Become the star sports writer on your local newspaper; then simply write to the BBC or an ITV company and say you want to work for them.

Every word of linkage and presentation has to be written—that's when those beautiful young men and women pop up on our screens between programmes to tell us of the delights in store later on if we stay with their channel. Writing promotional material can be a way in for the newcomer. You get yourself a three month contract and a little office down in the basement of the studio, and start to get to know something about the industry.

There is also a great deal of writing *about* television. *The Listener*, *Radio Times*, and *TV Times* employ a great many staff journalists, as as well as commissioning material from freelance writers.

It is interesting how many people, who now hold down important staff posts within television, started with very humble and often humdrum jobs in the industry. There are lady producers who started as PA's (which is little more than being a glorified shorthand-typist), and men producers who began as floor managers. Some of those talented interviewers you see daily in magazine programmes began as researchers, and some heads of script departments began as filing clerks. Almost no-one can enter the staff side of the television industry at the top, or even half way up. If you really want to work within the industry, the moral seems to be this: Forget your BA Hons. and those three foreign languages you speak fluently, and if someone ever offers you a job to make the studio tea, take it—but be sure that you make the best tea they've ever had, and that both you and it are always on time.

Chapter 16

WHAT NOT TO WRITE FOR TELEVISION

Is there any censorship in British television?

It is symptomatic of our times that the opening of this chapter has been re-written at least six times prior to the publication of this book. At one time the answer to that question—Is there any censorship in Britain television?—was a fairly emphatic 'no'. Then, suddenly, a cold wind started to blow across the editorial desks, and cautious producers re-sharpened long dull blue pencils. Some shows had pushed permissiveness too far; now programme chiefs were issuing lists of expletives that must no longer be used. At this moment in time the pendulum is swinging towards greater control. If the present tendency continues we may end up like Spain, where a television producer assured me they have no censorship problems at all: "It's all so simple for us. They tell us what to make, and by jove we make it."

All may be changed again by the time you read this book. The best I can do here is to give you some general pointers. Both the BBC and the IBA have codes about violence, and you can obtain copies by applying to the Head of Secretariat, British Broadcasting Corporation, Broadcasting House, London, W1A 1AA, and from the Independent Broadcasting Authority, 70 Brompton Road, London, SW3 1EY. Here are some of the salient points from both codes:

Children's Programmes

The worlds which children and grown-ups occupy, though they overlap, are different. Subjects with unpleasant associations for the one will often be taken for granted by the other. Guns and fist fights may have sinister implications for adults, but seldom for children. On the other hand, family insecurity and marital infidelity may be commonplace for adults, but to children these things can be deeply disturbing. The main danger points are:

Situations which upset a child's emotional security, arising out of adoptions, desertions, cruelty in the home, unwanted children, friction between parents. All these things apply more in contemporary than in historical settings, because the child is better able to identify with the present-day world.

Portrayal of injury, illness, or disablements, especially when used to sharpen a dramatic crisis (e.g. nightmares); and of embarrassing personal disabilities (e.g. stuttering).

Examples of weapons and other devices which the child can easily imitate. Few British children have access to guns or exotic poisons; but it is only too easy to stretch a piece of wire across a path which may result in the victim breaking a leg.

Bad habits in good characters. In children's shows, don't have your hero smoking cigarettes, drinking alcohol excessively, or hitting people below the belt.

Scenes in which pleasure is taken in the infliction of pain or humiliation on others. Suffering by children, women, and animals. (If it's a kids' show, and the story includes a ship sinking at sea, *save the ship's cat*.—MH)

Situations in which children get the impression that they are entering a world in which they can count on nothing as settled, reliable, and kind, in which they must make their way at the expense of others, resorting to physical or mental violence whenever it will pay them.

Scenes which children might copy with resultant injury to themselves. Years ago a number of small children imitated Batman and jumped out of windows.

Adult Programmes

Violence for its own sake is not permissable. There is a certain type of cheap paperback whose stories lead up to and dwell upon the calculated infliction of pain. It is this type of thing which neither the BBC nor the IBA will tolerate. A hand fight or a shoot up are perfectly acceptable, provided such physical confrontation is a natural development of the story. With fights, beware depicting a person held by another while a third hits him: people must not be under restraint while being hit.

Both the BBC and the IBA Contractors adhere to a watershed policy, whereby the more adult shows are not screened until after 9pm.

Most television producers and directors keep to both the spirit and the letter of the Codes. There was a time, during the big permissive push of the late Sixties and very early Seventies, when a series writer might find himself being asked to write in an unwarranted fight scene, or additional sexual references. Unless he was a big name there wasn't much he could do about it, any more than the young actress, grateful for the work, could protest if the director pointed his camera down her blouse front instead of at her face. But all that is changing at the time of my writing.

Don't run away with the notion that Mrs Mary Whitehouse is regarded as a figure of fun in television. Many would-be television writers seem to have this idea, and believe that the industry scoffs at her. That may have been true when she started her campaign. But by sheer persistence, plus no mean intelligence and a lot of personal charm, she has made her impact. The truth is that she really does put forward the feelings of a very great number of people in this country. For millions of people television means family viewing. They are not necessarily hidebound, and certainly they are not stupid, but bad language, nudity, and gratuitous sexual references embarrass them. Every time I go to give a talk to a group of people about television, someone in the audience raises this question; and, once the ice has been broken, almost the entire audience supports them. I have rarely heard complaints against an outspoken play, provided it was well-written and the outspokeness was necessary to make its point. But what they don't like is, to use that old fashioned word, smut.

Some producing organisations have their own rules. There is at least one which will not entertain any story about the improper use of illicit drugs, no matter how heavily the story is slanted against the users. The Bank of England has special regulations concerning the showing of bank notes on television, and for a pamphlet about this you can write to the Press Office, Bank of England, London, EC2R 8AH. It seems one of their fears is that a screened close up of a £1 note might be photographed by someone who would subsequently use the negative to make a forgery. Presumably there are a lot of people with both television receivers and cameras who are short of a £1 note from which they could make a forgery direct.

The big brake on what not to write for television is the law of libel. Every writer is at risk the moment he depicts a character unfavourably. Your story may include a character called Perigrine Augustus Larchpenny, a commercial traveller in Bolton; and it might be essential to your plot to mention that he drives a light-blue Ford Cortina motor car. Let us presume he is the villain of your story. Since his name is a trifle rare, if there is a real Perigrine Augustus Larchpenny living in Bolton he would have grounds to sue you for defamation, even though his occupation is that of hairdresser and he rides a dark brown bicycle. So, you might reduce your chances of a court action simply by giving him a less unusual set of names. There may be twenty or a hundred Tom Smith's in Bolton, and if you use those names none can claim you have singled him out to defame. But if one is a commercial traveller and drives a light-*coloured* Ford motor car, albeit not a Cortina, that Tom Smith might have grounds for action. There is no defence in law to say that you did not know this person existed (which is true), nor that you meant no harm (also true). The only safeguard is never to be more specific than is essential for your story. In our Tom Smith example, obviously the character had to have a name; possibly it was important to mention his job; even if the make of his car is never mentioned in dialogue, the car itself might be seen on the screen. So, what's the solution? Well, was it necessary to specify Bolton? Why not just refer to a northern town?

Whenever possible check that no-one exists with both the name and occupation of your intended character. All the professional bodies have lists of their members (the General Medical Council, General Dental Council; then there are trade associations, and trade unions— you use your imagination and do a bit of research); for Companies, there is the Registry of Company Names. Write a polite letter to the appropriate body, explain the situation, and always offer at least six imaginary names and ask them to check if any one of them is safe to use. This still may not protect you, because between writing your script and the transmission of the production any number of new dentists, clergymen, estate agents, and Companies, may have come into existence. But production of the correspondence will show to the Judge that you did your best, and he may go lightly with you.

You can also defame things. If your story is about a horse-race, you may want your characters to mention the names of some horses. Only one horse can win. What will your story do to the reputation of any existing horse whose name is used for one of the losers? The Jockey Club have the names of all existing race-horses. Defamation need not be only in dialogue, it can be visual. If your young housewife character complains that her sewing machine is always breaking down, and if we see a sewing machine whose shape identifies it as being of a particular make, the manufacture could be extremely angry, and with some justification.

Only use dead telephone numbers allocated to you by the post office. If in London, the people to ask are on 01-432 4722; out of London, phone your telephone manager and he will help. If the registration number of a motor vehicle is important to your story, write to your local Licensing Department and ask for a number you can use. Don't use the number of your own car, for two reasons. First, if you later sell it, and the teleplay is repeated, the new owner might sue. Second, writer Eric Paice once used the number of his own Volvo in a *Dixon of Dock Green* episode about a child molester with the result that he was attacked in the street by angry mothers and had to be rescued by the police.

All this sounds very restrictive. It is. The point is to protect the individual from intended or unintended harm. That individual could be you. There is a joke, which is really no joke, about a series of terrible murders in Bordeaux, France, and how every day the French newspapers ran stories about The Beast of Bordeaux. The first headlines read 'Police Seek Beast of Bordeaux', followed shortly by 'Beast of Bordeaux Captured'. Then the headlines read 'Beast of Bordeaux Stands Trial'. Finally they had to report, somewhat penitently, 'Beast of Bordeaux Proved Innocent'. That couldn't happen here.

What should you do if, despite your best efforts, you or your producer receive a letter which reads: "Character X in your play describes me, and this is causing me acute embarrassment with my neighbours"? There are two schools of thought. One is to reply immediately (a day's delay can deepen the wound), offer your sincere apologies, stress that you have never heard of this person before in your life, and invite them to show your letter of apology to all their neighbours. If the complainant is reasonably stupid they may accept your seemingly sincere apology and take the matter no further. However, if the angered viewer has typed his letter, has a double barrelled name, and has an address in London's literate NW3 or, even more formidable, in a Home Counties stockbroker belt, do not even send an acknowledgement but forward the complaining letter direct to the legal department of the producing organisation. In one instance reported to me, where the alleged libel involved one word, all existing scripts were recalled, the offending page was re-duplicated minus the word, and a copy of the revised script was sent to the viewer as proof that they must have mis-heard. Not very ethical, but that's show business.

While British law rigidly protects individuals, minority groups remain fair game so far as television is concerned. This is particularly noticeable in some of our light entertainment shows (see Adrian Mitchell's comments on page 153). Under the Race Relations Act of 1965 the use of 'abusive and insulting' words has to be in a public place, which, legally, may not necessarily apply to a television studio. Also it is necessary to prove intent to stir up race hatred. Things can be very different overseas. Jugoslavia prohibits films likely to cause war hate, and both American and Russian films have been banned for this reason. While outlawing films which depict certain "offensive" intermingling of white and non-whites, South African law prohibits entertainments which bring any section of their multi-racial community into ridicule or contempt. Presumably, therefore, if we hope to sell the tapes of some of our light entertainment shows to the new South African television service, we shall first have to tone down the racism. (Intermingling of whites and non-whites is, of course, permitted by British television if not by all members of the audience. When the plot of a continuing-story serial caused a well-known actress to be seen on screen in an embrace with a coloured man, she later received by mail a number of sheets of used toilet paper.) Most major American television series these days include the 'obligatory black' or 'statutory ethnic' because American sponsors are very conscious of not losing a single sale of a bar of soap. Except for a few 'enrichment stations' all American television is commercial, and many complete programmes are sponsored. This means a whole one hour drama or light entertainment slot is brought to you by courtesy of a manufacturer, and he is determined not to offend anybody with anything, while at the same time pandering to everybody with everything possible. This can have a disastrous effect on creativity. However, no American minority-group child is likely to grow up believing that they are inherently stupid because they are black, red, or yellow. We, on the other hand, seem to work on the basis that the sooner we can call our negro or Asian neighbours 'black bastards' and have them smile back at us over the garden wall, the better it will be. I have yet to hear this view endorsed by a black; nor, come to that, by anyone who happens to be a bastard, be they white, black, or polka dot.

247

GLOSSARY

The words included are peculiar to British television. Some are borrowed from the theatre and other arts, and of these some are given a slightly different meaning in television. Both slang and proper words are given; in some instances only the slang word is listed because that is the one everyone uses. The number in brackets following a definition refers to a page in this book where the word is used or is explained in more detail.

ACTT. Association of Cinematograph and Television Technicians (sometimes called 'the union').

ATV. Associated Television Limited.

ACTUALITY. Reportage of an event taking place at the time of showing, or recorded for showing at a suitable time with minimal editing.

ANTHOLOGY. A series of plays thematically linked (115).

BBC. British Broadcasting Corporation.

BCU. Big close-up (e.g. a section of a face).

BP. Back projection (44).

BACKING. A piece of scenery stood behind doors, windows, etc., to stop the camera 'shooting off', i.e. seeing the studio through some aperture in the set.

BOOK. The script.

BOOM. Sound boom (15).

BRIEF. The policy stated by a management regarding a production or series of productions, e.g. a programme may be intended to obtain high ratings cheaply—or expensively; or a programme may be intended to gain prestige for the organisation making it.

BUSINESS. Any activity for a character, e.g. pouring tea, polishing nails, dusting shelves, etc.

CSO. Colour separation overlay (45).

CU (AND C/U). Close-up, i.e. only the face, or a hand, or a hotel label on a suitcase.

248

CAMERA SCRIPT. In electronic television, the version of the script after the director has 'blocked out' his camera shots and moves. It is normally only distributed to the cameramen and other technicians (61).

CHEAT. A falsification in production giving an impression of truth, e.g. an actor looking off the screen to give the viewer the feeling that he is looking at an object, although he is in fact not doing so.

CHROMA-KEY. The ITV term for CSO (45).

CLIP. A short piece of film from a longer film.

CLOSED CIRCUIT. When both camera and receiver are linked by cable, and the electrical impulses are not transmitted through the air.

COPYWRITER. A writer who writes commercials.

CORNERPIECE. A very small set with a limited or non-existent acting area.

CREDITS. Same as 'titles' (see below), but 'credits' also refers to names in television programme journals as well as on the screen.

CUE. A signal to an actor or technician to take the action rehearsed. It can be the end of a line of dialogue (which is the other actor's cue to speak his lines), a wave, a nod, or a nudge.

CUT. (1) If your script is too long you may be asked to cut it, or to make a cut, or a number of cuts.

(2) In electronic television, to change from the view of one camera to that of another. In TV/film, to change from the view of one set up to that of another set up.

CUT AWAY. A quick shot of something away from the main action (37).

DIRECTOR. The person accountable to a producer for putting the show 'on the floor' (10).

DOCUMENTARY. A non-fiction programme other than a newscast or an actuality OB.

DRESS. (1) A set is dressed by its details, e.g. picture on the wall, flowers in vase.

(2) Prior to the production there is a full dress rehearsal simply called 'the dress'.

DROP. (Also back drop). A canvas curtain depicting the background to a set, e.g. houses opposite, garden, open country. It serves the same purpose as a backing (see above). However, a backing is a free-standing flat (18), whereas a drop is 'flown' (hung from the grid).

DRY. When an actor completely forgets his lines and stops altogether it is a dry, or you can say that he dried.

DUBBING MIXER. Only in filmed inserts, for which he gets a screen credit. After the film has been edited, he mixes in the appropriate sound tracks that were recorded at the time of the filming. There is a similar process for edited video tape; this is done by the sound supervisor, who gets no credit.

ETV. Educational television.

EDITING. (Film) The selection of disconnected shots and the assembly of those, or the parts of those, chosen for the final film.

EDITING. (VTR). An electronic process whereby material considered redundant can be cut out; the assembly by electronic means of separate scenes previously recorded, in or out of the final sequence.

EDITOR. (Features (see below)). The manager accountable for the material used in, say, a magazine programme.

EDITOR. (Film). The technician who edits film.

EDITOR. (VTR). The technician who edits vision tape.

EFFECTS. Sound effects.

ENTRANCE. The moment an actor appears on a set he has made an entrance.

EQUITY. Actors' Equity, the actors' and variety artistes' trade union. Also represents stage managers (SM's) and assistant stage managers (ASM's).

EXT. Exterior.

EXIT. The moments leading up to, and the actual moment of, an actor leaving a set.

EXTRA. Small part actor (28).

F/U. Fade up. Starting from a blank screen or silent sound, bringing up the picture and/or sound to the required level.

FX. Sound effects.

FEATURE PROGRAMME. BBC term for a documentary.

FLUFF. An actor who forgets a word or phrase, but covers it by continuing correctly, is said to have fluffed.

FORMAT. Document explaining an idea (115, 231).

FOURTH WALL. The non-existent fourth wall of a tape television or theatrical set (15, 101).

FRAME. The field of vision limited by the bounds of the picture.

FUDGE ROUND. To cheat (using that word in its television and theatrical sense) something in the plot or writing. If a writer hasn't the time or inclination to check a fact (e.g. date of the Battle of Waterloo), he can fudge round by not being specific. Given the choice, it's better to fudge round than to be inaccurate.

GET OUT. The time allocated for the removal of all the sets from a studio.

GRAMS. Generic term for sound sources playing back into the production (music, effects, etc).

THE GUILD. The Writers' Guild of Great Britain.

HAND PROPS. Properties carried by artists (wallet, handbag, gun) as different from properties which dress the set (telephone, flower vase).

HTV. Harlech Television Limited.

IBA. Independent Broadcasting Authority.

ITA. Independent Television Authority, forerunner of the IBA.

ITCA. Independent Television Companies Association.

ITN. Independent Television News.

ITV. Independent Television, which is an unofficial umbrella term for the IBA, all the members of the ITCA, and ITN.

IWG. International Writers' Guild.

IDIOT CARD. Slang for 'prompt card'. This term tends not to be used by actors who need them.

IN FRAME. For a person to be in the camera's view.

INLAY. An optical effect whereby something is added to the visual on the screen (41).

IN SHOT. Same as 'in frame'.

INSERT. (1) A short piece of film. (2) Script writer's term to denote a cut away (79).

INT. Interior.

INT/EXT. An exterior set located in the studio. An alternative is: EXT/STUDIO.

IN THE CAN. To have been recorded or filmed.

JICTAR. Joint Industry Committee for Television Advertising Research, which measures ITV audience ratings (see 'ratings' below).

LS. Long shot, showing the whole scene.

LAZY ARM. A sound boom with a limited field of operation.

LIVE. As you now know, there are three forms of television production in Britain: live, tape, and TV/film (99). Nowadays, only the news, weather forecasts, and some outside broadcasts (sport, coronations, etc) are live (i.e. transmitted as they happen). All drama is taped or filmed. But drama used to be transmitted live (14). Somehow the term 'live' has remained attached to any production which is not TV/film, resulting in this sort of thing:

WRITER A: Hello. What are you working on?
WRITER B: This new daily serial.
WRITER A: Film or live?
WRITER B: Live.
WRITER A: You mean really live?
WRITER B: No. Tape.
WRITER A: For a moment I thought you meant live.
WRITER B: Yes, that's right. It is.

MLS. Medium long shot (e.g. the whole figure).

MS. Mid or medium shot, e.g. cutting above the head and above the waist.

MU. Musicians' Union.

MAGAZINE. A type of regular, generally non-fictional, programme directed at a specific audience.

MIKE. Microphone.

MILEAGE. The amount of story material; twists and turns in the plot.

MIX. Transition from one scene to another, in sound and/or vision, by fading the end of one scene while fading in the beginning of another. In film they use DISSOLVE.

MONITOR. Television screens within the studio and control rooms, allowing those staff who need to see the action (director, lighting, sound mixer, floor manager) to do so.

MOVE. An actor's change of position within a set.

N/S. Non-speaking character.

NATKE. National Association of Theatrical and Kine Employees.

NODDY. A non-speaking character, because at one time low paid non-speakers were allowed to nod, but not to utter any sound, if spoken to. (See current Equity definitions on page 27).

OB. Outside broadcast (30).

OOV. Out of vision, not in shot.

O/S. Out of shot, not in vision.

ONE OFF. An original play, also called 'single shot'.

OUTLINE. A storyline.

OVER. If your script is too long for the slot, you may be told it is 'over' or, say, 'two minutes over'.

PA. A director's assistant (11).

POV. Point of view. Sometimes the term 'eyeline' is used.

PRS. Performing Rights Society.

PAN. Short for panoramic. Originally, and still in film, the act of turning a camera horizontally but now in television also applied to up and down movements of the camera.

PERIOD. A production placed in the historical past.

PICK UPS. Shots made in filming to assist in editing, e.g. the interviewer listening.

PIECE, THE. The script.

PLAY-TIME. The time scale within a play.

PRACTICAL. A property or part of a set required to function as real life, e.g. a door that opens and isn't simply painted on, a gas oven that really works, etc.

POST SYNCHRONISATION. Adding dialogue, music, or sound effects, after the mute or partially sound picture (tape or film) has been shot. Slang: 'post sync'. Slang past tense: 'post synked' or 'post sunk'.

PRODUCER'S RUN. A complete rehearsal in the rehearsal room for the benefit of the producer. By this time actors should be word perfect, don't need their scripts to remember.

PROMPT CARD. A card or note bearing the actor's lines, placed where the camera can't see it but the actor can.

PROMPT COPY. The producer's master copy of the script, in which all dialogue and other changes agreed during rehearsals have been noted.

PROPERTIES. Items used for dressing a set.

PROPS. (1) Same as properties. (2) Name given to the technician in charge of properties.

RATINGS. The estimated number of viewers of a particular programme. The figures are arrived at by checking the past week's viewing pattern of panels of viewers who are believed to be a cross-section of the population as a whole.

READER. A person employed to read unsolicited material.

READ THROUGH. The first time the cast of a play meet and read aloud the whole play. Normally the producer, director, wardrobe and make-up people will be present, as well as the writer.

REHEARSAL SCRIPT. The printed version of the script that is distributed to the writer, cast, and various non-technical departments. Pages 85 to 95 is rehearsal script. The term is used to differentiate it from the camera script (61).

RESIDUALS. Additional money the writer may receive from the producing company if they sell the tape of film abroad.

RIPPLE. An optical effect whereby the picture on the screen is seen as though through rippling water. It may be used for a subjective view by someone who is semi-conscious, or to go into a dream sequence or a flashback.

RUN, THE. The production, or VTR, from beginning to end.

RUNNING TIME. Length of a production.

RUSHES. The first rough prints of negative film.

STV. Scottish Television Limited.

SERIAL. A succession of drama presentations which unfold one complete story.

SERIES. A number of drama presentations using the same theme and leading characters. Each episode has a self-contained story.

SERIES/SERIAL. A number of drama presentations using the same theme and leading characters, each episode being an entity, but the series as a whole containing a serial element or overall story thread.

SET AND LIGHT. That period of time allocated by the producer in consultation with specialists for the erection of the sets and the basic lighting rig.

SET UP. The scene in the frame of a camera placed in a particular position.

SETS. Representations, stylised or realistic, of interiors or exteriors, in a studio.

SCENE HANDS. Operatives who set and strike the sets.

SINGLE SHOT. See 'one off'.

SLOT. Period of time allocated for a programme, e.g. one hour, thirty minutes, etc. However, the actual running time may be much shorter to allow for commercial breaks. This also applies to the BBC when they hope to sell the tape to commercial networks overseas where commercials will be introduced.

SPECIAL TALENTS. An actors' ability to sing, ride a horse, etc.

SPREAD. If your script is 'under' (see below) you may be asked to write a spread, i.e. an extra thirty or sixty seconds, or whatever is required.

STABILISE. Correct running speed for a VTR machine.

STAGE DIRECTIONS. The writer's description of sets, artists' moves and business, and in some cases thought processes.

STOCK. Film clips, obtainable from film libraries which may be inserted, e.g. busy street, storm at sea (43).

STOOGING. Characters in shot but without business or lines are stooging, i.e. doing nothing but stand around.

STORYLINE. An extended synopsis, but not as detailed as a treatment.

STRIKE. When the show is in the can (recorded) they strike (dismantle) the sets. In some cases, props may be struck during a production, if the story so requires.

STUDY. The act of learning lines; an actor who can learn quickly is a 'good study'.

SYNOPSIS. A brief outline of a story (130).

T/C. Telecine (37).

T/K. Telecine (37).

TAKE OUT. The rounding off of a scene.

TELEPHONE BACKING. A scene-heading term meaning a neutral backdrop for a close up of someone on the phone in a two-way telephone conversation, e.g.

3. INT. TELEPHONE BACKING.   DAY.

THREE SHOT. A frame in which only three people are seen. The term 'four shot' is used, but more than that number is generally termed a 'group shot'.

THROWN. An actor who is mis-cued, or has his concentration broken in some way, and is unable to react quickly enough to cover up the error, is said to have been thrown.

TIGHT. An actor who can't 'give' plays tight.

TILT. In film, the act of moving the camera vertically during shot.

TITLES. Your name, plus others, on the screen.

TOOK. An actor who gets a fit of the giggles is said to have been took, or to have corpsed.

TOM. Technical operations manager; the technician accountable for the technical operation of the studio and the studio staff.

TREATMENT. A detailed story synopsis, often describing the story scene by scene with scene headings. Some writers include a few lines of dialogue in their treatments if that helps to convey their story idea even more vividly.

TWO HANDER. A scene, or a play, in which there are only two characters.

TWO SHOT. A frame in which two people only are seen.

UNDER. The opposite of over (see above), meaning too short.

UNION, THE. ACTT (see above).

VTR. Video tape recording.

VIDEO TAPE. The tape on which is recorded both sound and vision electrical impulses.

VISON TAPE. Same as video tape.

WGGB. Writers' Guild of Great Britain.

WALK ON. Small role actor (27).

WHIP PAN. Instead of indicating a cut or mix from one scene to another, you can suggest a whip pan. This is a very fast pan blurring the scene, then cutting to another camera finishing a whip pan on to the new scene.

WILD TRACK. A clip of sound tape used for background effects, e.g. open air sounds, birdsong, airport concourse hubbub.

WING. Making up dialogue or business to cover a fluff, dry, or corpse.

WORKING TITLE. A temporary make-do title to help identify a script for discussion or commissioning reasons.

TECHNIQUE

A-Z of Movie Making, by Wolf Rilla. Studio Vista, 1970.

Agee on Film. Film scripts by James Agee in two volumes. Peter Owen Ltd, 1965.

The Anatomy of a Television Play, by John Russell Taylor. Weidenfeld & Nicholson, 1962.

The Complete Book of Movie Making, by Tony Rose. Fountain Press.

Dictionary of Cinematography and Sound Recording, by W. S. Sharps. Fountain Press, 1959.

Elements of Film, by Lee R. Robker. Harcourt, Brace & World Inc., 1969.

Encyclopaedia of Film and Television Techniques, ed. by R. Spottiswoode. Focal Press, 1969.

Film: An Anthology, ed. by D. Talbot. University of California Press, London, 1972.

Filmgoer's Companion, The, by Leslie Halliwell. Granada Publishing (paperback), 1972.

Grammar of Television Production, by D. Davis. Barrie and Rockcliff, 1960.

Informing Image, The: a career in radio and television, by R. Bennett. Educational Explorers, 1968.

Make Your Own Professional Movies, by Nancy Goodwin and James Manilla. Macmillan (paperback), 1971.

Making a TV Play: a complete guide from conception to BBC production, by Cecil P. Taylor. Oriel Press, 1970.

Making of a Feature Film, The, by Ivan Butler. Penguin Books Ltd (paperback), 1971.

Making of Doctor Who, The, by Malcolm Hulke and Terrance Dicks. Pan Books Ltd (paperback), 1972.

Making of Star Trek, The, by Steven Whitfield. Ballantine Books Inc (paperback).

Working in Television, by B. Brandenburger. Bodley Head, 1965.
Writer's Guide 1968/69, The, ed. by Malcolm Hulke. Kemp's Printing & Publishing Co Ltd, for the Writers' Guild of Great Britain, 1969.
Writer's Guide 1970, The, ed. by Malcolm Hulke. Kemp's Printing & Publishing Co Ltd, for the Writers' Guild of Great Britain, 1970.
Writing for Television and Radio, by R. L. Hilliard. Hastings House, New York, 1962.
Writing for the BBC: a guide for professional and part-time freelance writers on possible markets for their work within the BBC. Third revised edition. BBC Publications, 1971.

REFERENCE
Authors' and Writers' Who's Who. Burke's Peerage Ltd.
BBC Handbook. Annual. BBC Publications.
British Film and Television Year Book, ed. by Peter Noble. Annual. British & American Film Press.
Commercial Television Year Book, The. Annual. Admark Directories Ltd.
Contacts. Twice yearly. (Only obtainable from *The Spotlight*, 43 Cranbourn St, London, WC2. Send 35p).
ITV Guide to Independent Television. Annual. Independent Broadcasting Authority.
International Motion Picture Almanack. Annual. Quigley Publications.
International Television Almanack. Annual. Quigley Publications.
Kemp's Film and Television Year Book (International). Kemp's Printing & Publishing Co Ltd.
Stage and Television Today. Weekly.
World Radio and TV Handbook. Annual. Published in Denmark. UK distributors: W. Dawson and Sons Ltd.
Writers' and Artists' Year Book. Annual. A. & C. Black.

PLAYS
Belcher's Luck, by David Mercer. Calder & Boyars, 1967.
Chelsea Triology, A, by Kenneth Jepp. Calder & Boyars, 1969.
Conflicting Generations. Five television plays compiled by M. Marland (the plays are by Paddy Chayefsky, Ronald Eyre, John Hopkins, John Mortimer, and David Turner). Longmans Green (paperback) 1968.
Find Your Way Home, by John Hopkins. Penguin Books Ltd (paperback) 1971.
Generations, The, three plays by David Mercer. Calder & Boyars.
On The Eve of Publication: plays by David Mercer. Methuen, 1970.
Parachute, Let's Murder Vivaldi, In Two Minds, by David Mercer. Calder & Boyars, 1967.
Ride a Cock Horse, by David Mercer. Calder & Boyars, 1966.

Six Granada Plays. Faber & Faber, 1960.

Sleeping Dog, by Simon Gray. Faber & Faber, 1968.

Royal Foundation and Other Plays, by Simon Raven. Anthony Blond, 1966.

Son of Man, by Dennis Potter. Penguin Books Ltd (paperback) 1971.

Talking to a Stranger. Four television plays by John Hopkins. Penguin Books Ltd (paperback) 1967.

This Story of Yours, by John Hopkins. Penguin Books Ltd (paperback).

Three TV Comedies, by David Mercer. Calder & Boyars, 1966.

Z Cars. Four television scripts compiled by M. Marland. Longmans Green (paperback), 1968.

CORRESPONDENCE SCHOOLS WITH COURSES IN TELEVISION WRITING

The B. A. School of Successful Writing Ltd,
124 New Bond Street,
London, W1A 4LJ
(Director of Instruction: Hilary Johnson, M.A., Ph.D.)

International Correspondence Schools,
Intertext House,
Stewarts Road,
London, SW8
(Principal: E. R. Andrews, Assoc.M.C.T., C.Eng.,
            •   M.I.Mech.E., M.B.I.M., M.I.O.M.)

Writers' School of Great Britain and America,
Provident House,
St. Peter Port,
Guernsey,
C.I.
(Principal: Athelstan Ridgway)

The Writing School,
25 Catherine Street,
London, WC2B 5JS
(Principal: Malcolm Hulke)

MARKET INFORMATION SERVICE

Writer's Market Guide,
50 First Avenue,
London, SW14 8SR
(£1 for two issues)

INDEX